THE STORY OF CAMP DOUGLAS

Chicago's Forgotten Civil War Prison

DAVID L. KELLER

THE History PRESS

Published by The History Press
Charleston, SC 29403
www.historypress.net

First published 2015

Cover images courtesy of the Chicago History Museum.

Manufactured in the United States

ISBN 978.1.62619.911.8

Library of Congress Control Number: 2014958795

In memory of seventy thousand Union and Confederate soldiers on whom Camp Douglas left a lasting mark.

Contents

CONTENTS

Foreword

A few years ago, Dave Keller contacted me and asked a question that is not often heard: "Do you have a ground-penetrating radar?" Although unusual, I had heard it before—and yes, I did have one. After all, being an archaeologist and military historian put me in a position to receive such a question. Before I knew it, Dave had come to Kenosha to tour the Civil War Museum. Soon we were plotting ground-penetrating radar work to further efforts to locate the remains of Camp Douglas, the Chicago Civil War training camp and later prison for Confederate soldiers. Dave's enthusiasm for Camp Douglas was infectious. I was not a stranger to the subject, yet he told me things that I did not know about the camp. Not only was I intrigued; I was hooked.

When we think of the Upper Midwest and the Civil War, we think of far-off battlefields, not the agricultural products, meat, hides, clothing, shoes and other supplies that came out of the "West." Sometimes we think of Lincoln or Grant, but we rarely think about the nearly 250,000 men whom Illinois alone sent into battle. The importance of the homefront, and the need for prison camps, do not come to mind either.

Before the 1990s, even professional historians gave these camps little thought. Since then, their documentation has sometimes been uneven. Some works have been accusatory or apologetic. It is a difficult and unpleasant subject, especially during a time when the condition of soldiers in the field in terms of food, sanitation and crowding was not much better.

In this work, Keller looks at a camp that carries a bad reputation as an "Andersonville of the North." He looks beyond the facts and figures. He delves into the firsthand accounts provided by Confederate prisoners, Union officers, inspectors and others. Dissecting the often-dry official documents, he makes them interesting and relevant. He turns these varied sources into an investigation of Camp Douglas, bringing the camp to life subject by subject while also asking, "Why?" Here, the story inside the stockade is revealed. We are wise not to ignore the firsthand accounts of those who were there before the fort vanished from history in 1865 and became an archaeological site.

DAN JOYCE
Director
The Civil War Museum, Kenosha, Wisconsin
November 2014

Prefaces

David Keller shows conclusively that all history is now. *The Story of Camp Douglas: Chicago's Forgotten Civil War Prison* brings to life the realities of life and death during the Civil War (1861–65), America's most deadly conflict. It is one of the finest community studies one will read, with Camp Douglas as the community's center from 1862 to 1865. We meet Union and Confederate officers and soldiers as guards, prisoners and public enemies. We learn about the Chicago of that era and what modern Chicagoans are trying to do about it. In short, it is a marvelous book that has been expertly written and well researched by a knowledgeable and passionate author.

I first met David Keller when I gave a talk about my book *The Enemy in Our Hands* at the prestigious Pritzker Military Library in 2010. He told me about his project: the discovery of the lost remains of Camp Douglas, the largest Union prison camp in the North. I had visited several Union and Confederate prison camp sites during my own research, including Fort Delaware at the mouth of the Delaware River; Johnson's Island in northern Ohio; Camp Chase in Columbus, Ohio; and, of course, Andersonville in Georgia. But Camp Douglas was seemingly lost to historians forever. Not so. David Keller and his cast of loyal diggers and researchers are turning all this around in Chicago's South Side. This book shows just what has been achieved—history has again come alive.

The strong relationship that existed between the people of Chicago and Camp Douglas during the Civil War is a vital link in the story of the camp. We meet passionate Unionists and Copperheads in head-to-head conflict, all linked to Confederate plans to liberate Camp Douglas, Johnson's Island and possibly other camps in order to create a huge Confederate army in the north. The plan failed, but the effort remains impressive.

Lastly, one of the most contentious issues concerning Civil War prison camps in both the North and South involves the hideous death rates suffered by both sides behind the wire. Did both sides create POW policies that ensured so many deaths? Did U.S. Grant realize that the Confederacy simply could not sustain its Union POW population with the resources at hand when he and Abraham Lincoln canceled the Dix-Hill Cartel, which worked so well from 1862 to 1863? Did both sides understand medicine well enough to prevent unnecessary death from war wounds and diseases? Why were the food and provisions so bad on both sides? Did General Order 100, promulgated in July 1863, change anything in the field or the prison pen? These and other questions are addressed in this fine work. Thus, I salute David Keller and everyone involved with this project. It is well worth the effort and a wonderful contribution to POW history in general and Civil War studies in particular.

ROBERT. C. DOYLE, PHD
October 2014

What might well be the largest mass grave in the United States can be found in a peaceful, garden-like cemetery on the south side of Chicago. Beneath a forty-foot-tall granite-and-bronze memorial gathered together in a grass-covered earthen mound are the bones of between 4,200 and 6,000 soldiers of the Confederate States of America. These soldiers did not die at Gettysburg in the desperate charge at the high tide of their cause, nor were they among the fallen at Shiloh's harvest of death, after which it was said that "the South never smiled." Rather, these soldiers died far from the scenes of battle in one of the largest cities in the United States at the Camp Douglas prisoner of war facility. More Southern soldiers died at the camp than on any Civil War battlefield. The purpose of this book is to explore how and why this happened and to examine the significance of the true story of Camp Douglas as it relates to our understanding of the Civil War.

The story of Camp Douglas has been alternately distorted and neglected. In the city of Chicago, the existence of the massive prison camp, as well as the city's important role in the Civil War, has been all but forgotten. Only recently, through the efforts of the Camp Douglas Restoration Foundation, has this Civil War site even been graced with a historical marker. While the history of the camp is little appreciated in Chicago, it is well known among Civil War scholars and enthusiasts. Since the era of Reconstruction in the wake of the war, Camp Douglas has played a role in the "Lost Cause" mythology that paints the Southern Confederacy in heroic hues and condemns the Union war effort as unnecessarily brutal. "Eighty Acres of Hell" or "the Northern Andersonville" are phrases used in this genre to describe Camp Douglas.

The book before you is an attempt to cut through both the indifference and the invective that have shadowed our understanding of this important chapter of Civil War history. It is the most comprehensive study to date of the camp's history and a thoughtful effort to dispassionately place it in the larger context of the awful war that divided our nation. Through these pages, the bones in that all-but-forgotten mass grave take on new life in memory, not as tools in a partisan cause but as real men caught up in a tragic history.

THEODORE J. KARAMANSKI
Loyola University, Chicago

David Keller has single-handedly taken on the task of bringing the Civil War to Chicago. Few Chicagoans ever think of their city as being a significant spot where major Civil War events occurred. But Dave reminds us that 4,243 Confederate soldiers are buried at Oak Woods Cemetery. They died at Camp Douglas, the city's prisoner of war camp, where 30,000 Confederate soldiers were imprisoned at one time or another between 1862 and 1865. There are 4,243 names on the Confederate monument at Oak Woods Cemetery—these are the ones who could be identified. Due to poor record keeping, there were probably many more unaccounted for.

But housing Confederate prisoners is only part of the story of Camp Douglas. The camp started life as a training center for Union soldiers. Over forty thousand Union soldiers trained there. Another chapter in the camp's life was as a prison for Union soldiers who had been "paroled" after being captured by Confederates. They were exchanged for Confederate prisoners and served their terms at Camp Douglas. Yet another chapter in the camp's life was its role as a training center for African American soldiers when the Union army finally recruited and deployed its Colored Troops.

Chronicling the history of Camp Douglas permits Dave to explore how the treatment of prisoners of war evolved, how the parole system worked, how conditions in Union prisons compared with those in Confederate ones, the identities of those in command and how diseases, such as smallpox, were dealt with.

Daily life in the camp is also explored by allowing five prisoners to tell their own stories via their diaries and letters. This brings the reader closer to the reality of camp life.

Finally, Dave addresses the mystery of where the camp's boundaries are today. As an advocate for establishing an interpretative center at the site of the camp through the Camp Douglas Restoration Foundation, the Bronzeville community has been galvanized to join in the archaeological investigation of the site and to help promote educational efforts to bring the story of Camp Douglas and Chicago's role in the Civil War to the city's schoolchildren.

Tom Campbell
author of Fighting Slavery in Chicago

In a few months, the long sesquicentennial of the Civil War will come to a close. It has been a remarkable opportunity to memorialize through the lens of the twenty-first century the most divisive and bloody period in American history. Recognizing anniversaries of specific battles, recalling the heroic exploits of Confederate and Union men and women and contemplating the terrible loss and the shattering of lives that four years of bitter struggle brought into the homes of Americans across the North and the South has been an uplifting and sobering experience. Yet one could also argue that we did not need a sesquicentennial to acknowledge and remember the Civil War—the impact and legacy of that war is all around us today and still influences our politics, our race relations and our identity as Americans. And one might even wonder if, after four years of sesquicentennial events, lectures, programs, reenactments and a steady stream of new scholarly and popular books about all aspects of the war, there is anything left to say.

This volume on the history of Camp Douglas proves that we still have much to say and much to learn about the Civil War. Although Chicago was not the site of any battles, it had an enormous impact on how the war was waged and, ultimately, the North's victory. The city's strategic location at the center of national rail and water networks, its critical industries and its corps of Lincoln supporters were key factors in the Union cause. But the drumbeat of war in Chicago sounded loudest and longest at Camp Douglas, the training facility that was converted into a prison for Confederate soldiers. Letters and diaries provide intriguing glimpses into prison life and routine at Camp Douglas, but many of these details are unreliable at best. Although Camp Douglas was the most significant Civil War feature in Chicago, our knowledge about it is sadly scant.

In this remarkably researched book, David Keller aims to provide the most comprehensive overview of Camp Douglas published to date. He has brought together first-person observations and memories to give us a sense of what life in the camp was like and to place that experience in the broader context of the Civil War and specifically the war in Chicago. Seeking to address the misunderstandings, misstatements and confusion about Camp Douglas, this volume is a welcome addition to our understanding of this period in Chicago's history and our larger understanding of Civil War history. Yet as any good historian, Dave also understands the limits of his sources and laments the paucity of records to cross-reference and cross-check facts. Thus, to a great extent, the history of Camp Douglas remains shrouded in mystery.

This book is one piece of a larger enterprise that deserves special acknowledgement. In 2010, Mr. Keller founded the Camp Douglas Restoration Foundation, a nonprofit foundation devoted to bringing greater public awareness to Camp Douglas. Among its most exciting initiatives is archaeological research on the site of Camp Douglas to identify and map the buildings and features of the camp and to recover any material evidence that reveals aspects of the lives of prisoners and their guards. Like many projects where historical records lead to a dead end and professional historians abandon it for more fertile areas of inquiry, an independent historian taking a creative approach to historical research is more successful in moving the ball forward. David Keller is one of those tenacious historians who have succeeded in expanding our knowledge of Camp Douglas, and anyone who loves Chicago history or Civil War history will be grateful to him for this wonderful book.

RUSSELL LEWIS

Executive Vice-President and Chief Historian

Chicago History Museum

Acknowledgements

Writing my first book was a task for which I was not well prepared. Without the support and help of a lot of people, it would still be only an idea. The board of directors of the Camp Douglas Restoration Foundation—Gary Benson, Rob Girardi, Phil Grinstead, Andy Irvine, Leroy Malone, Dean Rodkin and Bernard Turner—gave me encouragement and picked up the slack while I was writing. The Chicago History Museum staff, especially Russell Lewis, Libby Maloney, Ellen Keith, Lesley Martin and Angela Hoover, were very helpful in providing resources and assistance in my efforts. At the American Civil War Museum (Museum of the Confederacy), CEO Waite Rawls, curator Randy Klemm and archivist Teresa Roane provided great encouragement and assistance. Thanks to Thomas E. Buffenbarger, library technician, Research and Education Services, U.S. Army Heritage and Education Center, for special assistance with the Burke diary.

Chicago historians Ted Karamanski, Tom Campbell and George Levy, along with Dan Joyce at the Kenosha Civil War Museum, not only gave me enthusiastic support but also offered valuable assistance during my research. Rick Kogan, writer, radio personality and Chicago icon, believed in my work on Camp Douglas from the start and never failed to say yes to any request. Michael Gray of East Stroudsburg University in Pennsylvania spent time with me to discuss Civil War prisons. Sharon Woodhouse of the *Lake Claremont Press* gave me a quick course on the publishing industry. Professor Robert Doyle at Franciscan University of Steubenville not only provided encouragement but also read an early manuscript and offered many suggestions that improved the message.

Mary Jane (MJ) Grinstead's friendly and positive edits and suggestions made this book into something readable, as opposed to the ramblings of an untrained writer and amateur historian. MJ, I'm not sure you were happy to have "volunteered" for this assignment. All I know is that I can't thank you enough.

Ben Gibson, Will Collicott, Hilary Parrish and the staff of The History Press made a novice feel like a veteran writer. Their gentle admonitions and understanding of my limitations showed professionalism seldom seen today. Thank you.

Last but certainly not least, thanks to my wife, Linda, who let me take over more than my share of our office while she stepped over books, binders and file folders. Linda also let me skip too many play dates.

With all of the support and encouragement from my friends and colleagues, any errors or omissions in this book are my own.

D. KELLER

Introduction

Camp Douglas, a major facility for the reception and training of nearly forty thousand Union soldiers, a prison for thirty thousand Confederates and the most significant physical presence in Chicago during the Civil War, is an often-misunderstood chapter in the history of the Civil War. In fact, the complete story of the camp remains shrouded in mystery.

Today in Chicago, the history of the camp ranges from unknown to badly misunderstood. Theodore Karamanski's *Rally 'Round the Flag* provides excellent background on Chicago, Camp Douglas and the Civil War, as does *Civil War Chicago: Eyewitness to History*, which he edited along with Eileen McMahon. In addition to known information on Camp Douglas, much of this work is based on the personal recollections of prisoners and contemporaries in Chicago during the war. These works are used with reservation. Letters, diaries and journals of Civil War veterans are often considered the best sources of contemporaneous information on the war. However, this material represents individual experiences and feelings. Letters often reflected what the writer thought the recipient wanted to hear. In addition, many journals were written well after the war and include the frailties of age and time. The journals are also colored by the times in which they were written and the social pressures of the post–Civil War period. African Americans in these written reports are often referred to as "negros" or "colored." These references have been retained in quoted material.

The "Lost Cause" proponents who emerged after the war created an atmosphere that was not conducive to the critical reporting of prior or current events. News articles of the time might represent the best information available but, without attributing intent, frequently contain factual errors and represent the editorial policies of the regional publications in which they appear.

The firsthand experiences documented within this work come from those who were there during the peak of Camp Douglas's existence. All were enlisted men who were involved in a variety of camp activities. In their own way, these men provide sometimes-conflicting descriptions of life at Camp Douglas. A majority of the writings come from:

Robert Anderson Bagby's Civil War diary. Born in 1830 or 1831, Bagby was a member of the First Northeast Missouri Cavalry and a prisoner at Camp Douglas from January 1863 to March 1865. He served as a "nurse" in the prisoners' hospital for nearly all of this time, and his writings provide an interesting perspective on health at the camp.

Curtis R. Burke's Civil War journal, published in 1915. Burke, a member of Morgan's Raiders, Fourteenth Kentucky Cavalry, became an inmate at Camp Douglas in August 1863 at the age of twenty-one and remained there until March 1865. Burke appeared to have significant resources, making his stay at Camp Douglas more comfortable than most.

John M. Copley's Civil War "Sketch," published in 1893. Copley, Forty-ninth Tennessee Infantry, was held at Camp Douglas from December 1864 until June 1865. His colorful writing style and vivid recollections, published thirty years after his stay, provide graphic details of camp life.

William D. Huff's diary. Huff, Thirteenth Louisiana Infantry, was a prisoner at Camp Douglas from October 1863 to May 1865. In addition to his written narratives, Huff's diary contained drawings made during his stay. He was a musician and engraver who sold his works to prisoners and guards for tobacco and other mediums of exchange at Camp Douglas.

James Taswell Mackey's diary. Born in 1842, Mackey, a corporal in the Forty-eighth Tennessee Infantry, was captured at Fort Donelson and arrived at Camp Douglas on February 22, 1862. He remained a prisoner until he was exchanged on September 7, 1862. After his exchange, he was promoted to second lieutenant and again captured in October 1863. He died of smallpox in prison at Fort Delaware.

The firsthand experiences of these five men often confirm traditional reports on life at Camp Douglas. In the same respect, their comments reflect inconsistencies of historic reports and add to the understanding of camp life. They provide a human face to life at Camp Douglas.

Reference is made in this material to the Camp Douglas Restoration Foundation, a nonprofit foundation organized in 2010 "to be a significant participant in increasing awareness of the Civil War in the Upper Midwest, especially Illinois and Chicago." Activities of the foundation include educational programs, archaeological investigations on the site of Camp Douglas and community outreach to provide information on Camp Douglas. The ultimate goal of the foundation is to develop a museum on the site of the camp.

My objective is to examine more closely the circumstances surrounding the camp's existence and history. Factors that resulted in the loss of over five thousand Confederate lives, along with the circumstances that led to high death tolls and poor conditions in all Civil War prisons, need to be reviewed with the clarity of twenty-twenty hindsight.

Too often we judge history based on current knowledge and standards. While reflecting in this manner might be meaningful in rewriting history, it does little to aid in the understanding of events as they unfolded. My purpose in writing this book is to expand the collective understanding of the conduct of activities at Camp Douglas based on conditions in the 1860s, especially through the eyes of those who participated in the Civil War.

The conditions of Camp Douglas are examined in light of the twenty-first-century writings of scholars on the history of prison camps during the Civil War. Works by Robert C. Doyle, Drew Galpin Faust, James M. Gillispie, Roger Peckenpaugh and Charles W. Sanders are critical to better understanding conditions that existed in these camps.

Questions relating specifically to Camp Douglas are addressed, including the location of the western boundary of Camp Douglas, which has been in question since 1878; camp improvements over time; and the controversy concerning the amount of camp land provided by the estate of Stephen A. Douglas.

When comparing official reports and the reports of prisoners and the media, dates and statistics relating to Camp Douglas and the Civil War are often conflicting. These inconsistencies remain in the text of this material, as they offer specific examples of the difficulty in reconciling various observations. This information results in my conclusions, based on the

150-year-old information available today as well as twenty-first-century hindsight. Readers are encouraged to review this material and reach their own conclusions.

David L. Keller
Chicago, 2015

Chapter 1

The Role of Chicago in the Civil War

Chicago's Camp Douglas was created as a reception and training center in September 1861. Growing from a population of 108,305 at the 1860 census to 298,997 in 1870, Chicago was the fastest-growing city in the country during the decade of the Civil War. Since the 1850s, the city had been developing its "broad shoulders" with a rich history regarding the question of slavery. It was transforming from a frontier town incorporated less than thirty years before to the most significant city in the West.

Fed by the influx of Irish, German and other European immigrants, along with the nucleus of founding pioneers, the city searched for its identity. More than any city in America, Chicago was defined by the Civil War, which left a mark on the city and its citizens that would remain for years to come. Social restructuring, economic development and Chicago's role in the conduct of the war were but a few factors that shaped the city.

As it turns out, the leading protagonists of the Civil War—Abraham Lincoln, Jefferson Davis and Robert E. Lee—indirectly established Chicago as the rail center of the West. Eventually, this resulted in Chicago taking the leading role in the West from the older cities of St. Louis and Cincinnati. Rail prominence drove an expanded role for Chicago in the Civil War.

In 1854, the first bridge across the Mississippi River was being built. The Rock Island Bridge was to span the river from Rock Island, Illinois, to Davenport, Iowa. The bridge would connect the Chicago and Rock Island Railroad over the Mississippi River with the Mississippi and Missouri Railroad, leading ultimately to Council Bluffs, Iowa, and the Missouri River.

The railway to the developing West from that point on was to come through Chicago. President Franklin Pierce's secretary of war, Jefferson Davis, was concerned that the bridge was unsafe and should not cross the U.S. military installation at Rock Island. The future president of the Confederacy took this position in spite of the positive recommendation from U.S. Army lieutenant Robert E. Lee that it be built.

More importantly, Davis was concerned that the Rock Island Bridge was placed too far north and would reduce the effectiveness of the South as a transportation hub. He wanted a bridge at Natchez, Mississippi, to serve the Mississippi Delta. Davis took the matter to court in *United States v. the Railroad Bridge Company* in April 1854. The Circuit Court for Northern Illinois, in Chicago, ruled that the military installation on Rock Island, Fort Armstrong, had been abandoned and therefore the United States had no standing in the court.

The Rock Island Bridge opened on April 22, 1856, with a train of eight cars filled with passengers crossing over to Davenport, Iowa. Subsequently, riverboat interests in St. Louis and New Orleans sued in *Hurd v. Rock Island Bridge* to stop all bridges over the Mississippi. Abraham Lincoln was engaged by the railroads to defend the suit. Using his personal knowledge of the river and the earlier data compiled by Robert E. Lee, Lincoln presented the case for the importance of east–west travel as equal to north–south river travel. His knowledge of river currents, coupled with Lee's data and study of the crash of the *Effie Afton* into the bridge in May 1856, led him to infer that the crash was caused on purpose by the riverboat interests. He prevailed.[1]

Pro- and Antislavery Forces in Chicago

While Chicago was by no means unanimous in its support of the antislavery movement, significant elements of the city encouraged and were actively involved in the Underground Railroad and the abolitionist movement. In November 1837, early abolitionist Dr. Charles Volney Dyer hosted a public meeting in Chicago to protest the murder of Elijah Lovejoy, editor of the *Alton Observer*, the leading abolitionist newspaper in Illinois.[2] Dyer would go on to be active in the antislavery movement in Chicago throughout the Civil War. He was instrumental in the formation of the Chicago Anti-Slavery Society and in convincing Zabina Eastman, editor of the *Genius of Liberty*, successor to the *Alton Observer*, to come to Chicago to become the editor of Chicago's abolitionist newspaper, *Western Citizen*.[3]

In 1851, Deacon Philo Carpenter of the First Congressional Church, along with Dyer, Eastman and other local abolitionists, including famed detective Alan Pinkerton, organized a section of the Underground Railroad that led to the freedom of many escaped slaves.[4]

John Jones, a free black tailor, and his wife, Mary, were also instrumental in the Underground Railroad in Chicago.[5] Jones had come to Chicago in 1845 and by 1860 was one of the wealthiest African Americans in the country. He was a founder of the Olivet Baptist Church that today is located on the northern edge of Camp Douglas. He and Abram T. Hall, a free African American from Pennsylvania, were leaders in the opposition to the Black Codes. These were laws that, among other things, prohibited blacks from suing whites, owning property or merchandise or gaining an education.[6] In September 1850, Jones and other African American leaders in Chicago, including Henry O. Wagoner and William Johnson, invoked the proclamations of earlier struggles:

> *We who have tasted freedom are ready to exclaim with Patrick Henry, "Give us liberty or give us death"…In the language of George Washington, "Resistance to tyrants is obedience to God." We will stand by our liberty at the expense of our lives and will not consent to be taken into slavery or permit our brethren to be taken.*[7]

While Chicago was considered a hotbed of abolitionism in 1850, the proslavery movement also had strong advocates. The Illinois law making harboring a runaway slave a crime was upheld by the Illinois Supreme Court in 1843. The Chicago Common Counsel, after passing a resolution in October 1850 calling the Fugitive Slave Act "a cruel and unjust law [that] must not be respected," reversed its position and, after an impassioned presentation by Stephen A. Douglas, who supported the act, repealed its earlier resolution.[8] Illinois statutes also included the Black Codes, which severely reduced the rights of free African Americans.[9]

In addition to Stephen A. Douglas's support of states' rights and thus slavery, other Chicago civic leaders, including former mayors Levi Boone (1855–56) and Buckner Morris (1838–39), were noted Southern sympathizers. Both Boone and Morris were imprisoned at Camp Douglas for short periods of time for their Southern sentiments.[10] Morris and his wife, Mary, were tried as conspirators for their participation in the Camp Douglas Conspiracy of

Buckner Morris, mayor of Chicago Mayor from 1838 to 1839. *Chicago Public Library.*

Levi Boone, mayor of Chicago from 1855 to 1856. *Chicago Public Library.*

1864.[11] Southern-sympathizing Copperhead organizations, including the Sons of Liberty and the Knights of the Golden Circle, were also active in Chicago.[12]

The passion of the abolitionist movement in Chicago was demonstrated in the city's reaction to the enactment of the Kansas-Nebraska Act in 1854. This act repealed the Missouri Compromise of 1820, which prohibited slavery in the western territories, and thus opened the territories to slavery. The new act, sponsored by Illinois's Senator Stephen A. Douglas, supported the concept that inhabitants should determine slavery in their territories. In August 1854, Douglas defended the Kansas-Nebraska Act before nine thousand people in Chicago. When the hostile crowd booed and hissed him, Douglas ended his two-hour justification speech with, "Abolitionists of Chicago! It is now Sunday morning. I'll go to church, and you may go to hell!"[13]

Without compromising his states' rights position, Douglas redeemed himself with the Union and Chicago when he unequivocally supported President Lincoln and the war effort after the Confederate attack on Fort Sumter. On May 1, 1861, at the Wigwam in Chicago, he accused the South of a conspiracy. He then asked for Union support, saying, "Every man must be for the United States or against it. There can be no neutrals in this war, only patriots and traitors." On June 1, Douglas died in Chicago of typhoid fever.[14] His final act in support of the Union was a significant factor in Camp Douglas being named in his honor.

Chicago and the Surrounding Region Supply Troops for the War

Chicago, the state of Illinois and the surrounding region played significant roles in providing manpower for the Civil War. Illinois ranked behind only New York, Pennsylvania and Ohio in the number of men who enlisted. Almost 260,000 soldiers for the Union effort came from Illinois, with approximately 40,000 of those from the Greater Chicago region and more than 17,000 from the city itself. Nearly 35,000 Illinois soldiers died in the conflict, the third-highest total of all Union states. Throughout the war, Chicago and Illinois consistently met recruiting quotas. During the course of the war and seven calls for volunteers, Illinois provided 237,488 volunteers compared to a quota of 225,791, or nearly 6,000 over the quota.[15] Illinois required draft registration; however, between volunteers and the hiring of replacements, virtually no draftees entered the military from Illinois.

In Chicago, as in other places, filling of quotas was not without controversy, even among those who supported the war. In February 1865, a delegation from Chicago headed by Joseph Medill, publisher of the *Chicago Tribune*, and civic leaders attorney Samuel S. Hayes and Roselle M. Hough (a wealthy meatpacker and former commander of guards at Camp Douglas shortly after the beginning of the war) called on Abraham Lincoln to protest the December 1864 Illinois volunteer quota. They complained that the earlier troops provided by Chicago and Cook County had been undercounted and that the quota should be reduced. After Secretary of War Edwin M. Stanton informed the party that the quota would stand, Medill and the others continued to object. Lincoln tried to convince them that his decision was proper, but as objections continued, he bitterly stated:

> *Gentlemen, after Boston, Chicago has been the chief instrument in bringing this war on the country. The Northwest has opposed the South as the Northeast has opposed the South. It is you who are largely responsible for making blood flow as it has. You called for the war until we had it. You*

> *have called for emancipation and I have given it to you. Whatever you have asked for you have had. Now you come here begging to be let off from the call for men which I have made to carry out the war you have demanded. You ought to be ashamed of yourselves. I have a right to expect better things of you. Go home and raise those 6,000 men. And Medill, you are acting like a coward. You and your* Tribune *have had more influence than any paper in the Northwest, in making this war. You can influence great masses and yet you cry to be spared at a moment when your cause is suffering. Go home and send us those men.*[16]

In the hallway after the encounter, one of them said, "Well gentlemen, the old man is right. We ought to be ashamed of ourselves. Let us never say anything of this and go home and raise those men."[17] They did.

As Lincoln so well reiterated, the political and business climate in Chicago supported the war effort. Medill's *Chicago Tribune* was a long-standing supporter of Lincoln and the Union effort. Only the *Chicago Times* was an outspoken voice for the anti-war Peace Democrats and Southern sympathizers. Editor Wilber F. Storey and publisher Cyrus Hall McCormick were harsh critics of Lincoln and the prosecution of the war.

In June 1864, Major General Ambrose Burnside, commander of the Department of Ohio (which included Chicago), on his own authority, ordered the suspension of publication of the *Times*. After significant unrest by Southern sympathizers in the city and communications with President Lincoln, which included a weak petition supporting free speech by William B. Ogden, first mayor of Chicago and head of the Chicago and Northwestern Railroad, a request was made to President Lincoln by Republican Senator Lyman Trumbull and Congressman Isaac N. Arnold to rescind Burnside's order.

Lincoln, who was unaware of Burnside's actions and in spite of his personal animosity toward the *Times*, requested that Burnside lift the ban. On June 4, just before a pro-suppression rally planned by the Republicans, the ban was lifted.[18]

Civilians in Chicago Support the War

The civilian population directly supported the war effort—not by being deprived of food and comforts, as happened in the South, but by supporting the troops mustered in in Chicago. Preparation and donation of uniforms, banners and flags were common before the troops went off to war. Women of Chicago were very active in their support of the medical needs of the Union military. When the first prisoners arrived at Camp Douglas in February 1862, the local population was interested in seeing the "secesh."[19] Local women conducted a drive to provide clothing, blankets and food for the prisoners when they first arrived. Churchwomen from Chicago opened a shelter in a renovated hotel for soldiers passing through Chicago in 1863. Before the end of the war, a Soldiers' Rest building was erected in Dearborn Park.[20]

The development of the U.S. Sanitary Commission traces its roots to New York, where Unitarian minister Henry Bellows created the basis for the organization shortly after the beginning of the war. A combination of today's Red Cross and the USO, the commission provided guidance on sanitation and soldier welfare, as well as inspecting military prison camps throughout the war and providing medical aid for the Union army. The Chicago branch of the Sanitary Commission was organized in October 1861 by Chicago civic and religious leaders. While the officers were men, the work of the commission was done mainly by the women of the community. Eliza Porter, wife of a Unitarian minister, was the first director of operations. She left after a few months to lead a group of nurses to Cairo, Illinois. Her group later followed Union troops to Vicksburg, Chattanooga and Atlanta. Jane C. Hoge and Mary Livermore replaced Porter and carried on the works of the commission through the end of the war.

The Soldiers' Home near Camp Douglas. *Chicago History Museum.*

The Chicago branch was one of the most successful of the Sanitary Commission and took a leading role in soldier welfare in the Western Theater. The Northwestern Sanitary Fair in July 1863 raised $86,000 for the war cause. For the 1865 fair, the commission received a copy of the Emancipation Proclamation written in the hand of President Lincoln. The proclamation was sold to Thomas D. Bryan for $3,000. Bryan then donated it to the Soldiers' Home, after which it was placed in the archives of the Chicago Historical Society for safekeeping. That fair raised $24,000.[21] Unfortunately, the proclamation was destroyed in the great Chicago fire in 1871.

In 1863, the Soldiers' Home was constructed as a hospital and convalescent home for Union soldiers. The building, located at Thirty-fifth Street and Lake Park Avenue, is the last remaining building in Chicago directly related to the Civil War and was designated a Chicago Landmark in 1966. After its use as a convalescent home, the facility served as an orphanage for the Catholic Church until the 1960s. After an extensive renovation in 2008, it now houses offices for seventeen archdiocesan agencies.[22]

Chicago and Illinois Soldiers Make Their Mark on the Civil War

Company C of the Eighty-second Illinois Infantry is a great example of community support for the war effort. The only all-Jewish force to fight in the Civil War, the unit was nicknamed the Concordia Guards because the men volunteered at a B'nai B'rith Ramah Lodge at the Concordia Club in Chicago. The unit was recruited largely through the influence of Henry Greenebaum, a Chicago banker and alderman. Within three days of the unit's formation, the initial 96 recruits (from a total Jewish population in Chicago estimated to be 1,500) raised $11,000 for the benefit of the men. It is likely that the Jewish community provided the largest proportional representation to the war of any ethnic community in Chicago.

Organized in Springfield on October 28, 1862, the unit was assigned to the Army of the Potomac, commanded by General Ambrose Burnside. After participating in many eastern battles, it was transferred to General Sherman and participated in his March to the Sea. The Eighty-second was mustered out in June 1865 in Washington, D.C.[23]

Chicago's first war hero was Colonel Elmer E. Ellsworth, who led the Chicago Zouaves to their win at the international drill competition in 1860. Ellsworth later returned to his native New York at the outbreak of the war to form the New York Zouaves. On May 24, 1861, while leading his unit, he saw a Confederate flag flying over the Marshall Hotel in Alexandria, Virginia. Ellsworth tore the flag down and was shot to death by the hotel manager, James W. Jackson. Colonel Ellsworth was the first Union officer to be killed in the war. President Lincoln wept when he heard the news.[24]

Illinois supplied 177 general officers during the war, including Lieutenant General Ulysses S. Grant from Galena. One of the most successful "political generals" was John A. Logan, who, at the end of the war, commanded an army corps in Sherman's Atlanta Campaign. On the other hand, Major General John A. McClernand, an Illinois Democrat and early appointee of President Lincoln, was an excellent fighter but an overly political officer. He was a constant thorn in the side of General Grant until he was relieved during the Vicksburg Campaign.

General Benjamin H. Grierson, a citizen-soldier from Jacksonville, conducted a six-hundred-mile, sixteen-day raid with two Illinois cavalry regiments across Mississippi while Grant maneuvered toward Vicksburg. (Ironically, Grierson had a strong dislike of horses.) Shawnee West Pointer James H. Wilson swept through the South at the end of the war, arresting Jefferson Davis. Other Illinois generals fought with distinction in both the Eastern and Western Theaters during the war.[25]

The growth of Chicago, a center for immigrants and African Americans, provided a significant source of volunteers for the Union military. Approximately 50 percent of Chicago's 1860 population was foreign born. Except for St. Louis (60 percent), this was the largest percentage of any major U.S. city. About 145,000 individuals, mostly Germans, Irish, Bohemians and English, immigrated to Chicago during the 1860s.[26] Of the total number of Illinois volunteers, 18,000 were from Germany, 12,000 were from Ireland and 2,000 were African American, most from the Chicago area.[27] In 1860, the Illinois population of "Free Negros" was 7,628, with 955 listed in Chicago. These "Free Negros" represented .46 percent of the state's population and .88 percent of Chicago's. Union states' population of "Free Negros" was approximately 1.2 percent, or 225,224, at the time of the 1860 census.[28] African American participation in Illinois units would have been greater if not for the delay in the state actively recruiting "Colored Troops." Massachusetts and New York were active in recruiting African Americans well before Illinois, and many Illinois African Americans went east to volunteer. Many of those joining Illinois United States Colored Troops (USCT) were escaped slaves from Missouri and Arkansas and free blacks from Wisconsin.

The Twenty-ninth U.S. Volunteer Infantry (USCT), an Illinois unit mustered in at Quincy, Illinois, in April 1864 (with Companies B and C and many of Company D recruited in Chicago), had the unenviable distinction of taking the greatest number of casualties at the Crater at Petersburg, Virginia, in 1864. Lieutenant Colonel John A. Bross commanded the regiment. Bross, from Chicago, was the brother of influential Republican and co-publisher of the *Chicago Tribune* William Bross. Lieutenant Colonel Bross had been assistant U.S. marshal and U.S. commissioner in Chicago. Early in the war, he raised two companies of the Eighty-eighth Illinois Volunteers and fought at the Battles of Perrysville and Murfreesboro. All officers of the Twenty-ninth USCT were white. Noncommissioned officers and privates were African American.

Initially, the Twenty-ninth USCT, part of Brigadier General Edward Ferrero's Fourth Division, Ninth Army Corps, and other USCT were selected by Major General Ambrose Burnside to lead the attack after the explosion at the Crater. They trained for several days, as the mission would require them to perform difficult maneuvers. But Burnside was overruled by Major General George Meade, Army of the Potomac, who did not want "untested" troops leading the attack. After a heated discussion, Meade agreed to present the matter to Lieutenant General U.S. Grant. Grant sided with Meade—not because he agreed with Meade but because he was concerned about possible political ramifications if the Colored Troops were to lead the assault and lose. The initial assault was carried out by the First Division, Ninth Army Corps, led by Brigadier General James Ledlie. Both he and Brigadier Ferrero, who was reportedly drunk, hid in a bombproof during the assault. The result was a disaster, with leaderless, untrained troops failing to meet their objectives. The men of the Twenty-ninth were in the second wave of the Union attack and ill prepared for this new assignment. They bogged down in the crater itself and took major casualties. In all, 3,475 of the Ninth Corps' 15,272 men lost their lives in the attack, including Lieutenant Colonel Bross. General Grant's consideration of the political ramifications of subjecting the troops to possible excessive losses resulted in the near destruction of the unit. Nineteenth-century values and the mistrust of the fighting ability of the African American soldier were misplaced. No one knows what would have resulted if these well-trained troops had been allowed to execute their original mission.[29] Chicago and Illinois suffered the loss of many fine African Americans forever to the community.

The performance of Illinois units in the Civil War is without comparison; 58 percent of military-aged men in the 1860 census in Illinois participated in the war compared to 48 percent for New York and 41 percent for Massachusetts. Illinois Union soldiers participated in nearly every engagement in the Western Theater and many significant battles in the East.

Commerce and Industry Support the War Effort

Chicago's growing industrial base provided great support to the war effort. The meatpacking industry was a primary supplier of meat for the armies, especially in the Western Theater. From 1859 to 1863, processed pork production grew sixfold. By 1862, Chicago had become the largest meatpacking city in the world, earning the title of "Porkopolis."[30]

Clothing and shoe manufacturers quickly changed their production to meet the needs of the military. From 1861 to 1863, the clothing industry in Chicago grew from $2.5 million to $12 million, while shoes and boot manufacturing grew from $2.5 million in 1861 to $14.5 million in 1864.[31] Sailmakers became providers of tenting material. Grain merchants provided food for men and animals, and tanners were important suppliers of tack for military horses. The overall amount of grain marketed in Chicago increased from two million bushels in 1856 to fifty million bushels in 1861.[32] In 1862 alone, the Chicago quartermaster purchased over $4.7 million in war materials from Chicago.[33]

Both Cincinnati and St. Louis, Chicago's greatest competitors in the West, had strong economic ties to the South. The loss of these markets during the war decreased both cities' influence and provided Chicago with additional opportunities. This changing economic condition was not only very profitable; it also provided a basis for industrial growth through the end of the nineteenth century. Chicago, the "city on the make," was making it big, thanks to the war.

When soldiers began to come to Chicago to volunteer or pass through during the war, the city was ready to receive them. Chicago had the reputation of being the "wickedest city in the country." The vice district along Randolph Street between State and Dearborn Streets was well established by 1860. Mayor Francis C. Sherman, elected in 1862, was flexible and tolerant,

Prisoners Square, Camp Douglas. *Illinois State Historical Society*.

imposing no crackdowns on beer or Sunday drinking. Both U.S. soldiers and Confederate prisoners would enjoy the benefits of Chicago's Levee District. In this setting, Camp Douglas began operations in September 1861 and continued as a significant military facility until December 1865.

Chapter 2

Creation and Development of Camp Douglas

On April 15, 1861, as the clouds of war reached the Midwest, President Lincoln called for seventy-five thousand ninety-day volunteers to put down the revolt; Illinois was faced with signing up enough men to meet its six-thousand-troop quota.

States were responsible for raising, equipping and providing initial training for volunteers. Illinois governor Richard Yates organized Illinois into three military districts. The Northern District included the area from Cook County on the south to the Wisconsin state line and from Lake Michigan to the Mississippi River. Governor Yates selected Judge Allen C. Fuller, later Illinois adjutant general, to recommend a site for a reception and training camp for Northern District volunteers. Judge Fuller, who had no military background, selected a site near the fairgrounds, just south of the Chicago city limits, that had housed the U.S. Agricultural Society's Seventh National Exhibition in 1859.[34]

Had Judge Fuller received the insight of military authorities, Camp Douglas might never have been located in the area bounded by Cottage Grove Avenue on the east, Giles Avenue on the west, Thirty-first Street on the north and Thirty-third Place on the south. The site, some four hundred yards from the Illinois Central Railroad and Lake Michigan to the east, was poorly drained, swampy land subject to the severe weather off the lake. These conditions were to plague the camp, its Union soldiers and its Confederate prisoners for nearly four years. Camp location and drainage were brought into question frequently over the years. In May

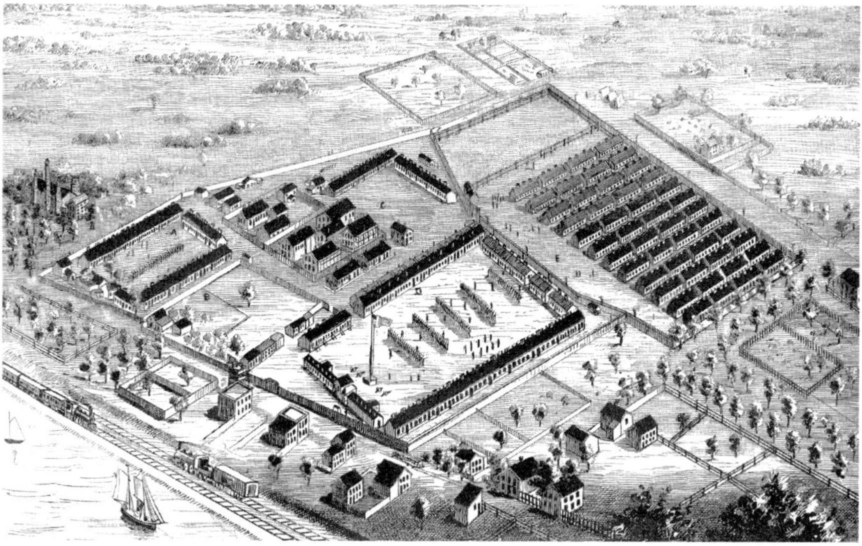

An aerial view of Camp Douglas showing the Illinois Central Railroad. *Chicago History Museum.*

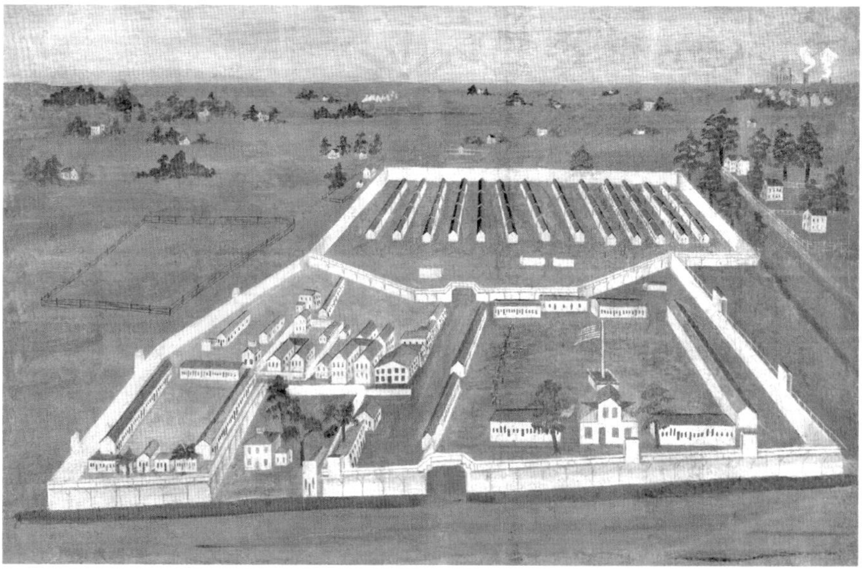

An 1864 painting of Camp Douglas by Albert E. Meyer. *Chicago History Museum.*

1863, Thomas Hun and Mason Cogswell, doctors for the U.S. Sanitary Commission, reported: "Ground at Camp Douglas is most unsuitable for a hospital or even for barracks, being wet and without drainage. We think it ought to be abandoned."[35]

Western Boundary a Controversy

The exact location of the western boundary of Camp Douglas has been in question since 1878 and is one of several of the camp's "mysteries." A drawing of the camp dated January 1, 1865, showed the western boundary as Kankakee Avenue (now Martin Luther King Jr. Drive); however, William Bross presented a paper to the Chicago Historical Society on June 18, 1878, that showed the western boundary as Forest Avenue (now Giles Avenue). Giles Avenue is located two streets west of King Drive, or about a quarter of a mile away. Bross had prepared the map with the assistance of Captain E.R.P. Shurley, assistant adjutant general at the camp; Captain Charles Goodman, chief quartermaster; and Captain E.V. Roddin, assistant quartermaster. The former officers walked the campsite in 1878 with Bross to retrace its boundaries.

Bross indicated that a number of streets had been "cut through," causing some confusion. The group concluded that the western boundary was Forest Avenue. After Bross completed his text for the presentation, Charles Cook, boss-carpenter at the camp, provided Bross with a survey that showed the western boundary as Calumet Avenue (one street west of King Drive), adding further to the controversy.[36] In 1885, A.T. Andres also located the western boundary at Forest Avenue.[37]

In 2012, the Camp Douglas Restoration Foundation and the Illinois Institute of Technology (IIT) began a project to create Virtual Camp Douglas. Students from IIT created a virtual map of the camp using historical maps, drawings, photographs and personal descriptions. A drawing of the camp (see page 45) prepared around 1864 by Colonel J.A. Potter, Chicago quartermaster, entitled *United States Q.M. Dept. Barracks, State of Illinois, County of Cook, West Side Camp Douglas* contained a detailed description of barracks in Prisoners Square, including measurements of buildings, streets and the distances between buildings, as well as the location of the stockade fence.[38] This detail was the basis for the creation of the virtual map. Using other data, namely a January 1, 1865 camp drawing probably done by J.A. Potter,

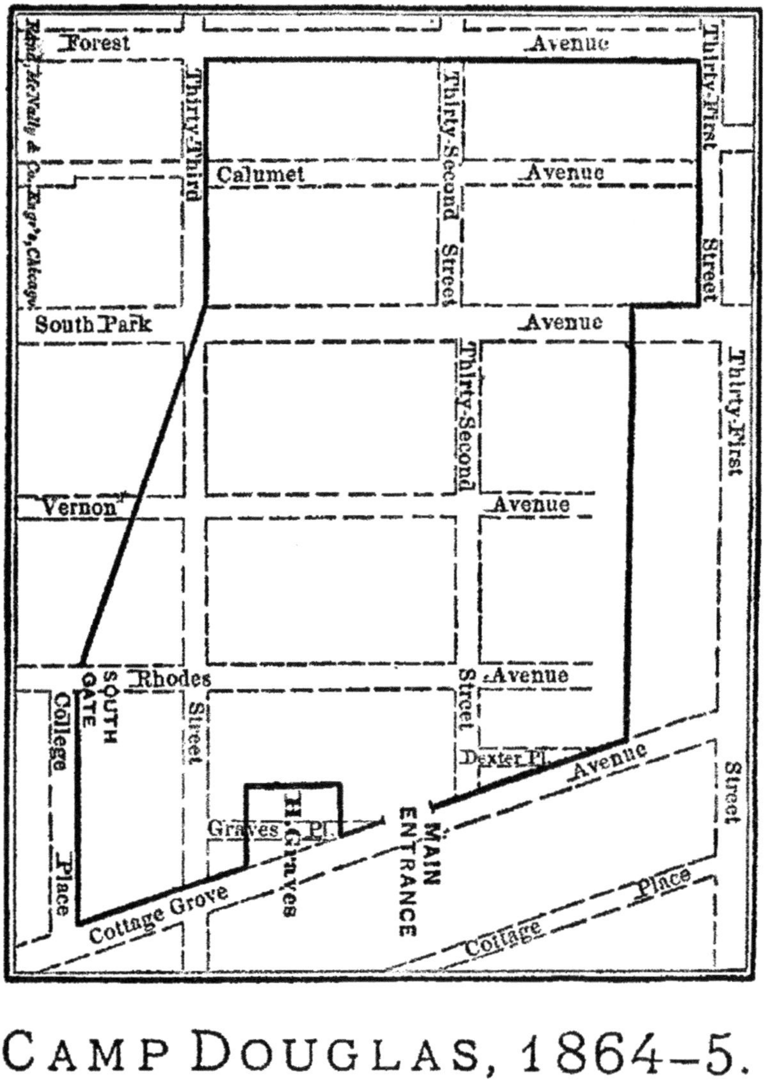

A map of Camp Douglas showing the western boundary at Forest Avenue. *Map by William Bross.*

students extrapolated the other building dimensions and placement. The completed virtual map of the camp was superimposed on current maps using the known eastern boundary, Cottage Grove Avenue, and the north and south boundaries. When viewed, the western boundary was clearly Giles Avenue, as described by Bross. This conclusion has been further

An overlay of Camp Douglas on a modern satellite map. *Author's collection.*

confirmed by the findings of archaeological excavations by the Camp Douglas Restoration Foundation and DePaul University in 2013 and 2014. This research supports the boundary at Giles Avenue and solves the mystery of the western boundary.

Camp Douglas Named for Stephen A. Douglas

Immediately south of the proposed site for Camp Douglas was the University of Chicago, located on College Avenue (Thirty-third Place) at Rhodes Avenue. The university had no relationship to the current University of Chicago (founded in 1890), which is located approximately four miles south of the site of Camp Douglas. Later known as Old Chicago University, this

Henry Graves donated approximately thirty-five acres of his land for Camp Douglas. *Chicago Public Library.*

first University of Chicago was founded in 1857 with a grant of ten acres of land by Stephen A. Douglas. After a variety of financial setbacks, and partly due to its proximity to Camp Douglas, the school closed in 1886, and the main building was torn down in 1890.[39] During the years of Camp Douglas, the school was in continuous operation.

Although most of the sixty acres of land for the camp was provided by other landowners, Camp Douglas was named for the late Stephen A. Douglas, whose home was southeast of the camp. The primary land donor was Henry Graves, who provided approximately thirty acres.[40] Mrs. Graves refused to give up her home at Cottage Grove and Thirty-second Street, so the camp was built around the Graves residence. Mrs. Graves was never known to comment on the impact some seventy thousand men and scores of horses, all lacking adequate sanitary facilities, had on her quality of life.

In 1865, the estate of Stephen Douglas petitioned the U.S. government for compensation for 45.00 acres of land used by Camp Douglas. A land plat provided in the petition showed land mostly south of the permanent camp. Some Stephen Douglas land might have been used by satellite camps, which were common in the early period of Camp Douglas. In March 1866, after an exchange of information between the U.S. quartermaster general, Chicago quartermaster Lieutenant Colonel L.H. Pierce and the Douglas estate, the estate agreed that its claim, now for 27.98 acres plus 5.0 acres used as the smallpox hospital, lay outside the southern edge of the main camp. The Chicago quartermaster reported that some of the property near the southern edge of the camp had been used from "Sept. 1860 to Aug 1862 for camping grounds for regiments and batteries."[41]

Pierce also confirmed that the bodies of five hundred who died in the smallpox hospital had been buried on the property in 1862. Also, a portion of this land had contained stables used by the Ninth Illinois Cavalry; the stables had been removed. This information indicates that virtually none of the Douglas estate was used for the main camp, other than the five acres of the permanent structure, the smallpox hospital.[42]

Crowded Conditions at Camp Douglas

Satellite camps were developed as a necessity, as the permanent Camp Douglas did not have sufficient facilities to house troops being mustered into the Union army. In the initial phase of the war, recruiting was carried out by filling regiments consisting of approximately one thousand men. Satellite camps such as Camp Dunne, Camp Song, Camp Mulligan, Camp Siegel, Camp Freemont, Camp Webb, Camp Ellsworth, Camp Mater and Camp Doggett, usually named after a commander or financial backer, were common.[43] For example, the Ninetieth Illinois Volunteers (Chicago Irish Legion) were at Camp Dunne, one mile south of Camp Douglas, but followed the routine laid out for soldiers at Camp Douglas and acted as guards for the Confederate prisoners.[44] These camps could be found as far south as Hyde Park and as far west as today's Dan Ryan Expressway. Approximately fifteen infantry, cavalry and artillery units were mustered into the Union army at Camp Douglas between May 1861 and February 1862.[45]

Area Near Camp Douglas

Cottage Grove Avenue was an improved road connecting downtown Chicago to the town of Hyde Park. Amenities along the avenue included a hotel near the camp and a horse-drawn trolley that, interestingly, offered transportation for escaped prisoners to visit downtown Chicago. In addition to the Graves home, which made the eastern boundary irregular, a Mrs. Bradley had property on the northeastern boundary of the camp. This property resulted in a setback from Thirty-first Street of approximately one hundred feet from

Cottage Grove Avenue west to the end of Garrison Square. There is no evidence that Mrs. Bradley had any problems with the camp other than encroachment from an unauthorized food vendor and wastewater from the camp flowing onto her property.[46]

Changes and Improvements at Camp Douglas

The permanent camp was hastily constructed and in a constant state of flux, with most buildings made of whitewashed wood unfinished on the inside. The only building built on a stone foundation was likely the camp headquarters. Construction of the camp was supervised by its first commander, Colonel Joseph H. Tucker, with much of the early construction completed by the Mechanic Fusileers, journeyman carpenters and apprentices from the Mechanics Institute of Chicago. On December 1, 1861, the Fusileers destroyed and burned part of the camp stockade fence in a mutiny over being reclassified as an infantry unit. They were put down by the camp guard force and required to repair their damage.[47]

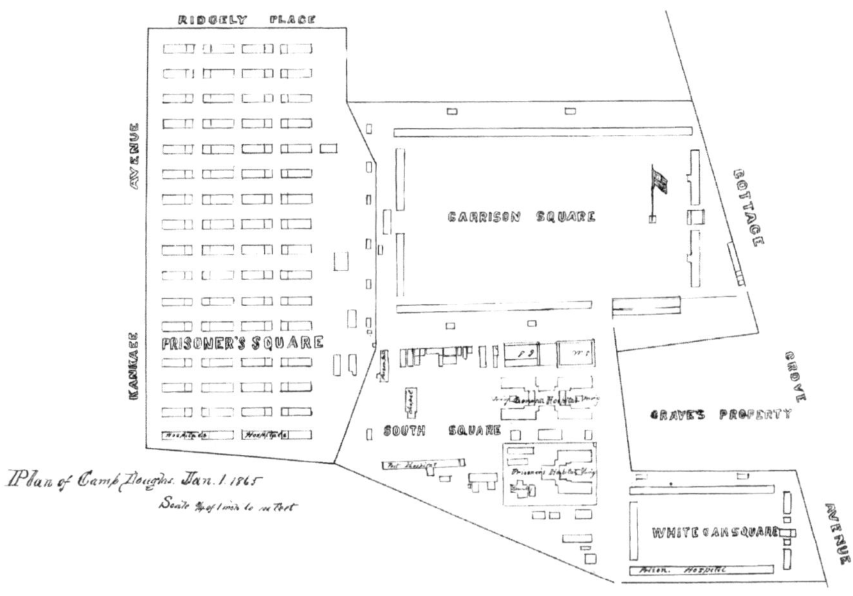

A drawing of Camp Douglas, January 1865. *National Archives.*

A common statement made by historians is that treatment of prisoners during the Civil War worsened as the war continued and that prison camps deteriorated during the war.[48] Contrary to that notion, Camp Douglas was constantly being improved. Additional barracks were erected, sewage removal was improved and water facilities were enhanced during the camp's existence. While these improvements might not have been as timely as desired or as extensive as warranted, they were improvements nonetheless.

The Four Squares

Garrison Square

Garrison Square, to the north fronting on Cottage Grove, contained the camp's headquarters, an eighty- by forty-foot building constructed on a stone foundation,[49] and barracks for officers and men permanently assigned to the camp. Officers' quarters consisted of individual rooms, and company barracks were approximately eighty-five feet in length by twenty-four feet wide.[50] Garrison Square was approximately twenty acres

The front gate of Camp Douglas. *Chicago History Museum.*

in area. The barracks surrounded a large rectangular parade ground, with the camp flagpole located west of the headquarters building. Stables were initially located at the southern end of Garrison Square, as were other administrative buildings.[51] The main gate was located on Cottage Grove at Garrison Square. The original water hydrant serving the entire camp was located in the northeast corner of the square. Over time, a total of three hydrants served the officers and men living in buildings in Garrison Square.

Prisoner Curtis Burke described his first view of Garrison Square on his arrival at Camp Douglas on August 18, 1863: "The Camp appears pretty large, with a high fence running around it. I saw a post office, barber shop, picture gallery, two sutler stores, a commissary house, and a chapel. The first square we entered [Garrison Square] was the Yankee quarters off to the left, with long barracks on the sides and a flag pole in the center."[52]

White Oak Square

The ten-acre White Oak Square, to the south fronting on Cottage Grove, contained one-story (nine feet high) barracks that were 105 feet by 24 feet and divided into three rooms. These barracks housed prisoners until early 1864, when Prisoners Square was opened. Upon the arrival of the first prisoners, Union soldiers were moved from White Oak—although prisoners and guards were sometimes housed together there. The exterior of the building was covered with twelve-inch vertical strips of wood (with three-inch boards covering the seams) and a tar-paper roof. This type of construction would continue throughout the life of camp. Three woodstoves (later converted to coal-burning stoves) heated each barracks. The latrines, also referred to as sinks or privies, were out back. In the early days of the camp, these latrines were simply shallow trenches—twenty feet long, six feet wide and four feet deep—that ran through the middle of White Oak Square. In October 1863, Dr. A.M. Clark, medical inspector of prisons, found the latrines with "no management at all [and] in filthy conditions."[53] One hydrant provided water service for the square. Also behind the barracks was a separate kitchen with long tables and benches for one hundred men.

In August 1863, Burke described White Oak Square as follows: "All the barracks were long one-story buildings, four of them forming a square with a cook house on the outside of the square to each barracks and the length of the barracks. The barracks were divided into little rooms with two to ten bunks in each and doors and windows to match, also one long room with a row of bunks on each side of the room, mostly three bunks deep or high, and room for about eighty men."[54]

William Huff described the barracks and camp in October 1863: "[We] were put in barracks…they were long low buildings partitioned off into rooms with a stove in each. They are as comfortable as could be expected for prison. In the rear of the barracks is a building intended for a kitchen, but there were so many prisoners when we arrived that most of the kitchens had to be used for barracks."[55]

In February 1864, Burke recounted, "The whole number of barracks [five] three hundred feet in all in length have the rollers under them and a capstan on each side near one end to pull them along."[56] These barracks and two others were moved into Prisoners Square. They were placed on "short legs" so that guards could view under them and inspect for possible tunneling.

There was also an underground dungeon in White Oak Square. Approximately eighteen feet square with a hatchway in the ceiling of the guardroom as access, the one-story building was shaped like a cross, with the guards located in a windowless area on the first floor. One small window provided the only light.[57] Dr. Clark reported twenty-four prisoners in the space and considered it "utterly unfit."[58] This dungeon was used to house both Union and Confederate soldiers guilty of misconduct.

By January 1, 1865, a prison hospital had been constructed on the south side of White Oak Square.

While another uncertainty (if not a mystery), it is likely that White Oak Square had limited use after the completion of Prisoners Square. The dungeon was probably used as confinement for Union soldiers who had violated regulations.

South (or Hospital) Square

South Square, or Hospital Square, was located on approximately ten acres west of White Oak Square along Thirty-third Place. This area contained the hospitals and various quartermaster and other support facilities. In 1865, by the end of the war, there was also a general hospital (100 feet by 80 feet) with four wings, a prison hospital (100 feet by 28 feet) with two wings and 225 beds and a large (204 feet by 28 feet) 180-bed post hospital.[59] The *Chicago Tribune* reported the construction of a new prisoner hospital in February 1864, noting that it would "accommodate about 300 men."[60]

The prison hospitals, according to prisoner-nurse Robert Bagby, were divided into three divisions. These administrative divisions consisted of the prisoner hospital, completed in January 1865; the hospitals in Prisoners Square; and the White Oak Square prisoner hospitals. The smallpox hospital appears to have been operated separately.[61] The exact number of hospital beds is unknown. It appears that there were no more than 550 to 600 beds available. In December 1862, the *Chicago Tribune* reported that the "General Hospital" could accommodate 400 patients "if required."[62] On January 18, 1865, Bagby reported that there were 744 patients in the prison hospitals.[63] George Levy states in his book that an 1864 medical study found 577 patients in all hospitals and 1,547 sick in barracks.[64] In his report on the history of Camp Douglas, I.N. Haynie, Illinois adjutant general from 1865 to 1868, indicated that each hospital could accommodate 300 inmates.[65] There is no evidence to support Haynie's numbers. Inspecting surgeon C.T. Andrews reported in July 1864 that there were 200 to 225 beds in the main prison hospital with a planned addition of 75 beds.[66]

A chapel was constructed in 1861 and converted to a prisoner hospital. Another chapel was constructed in December 1864. The government would not provide a bell for the new chapel, so prisoners and garrison personnel provided coins that were melted and used to cast the bell.[67] The bell is now held by the Chicago History Museum.

Coal sheds, an ordnance warehouse, a quartermaster warehouse, a butcher shop, a blacksmith shop, a tool house with a four-horsepower engine to operate a crosscut and rip saw and a bakery with running water were also constructed in the South Square.[68]

Prisoners Square

Prisoners Square, located on twenty acres on the western side of the camp, ran from Thirty-first Street to Thirty-third Street. Initially, it contained barracks in a square configuration similar to that of Garrison Square. When the newly constructed barracks opened in January 1864, there were thirty-six barracks completed; there would be a total of sixty-six by late 1864. The barracks were situated in four rows, with the building oriented with the long dimensions east to west. The one-story barracks, measuring ninety feet by twenty-four feet (with twenty feet of one end devoted to a kitchen), were raised on wooden legs approximately four feet tall. This construction reduced the ability of prisoners to tunnel out while also retaining a floor to

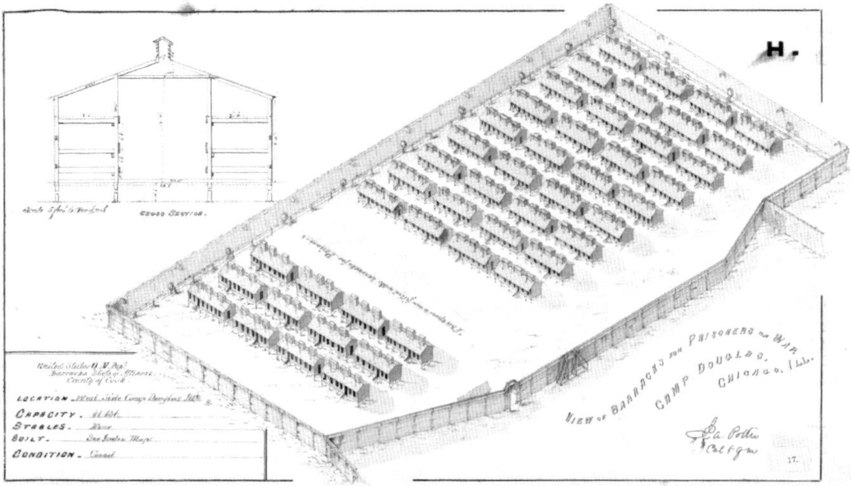

An 1864 drawing by Captain Potter showing details of the barracks in Prisoners Square. *National Archives.*

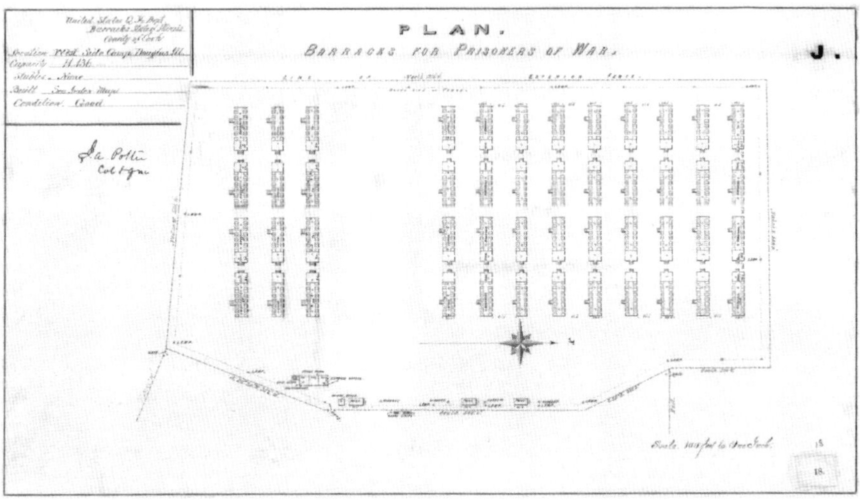

An 1865 drawing by Captain Potter showing the location of the stockade in Prisoners Square. *National Archives.*

keep out some dampness and cold. The buildings were twenty-five feet apart with fifty feet of street in front of each row. They were at least twenty-five feet from the stockade fence.

A variety of administrative buildings were also contained in Prisoners Square. These included washhouses, coal sheds, a sutler's store, a drugstore,

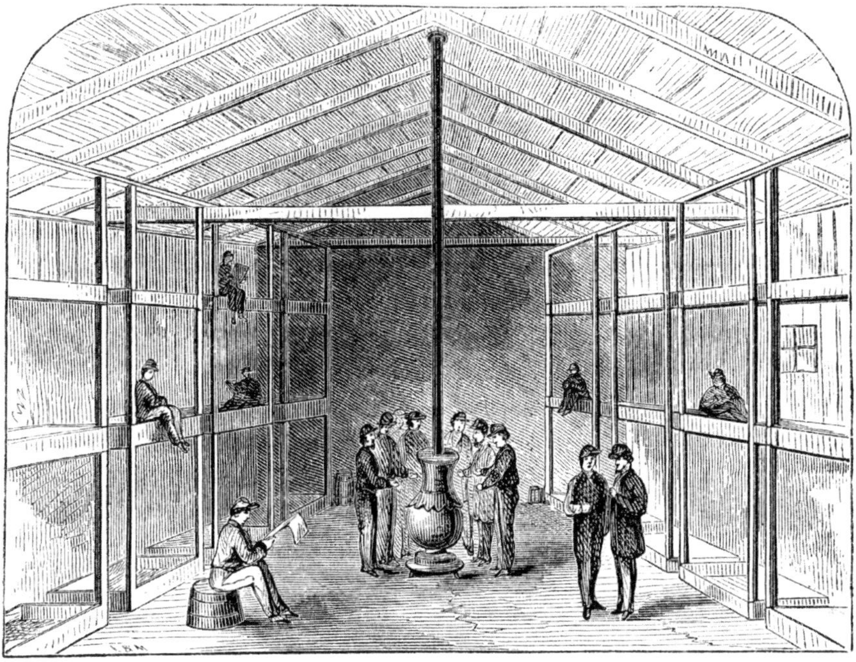

An interior view of the prisoners' barracks. *Chicago History Museum.*

a surgeon's office, a photo studio, a guardhouse and an express office. Hydrants were added, with a total of four serving Prisoners Square.[69] Quartermaster Porter reported that there were nine hydrants in the square by 1865. In addition, a fireplug was added with seven hundred feet of hose capable of sending a stream fifty feet.

A dungeon, known as "Four Diamonds" by the prisoners and "the Monitor" by guards, was constructed in Prisoners Square just inside the gate from Garrison Square. It was eight feet square and seven feet high with a door in front and two diamond-shaped windows on two sides.[70]

Construction of new barracks and repairs to existing structures continued through 1864, with prisoners providing work details for the construction. Improvements to the barracks included brick chimneys for the kitchens and air vents for the roofs, although the vents might not have been completed.

Prisoner John Copley arrived at Camp Douglas in December 1864 and gave this graphic description of his surroundings in Prisoners Square:

> *We will now take a bird's-eye view of all within this inclosure* [sic], *and see if we can find anything to admire, or strike the fancy, and note that*

which is most novel and interesting. Well, if our admiration of everything is to be judged by our silence and sullen looks, we admire everything. First, let's see of what this institution consists, or rather, what constitutes the prison. Here are near twenty acres of ground inclosed [sic] *by a plank wall sixteen feet high, upon the top of which a walk or parapet has been constructed four feet wide for the chain-guard, or sentinels, to walk.*

Near the ground, within ten feet of the plank wall, a strip of plank one inch thick by three inches wide, has been tacked upon the top of little posts about one foot high, the entire circumference of the prison grounds; this line is named and called the "Dead Line"; it means and signifies death to every living prisoner who attempts to cross it.

There is only one place of egress or ingress to this inclosure [sic], *and that through the aperture of the big gate, through which we have just entered. This gateway is large enough to admit easily a line of soldiers four ranks deep—that is, four abreast. Two guards are kept at this gate, one on the inside of the inclosure* [sic], *the other outside.*

The ground is nearly level…perhaps sloped towards the lake just enough to discover it with the natural eye and to make it drain very well. Our quarters consist of barracks, one story high and four feet off the ground upon posts. They were originally flat on the ground. While they were flat on the ground, every few days, one or more of the prisoners would escape from the prison, and after an examination it was discovered that the prisoners tunneled out under the barracks; this caused the Federal authorities to raise them off the ground, so that no one could tunnel out without being caught in the act, and before any success had been obtained. They were built of boxing plank, one inch thick by twelve inches wide, and twelve feet long. The barracks were not ceiled overhead; the cracks were stripped with pieces of plank one inch thick by three broad.

There are fifteen rows of barracks with four to each row, and number from one to sixty. Two hundred men are assigned to each barrack. The reader can see at once, that although there were so few barracks, they could afford quarters for quite a little army. Each barrack had a kitchen attached to one end, generally the north end, in which our beef and other meats were cooked. The main door or place of entrance to the barrack was near the center in one side, and so arranged that any one could enter or leave at any time during the day or night, and never be heard, and after night without being seen. The barracks had but one place of entrance to each, except that from the kitchens, which were not passable for the men. This entrance to the barracks had no shutter, and remained open; there were no windows in the barracks through which light could enter; sometimes the prisoners whittled out small light-holes between the planks of the walls large enough to admit some light, which enabled them to read such literature and books as could be obtained. These little apertures, or light-holes, sometimes were dangerous places to sit by, as when discovered by the Federal guards on the parapets, they possessed an attraction for minié balls.

A frame structure was erected on the inside, from the floor to the roof, in tiers or rows above each other the entire circumference of the barrack, divided by narrow strips of plank; on these structures we slept; they were called "bunks." Each bunk would contain two men comfortably; upon these we spread our bedclothing, and also kept many little trinkets of small value hid under our blankets. Everything here was not in season, but we dreamed at large and woke in prison. The barracks were supplied with heating stoves, two to each barrack, one placed at each end; that is, one stove to every hundred men.

The kitchen was separated from the sleeping apartment of the barrack by a partition wall, which extended from one side of the barrack to the other. The main entrance to the kitchen was at the rear or north end, which had a door with a shutter. The entrance into the barrack was through a square hole made in the partition wall, which cut off the kitchen from the barrack. This opening was about the size of the cashier's window in the National banks of the present day, perhaps it may have been a trifle larger, and was named and called the "Crumb Hole," from this fact, nothing except our rations ever passed through it, which were handed by the cooks through this for distribution, and we could obtain them through no other.

This crumb hole was closed by a slide door. When it slid back and left the aperture open, there would be a general rush to it by all the men in the barrack. After our rations were handed through from the kitchen to the inside of the barrack, this door would be closed and remain closed until the next meal. Stepping up to the cashier's window in a National bank to cash a check very forcibly reminds one of going up to these crumb holes at Camp Douglas, to receive our kitchen hash or slop; the cashier when he counts out the cash and pushes it through from the inside, reminds one of the head cook when he shoved our rations through the crumb hole to the sergeant of the barrack.

I have a perfect horror for these openings or windows, and I dislike the very thought of stepping up in front of these seeming crumb holes in National banks, they so forcibly recall the recollections of the crumb holes in our barracks at Camp Douglas, and to see them in the banks makes me feel like I am back within that prison barrack every time I enter a bank. I have a suspicion that the pattern and model for making these particular windows in the National banks at this day had their origin at Camp Douglas, were patterned after, and modeled from the crumb holes in our barracks at that place, they bear such a close resemblance to, and have such a similarity in workmanship. If I am correct in my surmises, the ingenious Yankee who invented those at Camp Douglas could make a fortune, if living, by prosecuting the National banks for an infringement of his patent. The kitchens were supplied with large pots or kettles for cooking purposes. They held from forty to sixty gallons of water each.

There were streets, between the rows of barracks, which were near twenty feet wide and thrown up in the middle from each side to make them drain.

Wash-houses were conveniently located on different parts of the prison grounds. They were box houses, the cracks being stripped same as the barracks, and one story high. These were supplied with hydrants, which conveyed the water to the inside, and also with tubs, buckets and soap, but minus towels.

Coal sheds had been erected on the inside of the inclosure [sic] *of the prison walls, and under these the coal we used for fuel was deposited. It was hauled from the outside by the Federals; sometimes a detail of prisoners would be sent out under guard to assist in hauling it. Near, and a little east of the entrance gate to the prison, a small barrack or office was located. This was comfortably arranged on the inside, and used by the officers of the guard, and occupied by them day and night. It was the headquarters of Lieutenant Fife, commandant of the police guard on the inside of the prison square.*

Not far from the officers' quarters a store-house had been erected, which was called a "Sutler's store," from the fact that the man who conducted and carried on the business there was a sutler. A short distance from the sutler's store, a post about four feet high was firmly set in the ground, on which were written little notices, advertisements and such general news as were allowed to come within the prison square. This post was called the bulletin board, and the news posted on it, grape-vine dispatches or grape-vine telegrams. News in our favor, or which they thought we would appreciate, never appeared on this bulletin board.

Within a short distance of the entrance gate, across the street and west of the officers' quarters, there was still another institution, which was one of the horrors of the prison, and more interesting than all the other institutions within the inclosure [sic] *of the prison walls. It was an underground room or place about ten feet deep, covered with plank and dirt, the top just above the surface of the ground. This institution was named and known as the dungeon, which meant and signified midnight darkness. It had the right name. We dreaded this underground abode equally as bad as some so-called Christians do a cyclone. Nothing within this gloomy cell could ever feel the gentle rays of the sun. It was all darkness—black-darkness to both soul and body of the poor victim*

> *who was so unfortunate as to be doomed to it. There was but one door or place of entrance, and it rather small. The furniture of this institution was very scarce, consisting mostly of a chain and two cannon balls chained together. The inhabitant of this room had to wear the chain and balls to his ankles while an inmate thereof. We often called this the doghouse.*[71]

The windowless barracks described by Copley might have been the barracks moved from White Oak Square. Barracks shown in various photographs of Prisoners Square clearly indicated windows in the buildings. The "doghouse" described by Copley was also known as Four Diamonds Dungeon.

At the south end of Prisoners Square, two barracks were converted into prisoner hospitals in January 1865.

The camp was surrounded by a stockade fence that was modified over time. Initially, the fence was approximately six feet high. As the prison compound developed, the stockade fence around Prisoners Square was replaced with one between twelve and fourteen feet high with a guard walkway and observation positions along the outside of the fence. Large reflector oil lamps were also added in 1864. In June 1864, inmate William Huff noted, "Lamps have been put up all around the fences and are kept burning all night that a guard may see a prisoner before he gets to the fence and fire at him."[72] Burke investigated the lamps in April 1864, noting, "Just at dark I took a walk through camp to see how the lamps at the foot of the fence threw their light. I found that the lamps were so close together and the light so brilliant that it would be almost impossible to get to the fence without being discovered by the guards on top."[73]

Approximately ten feet inside the stockade fence in Prisoners Square was a "dead line" (described by Copley) marked with a low (eighteen-inch) railing. Any prisoner crossing this line was subject to being immediately shot.[74] Water was provided by a three-inch city water line in Garrison Square; in October 1864, this line was increased to six inches.[75] Initially, sewer facilities were nonexistent, as the shallow latrines were simply used until full and then covered with dirt. In October 1863, a wooden sewer was placed along the southern edge of the camp along Thirty-third Place. The sewer was two feet high and eighteen inches wide. Water from the hydrants was used to flush sewage from the camp directly into Lake Michigan. The condition of the latrines continued to be a problem even with the added sewer facilities. Some latrines were converted to box toilets that had to be emptied by hand, producing an additional health hazard. Most of the construction of the sewer and additional latrines was done by prisoners, who were paid mainly in tobacco.[76]

Copley commented on the sewer facilities in Prisoners Square, writing, "At the north end of the streets, the water closets, more familiarly known to soldiers by the name of sinks, were located. The water was conveyed within the prison square by pipes leading from the lake to the reservoir, and from that to the prison. A sewer conveyed the filth from the sinks to the outside of the prison walls, the water being conveyed by hydrants into the sewers to wash off the filth from the prison."[77]

Throughout Camp Douglas' existence, mud and standing water caused problems. While the sewer lines helped, the nature of the land created water conditions that were both uncomfortable and unhealthy. Frequently, prisoners were required to dig ditches and perform other labor to reduce camp drainage problems. In addition, work details were organized to provide general cleanup of the camp.[78]

When the camp was razed in December 1865, it contained over two hundred buildings, including sixty-six barracks housing prisoners. Approximately 3,600 feet of water piping and 5,000 feet of sewerage were reported at the camp's closing.[79] The last healthy prisoners left the camp in July 1865. In November, government property was sold off. Buildings, barracks and fencing were torn down and the lumber sold. One row of barracks, probably officers' quarters, was sold and moved to the 700 block of Thirty-seventh Street in Chicago, where they remained as residential property through the early 1940s.[80]

The officers' barracks were moved in 1865 and used as private housing until the 1940s. *Chicago History Museum.*

Today, nothing above ground remains as evidence of the camp's existence. Recent archaeological excavations by the Camp Douglas Restoration Foundation have identified some artifacts from Camp Douglas. A historic marker was erected in 2014 on Martin Luther King Drive north of Thirty-third Street by the Illinois State Historical Society and the Camp Douglas Restoration Foundation.

Changes to the Camp

During the camp's existence, there were many buildings built, removed and modified. Modification included converting stables to barracks, converting the chapel to a hospital and modifications in reaction to prisoners' actions, such as removing flooring or raising barracks on footings up to five feet. In June 1863, after the camp population was reduced to nearly zero by an exchange, the camp was in deplorable shape. Damaged and burned buildings, deteriorating fences and an inadequate water and sewage system were clearly evident. The U.S. Sanitary Commission recommended that the camp be abandoned.[81]

Nonetheless, repairs were made, and the camp continued as a major prison facility. In December 1863, camp commander Colonel Charles V. DeLand ordered the floors in prisoner barracks removed to prevent tunneling. Later, barracks were raised about four feet to allow guards to see any activity under them.[82] Removing the floors created a very unsanitary condition, as water would seep through the soil, creating a mud floor. In late 1863, Colonel DeLand stated, "We have been building fencing, laying sewers, water pipe, etc. This has left large holes in the fence, openings in the ground, and during the day there have been large numbers of workmen passing to and fro among the prisoners. Of course all this has produced confusion. Prisoners have slid out the holes in the dark, have passed out as workmen, and in a variety of ways have eluded the vigilance of the guards."[83]

Contrary to comments that conditions in the camp deteriorated over time, physical improvements were made to the camp throughout its existence. Additional and repaired barracks and other buildings were evident until the camp was effectively shut down in the fall of 1865. Improvements in water and sewage over the life of the camp were significant and provided slightly enhanced sanitary conditions. However, none of these improvements and changes could keep up with the rapidly growing prison population from mid-1863 until the end of the war.

Chapter 3

Camp Douglas as a Reception and Training Center for Union Troops

Nearly forty thousand Union soldiers were received and trained at Camp Douglas during its existence. The first troops received in September 1861 were Brackett's Ninth Illinois Cavalry. Within a month, there were nearly five thousand men in the camp. From the arrival of the first troops, Camp Douglas and its satellite camps acted as a reception and training center for the Northern District of Illinois. Nearly two dozen infantry regiments, two cavalry regiments and a number of artillery units were mustered in at Camp Douglas. Almost half of that number had begun reporting to the camp by November 1861. Because of the number of troops arriving in the early stages of the war, satellite camps were used extensively.

The infantry regiment was the basic recruiting and maneuvering unit during the war. A regiment consisted of approximately one thousand soldiers, plus officers and staff. The last regiments to muster in at Camp Douglas were the 93rd and 127th Infantry in September 1862. These units remained at Camp Douglas until November 1862. The 113th Regiment mustered in at Camp Hancock (probably a satellite camp) near Camp Douglas in November 1862 and departed in December.[84] After Camp Douglas became a prison camp in February 1862, its ability to accommodate regimental-size units was significantly reduced. In October 1862, when the prison population was significantly reduced after a prisoner exchange, approximately three thousand Union soldiers were being organized and equipped at Camp Douglas.[85]

Well before prisoners were to arrive at the camp, the city was finding what it was like to have soldiers living in the community. After a series of incidents in January 1862, the *Chicago Tribune* ended an article on soldiers' behavior at "the Home" and other establishments on Clark Street with the following: "It is threatened by the City authorities to do something at the next session of the Common Council to prevent these infamies of the military. It is high time. If the commandants of the regiments and those in charge of the camp will not see to their men, it will fall upon the city fathers to take them in charge."[86]

Camp Fry, located in Chicago at what is now Clark and Diversey Streets, continued to provide mustering in for regiments through the end of the war. In December 1864, the 147th Infantry Regiment was the last to be mustered in.[87] Both Camp Douglas and Camp Fry were active in mustering out units after the war.

Camp Douglas continued to receive Union soldiers throughout its existence. These units were small, usually no more than company size (one hundred men). The Union army needed to get replacements to its regiments as quickly as possible; therefore, small units often remained at Camp Douglas and other reception centers for only a short period of time. Often, these men received little training. They might have been given a uniform, but rarely did they receive a weapon. They were immediately sent to the battle zones for training with the regiment.

The Concordia Guards (Company C) of the Eighty-second Regiment probably spent some time in Camp Douglas before moving to Camp Morton in Springfield for mustering in. It is reported that African Americans were received at Camp Douglas, although there is little evidence of this other than material provided by Ernest Griffin, who operated the Griffin Funeral Home on the site of Camp Douglas until his death in 1995. Griffin's grandfather Charles Griffin, a member of the Twenty-ninth USCT, was part of Company B recruited in Chicago. The elder Griffin stated that his company was housed at Camp Douglas before being mustered in at Quincy, Illinois. Ernest Griffin maintained a memorial to his grandfather at the funeral home until the home was closed in 2007. A majority of the artifacts from that display are now housed in the Chicago History Museum.

The camp operated on a daily routine established by the camp commander. This routine in 1862 was as follows:

Sunrise	*Reveille & Roll Call*
7:30 am	*Breakfast*
8:30 am	*Surgeon's Call*
9:30 am	*Guard Mounting*
10:30 am	*Drill & Roll Call*

Noon	*Dinner*
1:00 pm	*Fatigue Call*
2:00 pm	*Drill and Roll Call*
3:00 pm	*Battalion Drill*
Sunset	*Retreat and Roll Call*
9:00 pm	*Tattoo, Roll Call & Taps*[88]

Discipline of the new soldiers concerned the commanders. Colonel Joseph Tucker issued General Order 10 in mid-1862 in response to concerns about the Union soldiers accidentally wounding fellow recruits after failing to develop weapons proficiency. The order directed that "whenever arms are to be discharged the men should be sent to the Lake Shore." No one knows how effective the order turned out to be or how many soldiers marched the four hundred yards to the shore of Lake Michigan.

On September 10, 1862, Tucker issued his General Order 18. The order authorized Captain C.P. Bradley, Chicago's general superintendent of police, to "arrest all Soldiers from the Camp found in the City of Chicago without written passes in proper form and to report same to me."[89]

Paroled Union forces who surrendered to Major General Stonewall Jackson in September 1862 at Harpers Ferry, Virginia, in a prelude to the Battle of Antietam were sent to Camp Douglas to serve out their parole until exchanged. On September 28, Union brigadier general Daniel Tyler was in charge of delivering to Camp Douglas approximately eight thousand paroled soldiers from the 60th and 32nd Ohio; the 65th Illinois (commanded by Colonel Daniel Cameron); the 31st, 111th, 115th, 125th and 126th New York; and the 9th Vermont, as well as artillery units from the 1st Independent Indiana Battery, the 15th Indiana Battery, the 19th Ohio Battery, the 5th New York Battery and Phillips's Chicago Battery. Of the eight thousand, approximately one thousand were from Illinois.[90]

At this time, provisions for prisoner parole and exchange were being transferred from an individual commander's prerogatives to being established by the Dix-Hill Cartel, promulgated on July 22, 1862.[91] The individual commander's exchanges had been accomplished loosely under the provisions of the War of 1812 Cartel, in which paroled prisoners agreed, in writing, not to participate in military activities until duly exchanged.[92] Unfortunately, the timing of the parole of the troops from Harpers Ferry, so soon after the conclusion of the Dix-Hill Cartel provisions were announced, caused confusion in the administration of the provisions. The paroled soldiers knew nothing of the cartel until the terms were published in the *Chicago Tribune*.[93] Many of the paroled soldiers believed that, through parole, they were removed from any U.S. military authority. Brigadier General Tyler and the staff of Camp Douglas, on the other hand, expected the soldiers to act in a military manner, to respect military authority and to follow all military orders.

General Tyler anticipated problems with the paroled men when, on October 5, 1862, he asked the U.S. Army adjutant general for clarification of provisions of the Dix-Hill Cartel that prohibited the parolees from performing military duties. He wrote, "Indeed, under the last clause of article 6 the parole forbids performance of field, garrison, police, guard or constabulary duties. If we comply with this paragraph it appears to me it leaves little else for us to do with the men but feed and clothe them and let them do as they please." This concern set the stage for Tyler's continuing problems with the paroled Union soldiers.[94]

Conflict erupted when 150 members of the 32nd Ohio "escaped" by scaling and destroying part of the stockade fence. They were followed to downtown Chicago, where they were found enjoying "a good time." Captain H.R. Enoch, Camp Douglas provost marshal, captured and placed most of the escapees in confinement in White Oak Square.[95] This was to be the first of many such incidents with these Union troops until their exchange in December 1862. Court-martials were called for "mutinous soldiers" from the 9th Vermont and 125th New York for disobedience of orders, contempt of officers, assaulting officers, selling whiskey rations, tearing down enclosures and burning barracks.[96]

On October 23, 1862, General Tyler reported to Colonel Hoffman a mutiny of the Sixteenth Ohio Volunteers. Tyler had ordered the Sixteenth U.S. Infantry from Hyde Park to provide perimeter security for the camp. However, he eventually indicated that the men of the Sixteenth Ohio had "caved in" and that their behavior had markedly improved. After developing a plan to move all paroled units into the camp proper from the fairgrounds east of the camp within ten days, he believed the situation was under control and returned to normal camp operations.[97]

In a letter to his father on September 29, 1862, William L. Brown, Chicago Mercantile Battery, commented, "The paroled men from Harpers Ferry are nearly all here and a harder looking set of customers I never saw. Ragged, dirty and nasty with few exceptions and most of them have only been in the field about five weeks. I talked to several smart fellows and they say they are treated like dogs."[98]

On October 11, 1862, the first of three fires was set in the barracks of paroled units (32nd Ohio). The second fire, in the 65th Illinois barracks, occurred on October 18, and the third occurred on November 21 in the barracks of the 115th New York.[99]

All paroled troops had been exchanged and removed from Camp Douglas by December 1862. Only the Ninth Vermont was to remain at Camp Douglas as guards, eventually leaving in April 1863.[100] The paroled Union soldiers created more ill will and caused substantially more damage to government property than all of the Confederate prisoners housed at Camp Douglas.

With the announced arrival of the first Confederate prisoners in February 1862, remaining Union regiments (except guards) were moved from White Oak Square and eventually removed from Camp Douglas altogether. The camp was preparing to take on the role of one of the most significant and infamous prison camps in the Civil War.

Chapter 4

History of the Treatment of Prisoners of War in America

Before addressing Camp Douglas as a prison camp, it is important to consider the history of prisoners of war. Modern historians have provided significant insight into the social, military and political climate that has shaped treatment of prisoners of war from the founding of this nation. Not until the Hague Conference of 1899 was the question of treatment of prisoners of war adequately addressed by the United States, as part of the international community. General Order 100, issued by President Lincoln on April 24,1863, and authored by Francis Lieber, formed the basis for the 1899 Hague Agreement.[101]

Robert Doyle, in his excellent book *The Enemy in Our Hands*,[102] traces the history of prisoners of war in this country. Charles Sanders, in *While in the Hands of the Enemy: Military Prisons of the Civil War*,[103] provides a critical view of both the North and South in the administration of Civil War prisons. James Gillispie, in *Andersonvilles of the North: The Myths and Realities of Northern Treatment of Civil War Confederate Prisoners*,[104] effectively discusses the "Lost Cause" and its impact on the perception of Civil War prisons.

The phrase "prisoner of war" is inaccurate in describing enemy combatants captured prior to the late eighteenth century. Early war captives were killed, placed into slavery, ransomed or immediately paroled. In *Voices from Captivity*, Doyle indicates that in mediaeval Europe, only the wealthy or well connected were ransomed; the average soldier received a death sentence.[105] The needs of a moving army did not allow for the management of captives. The nature of gentlemanly wars and the very conduct of later wars encouraged parole of captive soldiers of equal political and social standings and slavery or death to the infidels. Imprisonment was often limited to senior officers or political prisoners.

In Carl von Clausewitz's *On War*, written in 1832, he stated, "Now, in the combat all action is directed to the destruction of his fighting force, for this lies in the conception of combat." Of prisoners, he advised, "Artillery and prisoners are therefore at all times regarded as the true trophies of victory, as well as its measure, because through these things its extent is declared beyond a doubt."[106]

With this backdrop, the conduct of war in the Americas was shaped by the French and Indian War (1754–63), the Revolutionary War (1775–83), the War of 1812 (1812–14) and the Mexican War (1846–48).

The French and Indian War was fought with relatively few soldiers supplemented by numbers of Native Americans. The British and colonial forces never exceeded about seventeen thousand men, and the French troops were rarely above seven thousand. Captives were frequently subject to massacres, with few treated as prisoners of war. This effect is attributed to the participation of Native Americans, who were considered savages, and the small-unit, mobile nature of the conflict.

In 1775, prior to the Continental Congress declaring war against England, Ethan Allen and his Green Mountain Boys attacked the British at Fort Ticonderoga, New York. After his capture and three-year imprisonment, Allen indicated that the British policy was to kill the prisoners. He believed that eleven thousand were killed during the Revolutionary War. According to Doyle, prisoners in the Revolutionary War were treated more like felons than soldiers.[107]

The American Revolution offered the first glimpse of the conduct of war on the North American continent in regards to management of prisoners of war. Parole or exchange was common during this time. The American Continental army captured an estimated fourteen thousand enemy soldiers and sailors. These numbers severely taxed the Americans' ability to house and feed the captives.[108] As a result, parole and exchange was the common practice throughout the war. British prisoners presented no moral, ethical or legal problems and most often were exchanged.

Hessians captured at Trenton in 1776, however, were another matter. There was little precedent for the treatment of foreign combatants or mercenaries. Nonetheless, the Americans conformed to common practice as much as possible. For example, wounded Hessians captured at Trenton were paroled and left in Trenton while able-bodied soldiers were moved out of Trenton and ultimately scattered in various places, where they took up civilian life in the colonies.[109] General Washington and Congress encouraged humane treatment of British prisoners. Officers were most often paroled locally to await exchange. Private soldiers were housed in simple barracks with little attention paid to security.[110]

After Kings Mountain (1780), General Washington wrote:

> *All prisoners taken by Colonel Campbell* [at Kings Mountain] *have been dismissed, paroled and enlisted in Militia Service for three months except 130. Thus we have lost by folly, not to say anything worse, of those who had them in charge up to 600 men. I am told Lord Cornwallis has lately made a proposition to General Smallwood for exchange of all prisoners in North and South Carolina. If it is upon terms that are just and equal, I shall avail myself of it for a great number of prisoners is a heavy weight upon our hands.*[111]

Based on the social and political climate at the time, British prisoners were treated fairly well. British officers were often honor-paroled to a local area, where they lived among the civilian population at their own expense.[112]

The worst treatment reported during the war was in the British prison ships that held American sailors or privateers. Often termed "death ships," these prison ships were located in Wallabout Bay, New York; Charleston Harbor, South Carolina; and St. Lucia, West Indies.[113]

The Treaty of Amity, ratified in 1785 between the United States and King Frederick the Great of Prussia, was the first time the United States addressed the treatment of prisoners of war. While not specific, Article 24 addressed prisoner treatment in general, noting that captors were to "furnish them with rations as they allow the common soldier in their own service."[114]

The War of 1812 contributed to the creation by British and American representatives of a cartel at a meeting in November 1812 in Halifax, Nova Scotia. This cartel addressed treatment of prisoners, exchange of prisoners, treatment of noncombatants and terms of parole. The 1812 cartel document became the cornerstone for the Dix-Hill Cartel of 1862 between the Confederate and Union forces. The Dix-Hill Cartel, however, was confined to the mechanics of parole and exchange and was silent on the treatment of prisoners. Most noteworthy was the provision that prisoners would be paroled within ten days of capture. This provision led to the notion that prisoners would not be held as prisoners of war for extended periods of time.

The Mexican War offers little insight into the handling of prisoners of war. The short, successive battles of this war produced many captives. As many as ten thousand Mexican captives were simply paroled home.[115]

In each of these wars, Americans were unprepared to deal with captured enemy military. Unfortunately for those fighting in the Civil War, nothing was learned from this unprepared state.

Looking at the Civil War in comparison with prior or subsequent American wars is challenging. The sheer magnitude of the Civil War resulted in unique problems. There were 211,400 Union prisoners of war in the South and 220,000 Confederates in the North. Of these, 30,218 Union prisoners and 26,436 Confederates died in captivity.[116] When considering the prisoner of war question with a twenty-first-century mindset, these numbers are even more revealing. In World War I, World War II, Korea and Vietnam combined, a total of 142,227 U.S. military members were captured and held; 125,171 were returned after the conflicts, while 17,034 died while prisoner.[117] This 11.9 percent mortality rate for these wars compares to 15.1 percent for Union internees and 12.0 percent for Confederate prisoners. The sheer number of prisoners held during the Civil War, over three times as many as in all twentieth-century American wars, demonstrates the magnitude of the problem facing civilian and military leaders in the North and South during the Civil War.[118]

The Lost Cause's Impact on the View of Prison Camps

The emergence of the Lost Cause justification by the South was best described by Gillispie when he wrote, "At the end of the Civil War, the South was faced with a rather serious intellectual dilemma. On the one hand there seemed to be evidence that the Richmond authorities, if the testimony given at the Wirz [commandant of Andersonville Prison] trial was to be believed, had been quite brutal and unchristian toward hapless prisoners of war."[119] The Lost Cause was a literary and intellectual movement intended to reconcile the loss by the honorable South to the brutal North. The movement intended to maintain the correctness of the Southern lifestyle and to interpret the Civil War as the North's unchristian and brutal treatment of the South and especially the Confederate prisoners. This model grossly overstated starvation, physical abuse and a broad conspiracy to kill Confederate prisoners.

The Lost Cause argument on prisoner treatment was, in part, based on Jefferson Davis's March 3, 1865 administration report describing prison conditions. In the report, Davis stated, "In nearly all prison stations of the North our men have suffered from insufficient food and have been subjected to ignominious, cruel, and barbarous practices, of which there is no parallel in anything that has occurred in the South."[120]

The lack of adequate healthcare was often stated as an example of the conscious action by the North to kill Southern prisoners. However, Lost Cause proponents failed to acknowledge that the recovery rate in Union prison hospitals was better than at Chimborazo Hospital in Richmond, the largest hospital treating Confederate soldiers.[121] For example, the recovery rate at Chimborazo was 88.61 percent compared to 94.29 at Camp Douglas.[122]

Lost Cause proponents also failed to acknowledge that the Confederate prisoner in the North was 29.0 percent less likely to die in a prison camp than in the Confederate army, while 68.0 percent of Union prisoners in the South were more likely to die in a Confederate prison than in the Union army.[123] Another fact the Lost Cause advocates failed to mention was that approximately 15.1 percent of Union inmates in Southern prisons died while incarcerated compared to 12.0 percent of Confederates who died in Northern prisons.[124]

Lost Cause advocates portrayed the Southern leadership as appalled that the exchange of prisoners was suspended by President Lincoln. They failed to adequately explain that the reason for Lincoln's decision was the Confederate position on the treatment of Union African American troops as escaped slaves and the threatened execution of the white leadership of "colored troops."[125] The Lost Cause also blamed General Grant for leading the movement to suspend the exchange. General Grant might have understood the military advantage of halting the exchange, but he had limited influence on the decision made in 1863. It was well into 1864 before General Grant attained a position that could affect this policy.[126] Lost Cause advocates fail to note that the inability of the U.S. government to control its own paroled prisoners might have contributed to the suspension of exchanges.

The Lost Cause doctrine was, in no small part, driven by the Union position during Reconstruction. Republican stronghold the Grand Army of the Republic (GAR) provided strong reminders of conditions at Andersonville, placing the Union as the morally superior side in the war.[127] This position continued in 1879, when James Garfield, future president of the United

States, raised the issue, blaming "from Jeff Davis down" for conditions at Andersonville.[128]

Chicago's part in continuing the tension between the North and South was evident when Charles Gunther purchased, dismantled and shipped the remains of Libby Prison to Chicago to be reassembled as a Civil War museum. The museum, opened in 1889, included in its collection shrunken Incan heads. Obviously, the museum was designed for pleasure and profit; however, the inference with non–Civil War artifacts was not lost on Gunther's critics. Any materials relating to Camp Douglas were conspicuously absent from the museum.[129]

The large volume of the Lost Cause material produced after the war has led to a misconception of Union treatment of prisoners that remains today. This and the defenders of Union actions have created an environment in which the argument becomes which side was worse. A more appropriate approach would be evaluating factors that contributed to the conditions in all prisons.

Leadership Blamed for Prison Camp Conditions

Charles Sanders places much of the blame for conditions in both Union and Confederate prison camps on senior leadership. He indicates serious deficiencies in standards as a major cause, placing little blame on the lack of training of commanders and soldiers on the conduct of prisoner of war activities and other factors. He dismisses the claim that the Confederates were restricted in their ability to properly care for prisoners due to a lack of resources. He reminds the reader that the South produced enough food to feed an army for nearly four years.[130] He also asserts that there was no attempt by the Confederacy to adequately prepare poorly selected prison camp sites for prisoners. The lack of wooden barracks at Andersonville was blamed on a lack of resources. There were sufficient stands of trees to provide adequate lumber for the camp. Camp officials could not obtain assistance from a local sawmill and took no steps to allow prisoner work details to obtain the needed material for shelter.[131]

Sanders comments on the reduction in rations by General Halleck and Secretary of War Stanton in retaliation for treatment of Union prisoners, particularly those ill prisoners released by the Confederacy in early 1864.[132] Even with the reduction, the rations authorized were sufficient for prisoners.[133] He further charges Stanton with responsibility for "measures that would result in the greatest amount of suffering and death in northern camps."[134] There is little basis for this conclusion.

Sanders also harshly criticizes Confederate general John H. Winder for his actions with prisons camps in the South even though Winder was not appointed commissary general of prisoners until November 21, 1864.[135] He faults U.S. commissary general of prisoners William C. Hoffman for ignoring provisions of General Order 100 and allowing "inhuman" punishment at Camp Douglas.[136] Sanders fails to note, however, that much of the punishment at the camp was similar to the punishment received by Union soldiers guilty of misconduct.[137]

While there is ample blame of senior military and civilian leaders to go around for the lack of planning and provisioning prison camps, there is very little evidence of any concerted effort by either government to intentionally kill or maim prisoners of war. Rather, failure to anticipate the need for prison camps, indifference and delays in responding to prisoner needs appears to be the primary factors behind both governments' actions.

Summary

Past history and the Dix-Hill Cartel were the bases for treatment of prisoners of war during the Civil War. The Union further documented prisoner treatment in General Order 100, promulgated by President Lincoln in April 1863.[138] The postwar frenzy caused by the development of the Lost Cause model and attempts to place blame have contributed to how we perceive Camp Douglas and other Civil War prisons today.

It will be seen that many factors, including the naïve approach by the Dix-Hill Cartel, significantly contributed to the treatment of prisoners in both the North and South. The Lost Cause has colored the way Civil War veterans perceived the war and prison conditions and has had a lasting impact on how modern Americans interpret history.

Chapter 5

Camp Douglas Selected as a Prison Camp and Prisoners Arrive

Near the end of 1861, it became apparent that the Union army required facilities to house Confederate prisoners who were not immediately paroled. In July 1862, the Dix-Hill Cartel came into effect. Article 4 of the cartel stated, "All prisoners of war are to be discharged on parole in ten days after their capture." This provision had a significant impact of the lack of willingness of the Union army to provide increased and improved facilities for Camp Douglas and other Union prison camps.

Selection criteria for prisoner camps were (1) a sufficient distance from the war to preclude raids to release prisoners, (2) a location with adequate transportation from the war and (3) proximity to a metropolitan area that could provide logistic support to the facility. Chicago met all of these criteria. Major General Henry Halleck, commander of the Department of Missouri, needed to find facilities for twelve to fifteen thousand prisoners taken after the surrender of Fort Donelson on February 16, 1862. The location of Fort Donelson on the Cumberland River, northwest of Nashville and within easy river transportation to Cairo, Illinois, made the movement of prisoners to Camp Douglas logical.

In 1861, the Chicago location was not prepared to accept prisoners. Colonel Joseph Tucker, Sixtieth Regiment, Illinois State Militia, was responsible for building Camp Douglas and would act as its first commander. Even though Colonel Tucker reported to General Halleck that Chicago could hold eight or nine thousand prisoners, the *Chicago Tribune* was unconvinced that Camp Douglas would be used to hold Rebel prisoners. On February 14, the paper reported:

> *An Absurd Rumor—The rumor was present upon the streets yesterday that an order had been received to put Camp Douglas in readiness for the accommodation of five thousand rebel prisoners. This is decidedly the joke of the season. The idea of keeping five thousand prisoners in a camp, where the strongest guard couldn't keep in a drunken corporal, is rich. The whole population would have to mount guard and Chicago would find itself in possession of an elephant of the largest description. If authorities will give Chicago permission to hang the whole batch as soon as they arrive, let them come.*

The next day, February 15, the *Tribune* modified its report:

> *New Use for Camp Douglas. In our yesterday's issue appeared a brief paragraph with reference to the use of Camp Douglas for holding prisoners of war, now that the time is near at hand when the troops will be withdrawn thence to active service. In the paragraph the real merits of the case were sacrificed to a little pleasantry. In reality, if prisoners are to be brought to this part of the State there is no better and more suitable accommodations than this very Camp Ground. Fitted as it is with Winter barracks and surrounded by high and closed board fences where a single battalion of armed guards could hold and keep safe and humanly several thousand prisoners. There are other points of advantage in favor of this location which the Government will consider, none of which are more apparent than the economy evident from the comparison of actual figures. Troops are now well and amply subsisted in Chicago at 11½ cents per ration, the cheapest figure known in the Northwest and so in the entire country. And the rations are pronounced equal to any furnished in the service. This too while 14 and 16 cents are the lowest prices known at Ottawa, Springfield and other points. These facts the Government will consider, giving them due weight, but there will be found no reason why Camp Douglas will not be found every way fit for the new use suggested.*

Finally, on the nineteenth, the *Tribune* read:

> *7,000 CONFEDERATES COMING TO CHICAGO. A new Use for Camp Douglas. We learned from Capt. Potter of the U.S. Quartermaster's Department, that the information has lately arrived in the city that as soon as the regiments now in Camp Douglas shall have departed, their place will be occupied by seven thousand confederate prisoners, captured by our forces at Fort Donelson. Their escort and guard will be detailed from troops engaged in the late victory in Tennessee, and will remain with them. All the rolling stock of*

> *the Illinois Central Road is now being collected at Cairo as expeditiously as possible for the transportation to this place of prisoners alluded to, and it is now confidently expected that their arrival here will not be delayed beyond Saturday of the present week. The exchange of six thousand brave Federal soldiers, but lately comfortably quartered at Camp Douglas, for seven thousand rebels, will prove an event of considerable interest—an event not without its effect upon the future of the confederates.*

It wasn't just the *Chicago Tribune* concerned about Camp Douglas's preparedness; Chicago mayor John Rumsey complained that seven thousand prisoners would endanger the city and that the small garrison would be unable to adequately guard the prisoners. He wired General Halleck on February 21, writing, "Our best citizens are in great alarm for fear that the prisoners will break through and burn the city." Halleck replied, "It is a great pity if Chicago cannot guard them unarmed for a few days. No troops can be spared from here for that purpose at present."[139] Chicago police and volunteer constables were pressed into service to assist the army with guarding the prisoners. These special police remained at the camp until February 27.[140] In part due to the poor condition of the first prisoners, there was little difficulty in managing them. Within a few weeks, Colonel James Mulligan's Twenty-third Illinois "Irish" Infantry Regiment arrived to take over running the prison camp.[141]

The first 1,258 prisoners arrived at Camp Douglas on February 20, 1862.[142] Prisoners were assigned to barracks in White Oak Square that had just been vacated by Union troops. Sergeant Charles Edwin Taylor, Twentieth Mississippi Infantry, recorded in his diary, "We were very well provided for having good passenger cars to ride in which was a good stove and plenty of fuel…Crackers, Bakers bread, chipped beef, fresh beef, coffee, already ground, sugar, beans, cheese and very good barracks." Private Ryan, Fourteenth Mississippi Infantry, commented on the reception: "Some would curse us and call us poor ignorant devils; some would curse Jeff Davis for getting us poor ignorant creatures into such a trap."[143]

Others traveling north from Fort Donelson were not as positive. Colonel Randal W. McGavock, Fifteenth Tennessee Infantry Regiment, commented on the trip to St. Louis, "The boat was very much crowded and very disagreeable to me." Andrew Jackson Campbell, Forty-eighth Tennessee, wrote, "At night we had to pile like hogs, scarcely any room enough for all on the floor, which was covered over with mud, slop, and tobacco spittle, well tramped through the day." He later complained that rations on the steamer *Hiawatha* were "loaf of bread, half-cooked beef and pickled pork-raw."[144] The trip from Fort Donelson was either by steamship to Cairo, Illinois, and then by Illinois Central Railroad to Chicago or by river all the way to St. Louis and then to Chicago via the St. Louis, Alton and Chicago Railroad. The Illinois Central's terminal was located in downtown Chicago, approximately four miles north of Camp Douglas. Shortly after the camp opened, a station was built approximately four hundred yards east of the main gate. The St. Louis, Alton and Chicago Railroad terminal was west of the Chicago River and the central city about four miles northwest of Camp Douglas. Prisoners reported exiting the train on Archer Avenue, which was parallel to the tracks. This reduced the march to the camp by approximately two miles.

The first prisoners were escorted from Fort Donelson by the Fifty-second Illinois Regiment, commanded by Colonel T.W. Sweeney. It was reported in the *Chicago Tribune* that the train from St. Louis was attacked by a "detachment of Eastern Cavalry [Union], a number of whom being intoxicated, assaulted the train with bricks and stones, breaking the car windows and injuring their inmates."[145] A large crowd of "thousands" of citizens came to the camp to view the prisoners. A reporter from the *Tribune* "circulated promiscuously" among the prisoners, who were characterized as follows:

> *A more woebegone appearing set of men it would be difficult for a reader to imagine. The uniforms were considered inadequate, and intended for a warmer climate with "some have coats of butternut." Many of them have no overcoats at all and supply their place with horse blankets, hearth rugs, coverlids, pieces of carpet, coffee sacks, etc. etc. Many looked pale and actually had attacks of ague chills as they stood awaiting the preparation of their barracks.*[146]

Similar stories appeared in the *Chicago Tribune* for the remainder of February as the paper reported the arrival of additional prisoners. The February 24 *Tribune* reported that "a contraband [slave]" of a prisoner was in camp.[147] There were at least seven African Americans captured at Fort Donelson, and three were considered the "property" of Confederate prisoners. The background of the others is unknown. All but one, who died at Camp Douglas, were released by September 1862.[148] It was not unusual for Confederate soldiers, especially officers, to require slave servants to accompany them into battle. Until later in the war, Union forces had no guidelines for handling these slaves when their masters were captured.

On February 27, the *Tribune* reported that there were 270 prisoners in the hospital, with 2 having died. Nearly 7,000 prisoners were reported in camp by February 28.[149] However, the total number of prisoners at the

Camp Douglas prisoners (probably from Fort Donelson), 1862. *Library of Congress.*

time was substantially less than the 7,000 reported by the *Tribune*. I.N. Haynie estimated the population at that time to be about 4,500.[150] The reported number of prisoners, deaths and escapes were often inconsistent. Newspapers, prison commanders and official records often differed, making it difficult to determine the exact numbers.

The second wave of prisoners, numbering approximately 2,450, began arriving in mid-April 1862 from Shiloh and Island 10.[151] As with Fort Donelson, Shiloh and Island 10 were located for direct transportation to Camp Douglas. Additional prisoners arrived throughout 1862 from hospitals in St. Louis and from other prison camps. About 800 of these were moved to Camp Douglas from Camp Randall in Madison, Wisconsin.[152] The camp's population continued to increase until the exchange of nearly 8,000 prisoners in September 1862. These prisoners were sent by the same rail that had delivered them to the camp to Vicksburg, Mississippi. Only about 100 sick prisoners remained in Camp Douglas.[153] After the exchange of the Confederate prisoners, Union troops numbering approximately 8,000 were all that remained in the camp and the satellite camps.

PRISONER OBSERVATIONS ON ARRIVING AT CAMP DOUGLAS

Arrivals at Camp Douglas were frequently documented by prisoners. Robert Bagby, captured at Fort Hindman, Arkansas, in January 1863, recorded his arrival from St. Louis in his diary on January 27, 1863:

> *We were still riding when the daylight came. I had slept but little during the night last. I smelt a terrible smell. We passed over some very fine country before we entered Chicago about 11:00. Before we got out of the cars many had crammed around the cars and one fellow remarked that the prisoners all should be hung. He had no more than said it until some Irishman had knocked him down. There liked to be a general riot. Finally we were marched out to Camp Douglas which* [was] *on or near* [the] *Lake Michigan shore. There were at least 170 or 180 prisoners of us. I was very much pleased with the prospects here. There were very many Federal paroled prisoners taken at Harpers Ferry. Some said they had been exchanged, some said they had not. I thought they had not.*[154]

Curtis Burke, captured at Buffington Island, Ohio, on July 19, 1863, recorded his arrival from Camp Morton, Indianapolis, Indiana, in his journal:

Officers imprisoned at Camp Douglas, 1864. *Chicago History Museum.*

Enlisted men imprisoned at Camp Douglas, 1864. *Chicago History Museum.*

Tuesday August 18th, 1863. Before sun up I noticed that we were going through a prairie country, level and without fencing. I could only see a few bushes as far as I could see on either side. After sun up I saw several trains on the tracks crossing the track that we were on. We stopped a few minutes at the town of Westville [Indiana]. *The country is much better wooded here. Just before reaching Michigan City* [Indiana] *I noticed that the country was getting very sandy. We passed the Penitentiary and entered the city. We got a glimpse of Lake Michigan. I saw several houses nearly covered with sand that had settled around them in the lake storm. Two kid-gloved negro gents of the city stopped and took a good look at us. The cars stopped about ten minutes. The guards at our door tried to hook some watermelons from a box car load that stopped near us, but our train moved too soon.*

We passed the Penitentiary again and took the Chicago road. The guards said that we were going to Camp Douglas near Chicago. The cars run along the lake shore for some distance before we got to the suburbs of Chicago where we got out. I could see the city and a few sailing boats but no large crafts. We were marched about four hundred yards inland and arrived at the gate of Camp Douglas on lake street [sic]. *I saw two street cars and several carriages of city folks waiting to see us. The gates swung open and in we marched. The camp appeared pretty large, with a high fence running around it. I saw a post office, barber shop, picture gallery, two sutler stores, a commissary house, and a chapel. The first square we entered was the Yankees quarters off to the left, with long barracks on the sides and flag pole*

> *in the center. Then we marched to another square that was vacant and they called it White Oak square.*
>
> *All of the barracks were long one-story buildings. Four of them forming a square with a cook house on the outside of the square to each barrack and the length of the barrack. The barracks were divided into little rooms with from two to ten bunks in each, and doors and windows to match, also one long room with a row of bunks on each side of the room, mostly three bunks deep or high, and making room for about eighty men. There was a general stampede of our boys to secure the little rooms. My mess of four decided to go in a little room with three of company C to fill it up making seven in all in the room. It was* [illegible] *feet wide by twenty-five feet long. A door and window front and a window back.*
>
> *We nailed up a cracker box and three shelves to put our rations and other tricks on. There was a table ready made in the room when we came. I made a stout bench about seven feet long from planks I found laying around. We opened both windows and door to let the fresh air pass through. There was a plank pavement in front of our door about three feet wide. We received rations of crackers, bread, bacon, pickelled* [sic] *pork, coffee, sugar, potatoes, hominy, salt, soap, and candles. Of course, a man only got a handful of each when it was divided, but we received better rations here than we did at Camp Morton, Ind.*
>
> *I got Sergeant* [William] *Miller's coffee pot and we made a little chip fire in the square, and we had some coffee, crackers and broiled bacon for supper. Col. DeLand, commanding the post, came to our quarters and had a chat with the boys. They had a thousand or more questions to ask about writing, receiving things, etc. A lot of us hastily wrote home and a Yankee captain took them to headquarters to be mailed. A heavy dew fell during the night. I slept better than I expected in my bunk without any blankets.*[155]

William Huff was captured at Chickamauga on September 20, 1863, and arrived at Camp Douglas on October 4, 1863. He noted of his arrival, "October 4, 1863—Arrived at Camp Douglas. The day was very cold and we were kept standing in the open square for about four hours. Had had nothing to eat for two days. Were put in barracks…they were long low buildings partitioned off into rooms with a stove in each. They are as comfortable as could be expected for prison."[156]

As the war progressed and Camp Douglas was established as a major prison camp, prisoners came from the Eastern Theater as well as the West. Some came from as far away as Chickamauga, Georgia. On July 16, 1864, Burke reported the arrival of additional prisoners to Camp Douglas:

> *The first thing that I noticed this morning was a crowd of new prisoners in the open square with a guard around them. The most of them were still sleeping on the ground. No one was allowed to speak to them till they were drawn up in line and searched for their money, papers, etc. Then they were put in barracks. They arrived last night and number about 330. They were captured at Kennysaw* [sic] *Mountain, Ga. near the first of this month, and from long fighting, digging and traveling, they are a very dirty looking set. They report that our army is in the best of spirits with plenty of eat. It rained at night.*[157]

On August 24, 1864, Burke reported on the arrival of prisoners transferred from an Alton, Illinois prison: "Wednesday August 24th, 1864. 480 prisoners arrived from Alton, Ill. Prison, twenty escaped on the way here. They are a good looking lot of men and bring exchange rumors. They are quartered in barracks 41, 43, 44. The workhands dining room being broken up to make room for them."[158]

Both Bagby and Burke commented on prisoners arriving from Nashville in December 1864. Burke wrote, "Friday, December 23, 1864. Another lot of new prisoners arrived, some of them suffering severely from frost bitten feet and hands. Some has to be hauled in on account of frozen limbs. Henry White sold a grey jacket for $1 and got 1 qt. molasses, 75 cts and 18 onions 25 cts."[159] Robert Bagby's diary entry on January 15, 1865, recounts the results of new prisoners waiting in snow until they could be processed. Throughout Camp Douglas's existence, severe Chicago winters would plague prisoners and guards alike. In several instances, guard tours were cut from two hours to a half hour because of the cold weather.

> *January 15, 1865. We had a good many that were badly frosted. One poor fellow had all his fingers frosted so they had to be taken off, leaving nothing but what would be called club hands. Samuel had all his toes taken off. Those that were so frosted came with the last squad of prisoners. The weather was so cold as they came into camp at daylight and were kept standing in the square until late in the day to give time to search them and not been fit for several days before. A good deal of their clothing had been taken from them before they were led into Prisoners Square. Consequently a great many were badly frozen.*[160]

John Copley, one of the most prolific and colorful Confederate diarists, could have been a prisoner at Camp Douglas with those who surrendered at Fort Donelson in 1862, had it not been for a "severe attack of pneumonia" that landed him in a hospital in Confederate-controlled Nashville. Near the end of the war, in November 1864, he was captured at Franklin, Tennessee. After being moved to Nashville, he recounted his travel to and impression of Camp Douglas:

> *After spending one night in the city of Louisville, we were marched to the proper depot and ordered on board a train of box cars and were packed in them like beef cattle for shipment, after which, two large engines pulled us out of the city. We were soon carried far beyond the reach of* [Confederate general John Bell] *Hood, or the sound of his cannon, steaming away for the place of our destination, where about daylight on the morning of the 5th of December, 1864, we found ourselves landed on the shores of Lake Michigan, and near a place called "Camp Douglas." As we came on the borders of the lake, its waves lay dark and voiceless; only at intervals the surf fretting along the pebbles, made a low and dreary sound.*
>
> *The beach and grounds were covered with snow and ice nearly twenty inches deep. The beautiful white snow, the pure azure-colored waters of the lake, and the appearance and feelings of this little handful of ragged, half-starved, wornout* [sic] *prisoners, presented a sorrowful and pitiable contrast. We were now placed in charge of a different set of guards. The guards now ordered us to march out of the box cars upon deep snow and ice, form open ranks* [and] *take off our outside clothing, including our shoes and boots—in other words, undress. But few of this little crowd wore shoes or boots, the majority of them being barefooted, and had been for some time previously, and not many of us wore anything except outside clothing.*
>
> *In the warm climate of the South, some two years prior to this the army of Tennessee had dispensed with such unnecessary luxuries, for the reason that the Confederate States Government was financially unable to furnish that class of clothing to its soldiers. We were required to stand upon this deep snow and ice, facing an icy breeze of mist, which was flying from the lake propelled by a strong gale of wind, for several hours, without fire or anything to eat, for the purpose of undergoing an examination, a close and rigorous search for all arms of offense or defense, which might be found on our persons or in our possessions. When the search was finished, we donned our clothing, were ordered to form in two ranks and face to the front. We can see a plank wall in which there is a large gate, on the inside of which, we understand, our quarters are located.*[161]

Little has been written about the reaction of Union soldiers on the plight of arriving Confederate captives. Since most of the guards were wounded or incapacitated campaign veterans, it can be assumed they had some

Prisoners from Franklin, Tennessee. *Mike Miner.*

compassion for the prisoners. Nonetheless, these guards appeared to follow their officers' instructions in handling the prisoners.

Clearly, the first prisoners drew the most attention from the community at large; however, many Chicago citizens continued to be curious about later prisoners and some of their guards. In May 1862, near the camp's main gate on Cottage Grove, entrepreneurial-minded folks erected a privately funded tower, Union Observatory, that was fifty feet high and painted red, white and blue.[162] For five cents, anyone could climb the tower and observe the prisoners. A second tower, a twenty-foot structure known as the Free Observatory, was built on the roof of the Cottage Grove Hotel and provided views of Camp Douglas.[163]

In August 1863, Colonel Charles DeLand and the First Michigan Sharpshooters stirred up a considerable interest when they arrived at Camp Douglas to act as guards. Company K of the First Michigan Sharpshooters was composed of Native Americans from the Chippewa and Ottawa tribes in Michigan. Citizens of Chicago came to the camp to view the "savage" guards.

Chicago Community Support of the Prisoners

When the prison camp first opened, women of Chicago took up collections of clothing, bedding and food for the prisoners. Visits to Camp Douglas to see these misguided youths were a popular activity until March 1862, when Lieutenant Colonel William Hoffman, commissary general of prisoners, ordered camp commander Colonel James A. Mulligan to put a stop to visitors. Hoffman believed these visits led to the smuggling of items such as knives and guns and generally led to poor discipline in the camp. Colonel Mulligan ignored the order until April, when he put an official halt to civilian visits.[164]

Colonel Mulligan might have had reason to stop visits when initially ordered when former Chicago mayor Levi Boone, a noted Southern sympathizer, was ordered arrested in August 1862 for providing money that was used to bribe guards to aid in a Confederate prisoner escape.[165] In addition, another Southern sympathizer, former mayor Buckner Morris's wife, Mary, was known to visit the camp frequently. Robert Bagby reported ongoing contact with Mary Morris, including Mrs. Morris delivering writing paper and postage to Bagby for distribution to prisoners. Bagby provided her with lists of prisoners who had died.[166] The purpose of providing this information is unknown, but perhaps Mrs. Morris was communicating this information to the families of the deceased.

Visits were again authorized by Colonel Hoffman in a June 29 communication with Colonel Tucker. Mail and packages was also permitted to be received by prisoners, and prisoners could write one-page letters.[167]

On March 1, 1862, the *Tribune* reported that the U.S. Sanitary Commission delivered to the prisoners corn meal, clothing, eating utensils and "in fact everything that could add to their welfare."[168]

On March 2, a committee of Chicago citizens was appointed "to furnish relief to the sick and destitute at Camp Douglas." Duties included visiting the camp hospitals, including those holding prisoners.[169] This committee continued its work with the support of Colonel Mulligan during his tenure and beyond.[170] The editors of the *Chicago Tribune* complained that while citizens had provided much-needed support to the Confederate prisoners, they had ignored the Union soldiers at Camp Douglas. The editors recounted the large amount of support they said was provided the prisoners by the U.S. government and noted that washtubs and wooden pails were needed by the Union soldiers.[171]

This community support was one of the many ironies of the Civil War. While some were, undoubtedly, Southern sympathizers, many expressed concern for their fellow man. As in many wars, the individual soldier was not held accountable for the actions of his leaders.

Women visiting Camp Douglas, circa 1864. *Chicago History Museum.*

Chicago citizens rallied support for both Union soldiers and Confederates. Individual efforts as well as religious organizations and the Sanitary Commission provided ongoing support to Camp Douglas throughout the war.

This, then, was Camp Douglas. Prisoners began arriving in February 1862 principally from the Western Theater. The prison population had grown to nearly eight thousand by the time of the first exchange in September 1862. Only a handful of sick prisoners remained until additional prisoners began to arrive at year's end. The peak of recruiting and receiving Union regiments took place during the year. Satellite camps from Hyde Park to a mile or so north and west of the camp were busy with Union soldiers. After the departure of the destructive paroled Union soldiers, Camp Douglas settled into a period of reconstruction and rebuilding in anticipation of the arrival of additional prisoners. The camp had transitioned from a Union reception center to a prison camp and then back to a Union camp handling paroled prisoners before ultimately returning to a prison camp, all while continuing to provide facilities for the reception of small Union units. Commanders were challenged to meet the needs of soldiers, both Confederate and Union, who were assigned there.

Chapter 6

Camp Douglas and U.S. Prison Camp Leadership

Leadership of Union prisons was under the responsibility of the U.S. Army Quartermaster Corps. Additionally, a commissary of prisoners was appointed for day-to-day operations of prisons that held Confederate captives. Individual camps, such as Camp Douglas, were commanded by Union officers who, for prison matters, reported to the commissary of prisoners.

U.S. Army Prison Leadership

General Meigs

Brigadier General Montgomery Meigs was appointed quartermaster general of the U.S. Army on June 16, 1861. Before his appointment as quartermaster general, he identified the impending need for handling Confederate captives. On June 12, 1861, he wrote to Secretary of War Simon Cameron, "As in the conflict now commenced it is likely to be expected that the United States will have to take care of a large number of prisoners of war."[172] In view of the history of captives in earlier wars, Meigs was unusually perceptive of the situation in the Civil War.

Montgomery Cunningham Meigs was born on May 3, 1816, and graduated from West Point in 1836. Prior to the Civil War, he served in a number of engineering capacities for the U.S. Army. From his appointment in 1861 until his retirement in 1882, he served with distinction as quartermaster general.[173] General Meigs was responsible for all Union prison camps and was keenly aware of the costs of maintaining these facilities. However, Meigs was of the opinion that housing the Confederate prisoners would be temporary until paroled under the Dix-Hill Cartel and that funds for enlarging or improving facilities were limited. After the suspension of exchange in the fall of 1863, Meigs was more willing to approve expenditures to modify the prison camps.

Colonel Hoffman

Lieutenant Colonel William Hoffman was appointed commissary of prisoners on October 3, 1861. He retained that office until the end of the war and was promoted to colonel and later brevet (temporary) brigadier general.[174] His duties and responsibilities were specific and sweeping:

> *GENERAL ORDERS, WAR DEPT., ADJT. GENERAL'S OFFICE,*
> *No. 67.* *Washington, June 17, 1862.*
> *The supervision of prisoners of war sent by generals commanding in the field to posts or camps prepared for their reception is placed entirely under Col. William Hoffman, Third Infantry, commissary general of prisoners, who is subject only to the orders of the War Department. All matters in relation to prisoners will pass through him.*
>
> *He will establish regulations for issuing clothing to prisoners, and will direct the manner in which all funds arising from the saving of rations at prison hospitals or otherwise shall be accounted for and disbursed by the regular disbursing officers of the departments in providing under existing regulations such articles as may be absolutely necessary for the welfare of the prisoners.*
>
> *He will select positions for camps for prisoners (or prison camps) and will cause plans and estimates for necessary buildings to be prepared and submitted to the Quartermaster-General upon whose approval they will be erected by the officers of the Quartermasters Department.*
>
> *He will if practicable visit the several prison camps once a month.*
>
> *Loyal citizens who may be found among the prisoners of war confined on false accusations or through mistake may lay their cases before the commissary-general of prisoners, who will submit them to the Adjutant-General.*

The commissary-general of prisoners is authorized to grant paroles to prisoners on the recommendation of the medical officer attending the prison in case of extreme illness but under no other circumstances.

By order of the Secretary of War[175]

Colonel Hoffman was an 1829 graduate of West Point and had extensive prewar experience in constructing forts in the Indian Territories. He was characterized as being preoccupied with thrift, including instructing the construction of only the "cheapest kind" of buildings in the prison camps.[176] Along with Meigs, Hoffman was willing to spend little money on prison camps, and only with reluctance did he recommend such expenditures.

Confederate Prison Leadership

General Winder

The Confederate counterpart of Colonel Hoffman, Brigadier General John Henry Winder, was an 1820 graduate of West Point. Winder joined the Confederate army on April 27, 1861. He was appointed provost marshal of Richmond, Virginia, in June 1861 and had responsibility for all prisons therein. Unlike the Union army, the Confederates delayed naming a commissary general of prisoners until November 21, 1864, when Winder was appointed.[177]

Like the U.S. government, the Confederates assigned the general responsibility for prisons to the army

Brigadier General John Winder, CSA. *American Civil War Museum.*

quartermaster. Since Confederate prison camps were concentrated in the Richmond area, Jefferson Davis's government saw no need for anyone but General Winder to manage its facilities. As the provost marshal, Winder did not report directly to the quartermaster general, making communications and decision-making difficult. Factories, warehouses, mills and former jails in and around Richmond formed the nucleus of the Confederate prison system, all under his control. The South never developed a comprehensive centralized organization to administer its prisons.[178]

As the system grew and prisons began to be located outside Richmond, General Winder was spread very thin and lacked the authority of commissary general of prisoners until late 1864. Even after Winder's appointment, the system was virtually unmanageable.

Camp Douglas Leadership

The U.S. Army's thriftiness and belief in the temporary nature of prison confinement would be the source of conflict between Meigs/Hoffman and the commanders of Camp Douglas.

Command of Camp Douglas was constantly turning over. Colonel Hoffman acknowledged the problem of command turnover when, in May 1863, he reported to Secretary Stanton, "It is almost impossible to have instructions carried out at Camp Douglas because of the frequent changes of commanders."[179]

The high turnover rate was a result of early confusion regarding the organization and reporting of the military in the Civil War. Initially, Camp Douglas was under the control of the State of Illinois as a reception center. As the camp evolved into a prison camp, control passed to the U.S. Army. Early commanders were senior Union officers who were selected simply because they were there. These active-duty officers were eager to "get to the fighting" and left Camp Douglas as soon as possible. Not until the Invalid Corps units were assigned to guard duty in late 1863 was turnover reduced. The Invalid Corps were made up of soldiers and officers who were wounded in battle or otherwise had limited ability to engage in active combat.

From its beginning as a prison camp in February 1862 until its closing in December 1865, Camp Douglas had no fewer than twelve commanders represented by eight different officers when holding a significant number of prisoners. Captain John C. Phillips (May 1863), Captain J.S. Putman (May–

August 1863), Captain Shurly (September–October 1864) and Captain E.C. Phetteplace (October 1864–March 1865) commanded Camp Douglas when there were few prisoners as a result of the exchange of 1863 and releases at the end of the war.

Colonel Tucker—First Commander

Colonel Joseph H. Tucker, Sixtieth Illinois State Militia, was chosen by Governor Yates to construct the camp. Having lived in Chicago since 1858, Tucker was a successful commodities trader before the war. He had no experience managing a military facility. In addition, he had little experience with his other raise-a-camp duties, which included recruiting, transporting and overseeing the downstate prisons of Alton and Camp Butler. Colonel Tucker initially developed Camp Douglas as a receiving and training facility for the Northern District of Illinois, not as a prison camp. He was inadequately trained to manage the facility. While he handled the construction sufficiently, his lack of leadership skills was telling.

Tucker remained in command until replaced on February 14, 1862, by Colonel James Mulligan, Twenty-third Illinois Infantry (Irish Brigade). Tucker took temporary command again on February 21, when Colonel Mulligan refused to accept responsibility for the camp. Until Colonel Tucker could return to Camp Douglas from Springfield for that command, Colonel Arno Voss, Twelfth Illinois Cavalry, who was preparing to move his regiment from Camp Douglas, remained to prepare for the prisoners. The first prisoners arrived on February 20. Mulligan, technically in command of the camp as of February 14, officially accepted responsibility on February 26.

Camp Douglas was under the jurisdiction of the State of Illinois, not the U.S. Army. This dispute and confusion was settled when Colonel Hoffman sent a telegram to Captain Joseph A. Potter, the camp's assistant quartermaster, on February 24, 1862. "The prisoners are the prisoners of the United States!" he declared. "The supplies to be issued are the property of the United States. You are an officer of the United States. The State of Illinois has no more right to give you orders than the State of Massachusetts. State Authorities have no right to give orders to an officer of the United States."[180]

Colonel Mulligan Takes Command

Above all else, Colonel James A. Mulligan wanted to be a soldier and leader of the Irish Brigade. He was born in 1830 and educated as a lawyer. He had edited a Catholic newspaper in Chicago before raising the Twenty-third Illinois. In September 1861, the Twenty-third was captured in Lexington, Missouri, and Colonel Mulligan was exchanged in October 1861. The rest of the regiment had been paroled and was awaiting exchange. Since no exchange was completed, the regiment was discharged on October 8, 1861, but was declared exchanged by Major General George B. McClellan.

The regiment was then reorganized and placed on guard duty at Camp Douglas, with Colonel Mulligan in command. Mulligan was not known for his recordkeeping, and after his unit returned to the battlefront in June 1862, $1,450 of the prisoners' fund at Camp Douglas was missing. Colonel Mulligan was ordered arrested on July 20 as a result of the loss and charged with disobeying an order to account for prison funds. On August 25, he contacted the adjutant general, seeking an immediate trial to clear his name. The matter was ultimately referred to Colonel Hoffman, who judged that Mulligan should make restitution. General Halleck, U.S. Army chief of staff, ordered Mulligan to report to the adjutant general and "settle his accounts at Camp Douglas." Mulligan made restitution, and the matter ended.[181] Not unlike today, Mulligan made restitution without admitting any guilt.

Colonel Mulligan managed the prison compound with little experience. He added security and rallied medical support, including local doctors, for the sick and injured Confederate prisoners. In allowing civilians access to the prison, Colonel Mulligan was unable to adequately control escapes, and sanitary conditions remained well below acceptable standards.

The first contact at Camp Douglas with Colonel Hoffman took place on March 1, 1862, when he visited. Hoffman praised Mulligan for his efforts to obtain medical care for sick inmates. Colonel Hoffman left the camp on March 7 generally pleased with Mulligan and the facilities.[182] Colonel Hoffman recommended construction of a two-story barracks for prisoners before winter. General Meigs rejected this in favor of one-story buildings without insulation and no interior ceilings.[183]

Colonel Tucker Returns to Command

On June 19, 1862, Tucker returned to command of Camp Douglas upon the departure of Colonel Mulligan. Mulligan had turned command over to Colonel Daniel Cameron five days earlier. Approximately eight thousand prisoners were at the camp. Tucker's first contact with Colonel Hoffman was after the Sanitary Commission, in July 1862, had indicated that a proper sewage system was needed in the camp. Hoffman proposed the construction of a sewer system as soon as possible. Meigs turned down the request, stating that it was too "extravagant."[184]

The summer of 1862 was a difficult time for the unqualified commander, who lacked confidence in himself and the garrison at the camp. The Sixty-seventh Illinois Infantry, ninety-day volunteers, commanded by Colonel R.M. Hough, a well-connected Republican businessman, was assigned to guard the camp in early June.[185] Tucker was preoccupied with security and managing this Union garrison. On June 24, he enlisted thirty-five Chicago police to conduct a search of the prison barracks for weapons. Few, if any, were found, but a large quantity of contraband articles, such as knives, extra clothing and money, were seized.[186]

Tucker, concerned that he was without authority, contacted Colonel Hoffman on July 11 seeking clarification and authority to hire necessary horses and men to improve the prison facilities. On July 12, Hoffman indignantly responded that necessary authority had been given and that Colonel Tucker should contact Captain Potter, Chicago quartermaster, for support.[187]

On July 23, an escape attempt, assisted by outsiders, caused a panic in Chicago and added to Colonel Tucker's problems.[188] To reduce the involvement of outsiders in escape attempts, martial law was declared for an area one hundred feet beyond the camp perimeter. Anyone violating military rule could be confined by the military and tried by military court-martial.[189] Colonel Tucker soon extended the martial law line as far west as State Street and south to include the University of Chicago property. This effectively extended the authority of Colonel Tucker to all areas around Camp Douglas except the east side of Cottage Grove Avenue.

To further add to Tucker's woes, he became host to former Chicago mayor and Southern sympathizer Levy D. Boone. Tucker accused Boone of "furnishing comfort to the enemy" by providing money to Camp Douglas prisoners and arrested and imprisoned him on August 5, 1862.[190] Arresting someone on near-treason required Tucker to seek instructions from the secretary of war on how to proceed. On September 1, Secretary Stanton received a personal endorsement of Boone from President Lincoln. This was communicated through Colonel Hoffman to Colonel Tucker, who then released Boone.[191]

Tucker was further unprepared for the demands for better medical care for the prisoners and the shortcomings of the camp. Throughout June and July, problems regarding medical treatment and sanitation were evident. Foul sinks, standing water and general filth were reported by the U.S. Sanitary Commission. In spite of requests by Colonel Hoffman to seek funding for a sewer, General Meigs refused, indicating that "the ten thousand men should certainly be able to keep this camp clean."[192] Subsequent improvements were curtailed with the Dix-Hill Cartel in July, which contemplated an immediate general exchange of prisoners.

Tucker continued to be clearly out of his element, demonstrating poor administrative skills. Escapes, collapsing buildings and ineffective guards were consistently evident during his summer of command. As his tenure ended, deaths between February and September 29, 1862, totaled 976.[193] By the end of September, Tucker had managed the exchange of nearly eight thousand prisoners, leaving only about one hundred sick prisoners in camp.

While his problems with Confederate prisoners were behind him, the arrival on September 28 of some eight thousand paroled Union soldiers captured at Harpers Ferry, Virginia, would offer Tucker a separate and difficult set of problems. Not wishing to accept military orders, Tucker clashed immediately with the Ninth Vermont when its men refused to obey him.

General Tyler Takes Command

On September 30, 1862, Tucker was replaced by General Daniel Tyler, who escorted the parolees from Harpers Ferry.[194] Tucker remained to organize and train volunteers at the camp.

Daniel Tyler, born in 1799, was an 1819 graduate of West Point. He was highly successful in civilian life in railroad and canal companies. At the outset of the war, he became a colonel in the ninety-day First Connecticut. In March 1862, he was appointed brigadier general of volunteers. Known for his rigid honesty and business acumen, he had excellent credentials for his assignment at Camp Douglas.[195]

General Tyler took a hard stand with the parolees, banning passes and requiring the men to stand guard duty and perform other military activities. He was faced with great discipline problems and misconduct by the parolees. The *Chicago Tribune* reported the men's misconduct in articles from September until their departure in November. On October 1, 1862, the paper noted there was "Outrage by the Military" over assaults, theft and beatings of "unoffending civilians." The *Tribune* closed its article by stating, "We sincerely trust that Gen. Tyler, who assumes command this morning, will remedy the evils."[196]

Unfortunately for Tyler, the *Tribune* published the full text of the Dix-Hill Cartel on October 6. The provisions of Article 4 of the Dix-Hill Cartel prohibiting parolees from performing military duties was not lost on the men from Harpers Ferry.[197]

On October 10, 1862, General Tyler directed the following to A.C. Coventry, Chicago police commissioner:

> *Sir: I desire that you will direct your police to arrest any persons connected with the military service, without regard for rank, who may be found intoxicated, riotous or disorderly, in the streets of Chicago, and to confine them until released by my order. In the meantime, I wish these men to be treated exactly as citizens would be when arrested by the police for similar offenses. While these men are in confinement I will see that the city authorities receive any army ration or commutation in cash, provided they are fed by the city.*[198]

The *Tribune* reported three fires in the paroled soldiers' barracks on October 1, October 18 and November 21. The U.S. Sanitary Commission reported deplorable conditions during the parolees' stay. The lack of discipline continued until the troops were exchanged in December 1862.

It was claimed that Tyler violated the conditions of the Dix-Hill Cartel by drilling and training parolees, and he was relieved of command. The behavior of the paroled troops caused the physical facilities at Camp Douglas to deteriorate significantly. Command of Camp Douglas was given to Colonel Daniel Cameron, Sixty-fifth Illinois Infantry, on November 20, 1862. At the same time, former camp commander Colonel Tucker saw no future in the army and resigned his commission on January 1, 1863, returning to the Board of Trade. This was the second time Colonel Cameron had interim command of Camp Douglas. Cameron's command of six days was to accomplish nothing.

General Ammen Takes Command

Colonel Cameron was replaced in command by Brigadier General Jacob Ammen on January 6, 1863. General Ammen was greeted on January 26, 1863, by 1,500 prisoners from the Battle of Stone River.

Jacob Ammen was born in Virginia in 1806 and graduated from West Point in 1831. He resigned his commission in 1837 and taught mathematics at various colleges in Kentucky, Indiana and Mississippi. He re-entered service as a captain shortly after the surrender of Fort Sumter and was later appointed colonel of the Twenty-fourth Ohio. He served in West Virginia and at the Battle of Shiloh. He was promoted to brigadier general on June 16, 1862. Ammen had administrative experience as commander of Camp Dennison in Ohio when he took on command at Camp Douglas.[199]

Ammen, a strong disciplinarian, faced the arrival of 1,300 additional prisoners from Arkansas's Fort Hindman on January 27, 1863. Before capture, these prisoners had been subjected to conditions similar to those in Fort Donelson. As a result, illness and the subsequent death rate were high. Ammen had ordered quartermaster Captain Charles Goodman to repair barracks damaged in the earlier fires when the new prisoners arrived. They were described as "poorly clad, dirtier, and more cadaverous than any that have been in camp before."[200]

On January 28, 1863, Robert Bagby, who had arrived with the group of Arkansas prisoners, described his quarters thusly: "There were about 100 of us in one room and the boys sat with their stories and pipes. Conditions were extremely severe during January and February. Weather was extreme; temperature was reported at twenty degrees below zero, with barracks stoves barely being able to keep out the cold. Rags and clothing were used to block cracks in the walls, windows, and doors with little effect."[201]

In February 1863, 387 deaths were reported among the prisoners, with 262 prisoners in the hospital and 125 cases of smallpox in the barracks. This was the highest monthly total during the camp's existence.[202] Most of these deaths can be attributed to the severe weather and the poor condition of the prisoners when they arrived.

General Ammen was most interested in maintaining proper security. As a result, outside visitors were severely restricted, and passes to leave the camp were reduced. His measures seemed to be effective, as only fourteen escaped during his three months in charge.[203] Ammen's administrative skills were acknowledged by Captain Freedley, Colonel Hoffman's assistant. Books and records were properly maintained and barracks and fences repaired.

Freedley stated on March 11, 1863, "I find the condition of prisoners at Camp Douglas much improved."[204]

In response to the spread of smallpox, General Ammen had a "pest house" constructed approximately four hundred yards south of the camp and west of the University of Chicago in early 1863. Excessive deaths during General Ammen's command continued through the spring of 1863. The exact number of these deaths is unknown due to poor record-keeping or a cover-up by General Ammen and his medical staff. The deaths from January 1863 to May 1863 range in totals from the 464 noted in the *Official Records* to the 700 estimated by the *Chicago Tribune*.[205]

General Ammen managed the second major prisoner exchange beginning on March 31, 1863, when 700 prisoners left Camp Douglas. Approximately 2,500 more left camp in April, with 350 patients remaining. By July 1863, only about 50 sick prisoners remained at the camp. During this exchange, General Ammen was accused of transferring prisoners with smallpox.

Responding to the damage done by paroled Union soldiers while overseeing the arrival of additional prisoners and a general exchange all in just a few months would be a challenge for any commander. In January 1863, General Amen was faced with yet another situation of an entirely different nature.

Mrs. Finley opened an enterprising operation selling food and beverages to anyone in Camp Douglas through a hole she cut in the stockade fence. She had a shack near the northeast corner of the camp, just outside Garrison Square. Unlike the official sutlers, Mrs. Finley paid no tax to the prison fund. When the military repaired the fence, she would reopen the hole and continue to sell her wares, much to the pleasure of garrison soldiers and prisoners and much to the consternation of General Ammen.[206]

General Ammen knew how to impose discipline and handle administration. The number of ill prisoners, the conditions of the camp and harsh weather in Chicago made managing medical treatment particularly taxing. General Ammen's training at West Point had not prepared him for this task. He was forced to accept the work of unreliable medical personnel, and medical conditions improved but little. General Ammen became commander of the district of Springfield in early April 1863.[207] In May 1863, he was replaced by Captain J.S. Putnam.

Colonel DeLand Takes Command

On August 18, 1863, Colonel Charles V. DeLand was ordered to assume command of Camp Douglas by General Ammen without the consultation of Colonel Hoffman.[208] DeLand's strong military background, including his time as a prisoner after being capture at Murfreesboro, Tennessee, while a captain in the Ninth Michigan Infantry, made him an excellent choice as commander of Camp Douglas.

Colonel DeLand was a thirty-five-year-old volunteer officer in command of the First Michigan Sharpshooters, which included the company of Chippewa and Ottawa Indians from tribes in Michigan. This unit had been pursuing John Hunt Morgan's Raiders in Indiana and Kentucky. Ironically, the more than two thousand enlisted men of Morgan's Raiders were captured at Buffington Island, Ohio, on July 19, 1863, and sent to Camp Douglas, arriving there in August and September 1863 as prisoners with DeLand's men as guards.[209] With the suspension of exchanges under the Dix-Hill Cartel in mid-1863, these prisoners were destined to remain at

Morgan's Raiders at Camp Douglas. *Chicago History Museum.*

Camp Douglas for the duration of the war unless they signed the oath of allegiance, escaped or died.

DeLand commanded about 500 First Michigan and 150 Sixty-fifth Illinois to guard approximately 4,200 prisoners in late September. These troops were supplemented by 300 men from the Invalid Corps on September 27.[210] The Invalid Corps, re-designated the Veteran Reserve Corps (VRC) on March 18, 1864, would typically serve as prison guards throughout the remainder of the war. This relatively small garrison of guards who, at times, were corrupt and subject to prisoner bribes was a constant source of problems for DeLand.

Physical problems at the camp continued to be common. The one hydrant supplying water was not working, rations for the prisoners were slow in arriving and the barracks needed repairs. In October 1863, Colonel DeLand spent considerable time and effort (with mostly prisoner help) improving the barracks and installing the water and sewage system that General Meigs had provided belated approval for in June.[211]

DeLand was constantly in conflict with U.S. prison authorities and was frequently justifying his actions to Colonel Hoffman via telegraph. Colonel Hoffman's concerns about prison conditions and excessive escapes led him to have Dr. A.M. Clark, medical inspector of prisons, visit the camp. This visit led to a series of communications between DeLand and Hoffman. DeLand consistently justified his actions and requested more support from Hoffman. A lack of guards, inadequate security and other factors resulted in escapes, according to DeLand.[212] Hoffman continued to demand additional action to improve conditions and reduce escapes while offering little support to DeLand. This exchange between the two did little to improve Camp Douglas.

DeLand continued to manage the camp with an iron hand while working to improve conditions.

General Orme Takes Command

On December 16, 1863, the U.S. War Department gave command to the Northern District of Chicago, including Camp Douglas, to Brigadier General William W. Orme. Colonel DeLand had been relieved of duties on December 2, 1863, but remained in charge of the garrison. Colonel James C. Strong, Fifteenth Regiment of the Invalid Corps, was placed in command of the prison. Colonel Strong had been commander of the Thirty-eighth New York Infantry when he was seriously wounded at Williamsburg, Virginia, on

May 5, 1862.[213] Strong, who was responsible for day-to-day prison operations, began his command while residing in Chicago rather than Camp Douglas. As a result of this reorganization, General Orme was not responsible for the day-to-day operations of the prison.

General Orme was born in 1832 in Washington, D.C.; moved to Bloomington, Illinois; and was admitted to the bar in 1853. He was a law partner of Leonard Swett, who was a close associate of Abraham Lincoln. Lincoln regarded Orme as one of the most promising attorneys in Illinois. A colonel in the Ninety-fourth Illinois Infantry, Orme was promoted to brigadier general on March 13, 1863, and assigned, with the Ninety-fourth, to U.S. Grant's army at Vicksburg. During the siege of Vicksburg, General Orme contracted a tubercular condition that would result in his resignation in April 1864 and his death on September 13, 1866.[214] His frail health undoubtedly affected his ability to be an effective commander of Camp Douglas.

In November 1863, as a prelude to taking command of Camp Douglas, Orme was assigned to inspect a number of prison camps in New York, Pennsylvania, Ohio, Illinois and Indiana.[215]

Orme left daily operations of Camp Douglas to Colonel Strong, who continued to reside in Chicago. Colonel Benjamin J. Sweet's Eighth Regiment of the Invalid Corps joined the Fifteenth Regiment of the Invalid Corps and the First Michigan Sharpshooters as camp guards.

Colonel Strong continued his efforts to make the prison efficient. He established a camp regiment and time schedule that accounted for prisoner time from sunrise until 7:00 p.m.[216] He was obsessed with roll calls and accounting for prisoners.[217] He employed forced labor from prisoners to improve barracks, reduce mud and flooding and improve the general policing of the camp.[218]

Colonel Strong provided some continuity to the management of prisoners. Strong organized camp patrols and stockade guards into separate units for the first time, each with specific duties. Actions of some of these patrols were extremely brutal and repressive.[219] Overall discipline during Colonel Strong's command of the prison was heightened. A new dungeon in Prisoners Square, the use of the ball and chain and other measures were encouraged for various offenses.

The relationship between Orme and Strong was strained, as reported by Colonel James A. Hardy, U.S. Army inspector general, in his April 16, 1864 report: "General Orme gives very little personal attention to his command at Camp Douglas. The result is a want of harmony and efficiency in the management of every department of this command. There is also a want of courtesy on the

A prisoner pulling a ball and chain at Camp Douglas. *Illinois State Historical Society*.

part of the commanding officer toward the commander of the garrison. Colonel Strong and Major Skinner would be valuable officers serving under an efficient commander." General Orme was ordered to assume more personal responsibility for prison affairs after Hardy's report.[220] On April 29, he resigned.[221]

A high point at the camp during General Orme's tenure was the development of a remodeled and modernized Prisoners Square, including plans for new barracks, a lighted stockade fence, new latrines, a new water supply and new support buildings. A more difficult time was his embroilment in the controversial beef scandal involving Ninian Edwards. Ninian Wirt Edwards was the aristocratic, wealthy son of a former Illinois governor. He was associated with the elite of Springfield and known to be snobbish. He was married to Elizabeth Todd Edwards, the elder sister of Mary Todd Lincoln. Edwards was deeply involved in Illinois politics and an active supporter of President Lincoln, who had been instrumental in Edwards's appointment as commissary of subsistence for Illinois with the rank of captain.[222] In November 1863, Colonel DeLand had reported that he had no influence over Edwards and the support Edwards provided Camp Douglas, including the contracting of commissary supplies.[223] Curtis Burke reported poor quality of beef that was "mostly neck, flank, bones and shanks."[224] Colonel Hoffman ordered DeLand to bypass Edwards's contractors for providing bread for the camp.[225] DeLand clearly did not monitor the contractors who were providing provisions, especially meat products, to the camp.

General Orme conducted an investigation and reported his results to Colonel Hoffman. He found that one subcontractor's beef had been short "for some time back." However, he noted that he lacked sufficient evidence of the "fraud" and "cheating of weight" to warrant prosecution. He required Mr. Curtis, the subcontractor, to make restitution for the shortages. He found that Edwards and all other contractors were not involved in the matter.[226]

Colonel Sweet Takes Command

General Orme relieved Colonel Strong on April 27, 1864, and replaced him with Colonel Benjamin J. Sweet. After General Orme's resignation, Colonel Sweet was given command of the district and Camp Douglas on May 2, 1864. He reinstated Colonel Strong as commander of the garrison.

Colonel (Brevet Brigadier General) Benjamin J. Sweet would remain commander of Camp Douglas until nearly all Confederate prisoners were released in 1865. Born in 1832, Sweet moved from New York to Wisconsin, practiced law and was a member of the Wisconsin legislature. In May 1861, he joined the Sixth Wisconsin Infantry as a major and was later promoted to lieutenant colonel. He became engaged in conflict for undermining his commanding officer, Colonel Lysander Cutler. This resulted in his resignation from this storied unit of the famous Iron Brigade in June 1861. On July 21, 1862, Sweet was named colonel of the Twenty-first Wisconsin Infantry. Colonel Sweet was severely wounded in the right arm at the Battle of Perrysville (Kentucky) in October 1862. He resigned his commission on September 8, 1863, and on September 28 was appointed colonel of the Invalid Corps.[227]

The earlier Camp Douglas commanders—General Orme, General Ammen and General Tyler—had earned their general stars in combat. Colonel Sweet believed he could earn his star by managing Camp Douglas. While he received a brevet promotion on December 20, 1864, this temporary rank was never made permanent. He chose many actions at Camp Douglas that were intended to place him in the best possible light with superiors and enhance his chances for promotion and a postwar legacy.

Colonel Sweet's ambition was not reduced by his assignment at Camp Douglas. Orders to guards to "shoot to kill" and the incorporation of a variety of corporal punishments were typical of his approach. He also introduced "Morgan's Mule" to the camp. This carpenter's sawhorse on steroids was nearly fourteen feet tall and could accommodate several soldiers. It was used extensively by guards, who required prisoners to straddle the mule for several hours. While the device was notorious at Camp Douglas, similar horses were used throughout the Union army to punish prisoners and Union soldiers alike.[228]

Colonel Sweet's thirst for discipline included insistence on cleanliness of the prison area and the prisoners. Daily sweeping of barracks and weekly scrubbing were required. Prisoners were not permitted to empty dirty water in the streets and were expected to wash themselves and their clothing every

Friday. Failure to meet these requirements resulted in a two-hour ride on the mule.[229] While these measures might have seemed harsh to the prisoners, they resulted in the overall improvement of sanitary conditions in the camp and undoubtedly reduced deaths.

Initially, both Colonel Sweet and Colonel Strong established their headquarters in Chicago rather than at Camp Douglas. Captain Shurley, assistant adjutant general of Camp Douglas, was effectively in charge of the camp at this time. The secretary of war ordered Sweet to move his headquarters to Camp Douglas on July 1, 1864.[230] On July 27, Colonel Strong was ordered to establish residence at the camp by the U.S. adjutant general.[231] Neither of these orders were followed, and Sweet sent a letter to Colonel Hoffman on August 8 justifying keeping his headquarters in Chicago. On August 21, Hoffman responded in a somewhat patronizing manner, stating that the headquarters would indeed be moved to the camp.[232] Sweet was faced with circumstances that no other commander had faced. With the suspension of prison exchange in mid-1863 and the realization by the prisoners that exchange was not likely, he was faced with elevated prisoner discontent, more escape attempts and a growing prisoner population. A facility rated for 11,000 prisoners by Captain Potter, Chicago quartermaster, peaked at 12,092 in December 1864. The arrival of another 2,000 Morgan's Raiders in August 1863 posed additional challenges for Colonel Sweet. These men knew they would not be exchanged. They refused to sign the oath of allegiance or cooperate with prison authorities. Their actions made life for the guards miserable and were a constant challenge for the colonel.

With the increase in prisoners and the unlikely reduction through exchange, Colonel Sweet had to place a priority on completing the construction of additional barracks and other facilities in Prisoners Square. Work on the square, done mostly by prisoners, continued through 1864, including the addition of a six-inch water line to replace the three-inch line. This was finally approved by Colonel Hoffman in September and completed in November.

Overall, conditions in the camp improved as Prisoners Square was expanded. Inspection reports in August, September and November 1864 indicated satisfactory conditions of the prison facilities and the prisoners. These same reports showed concern for security and recommended additional guards and the issue of two cannons to control prisoners. Reports stated that five hundred pistols had been provided the guards.[233]

Prison security concerned Colonel Sweet as well. Veterans Reserve Corps troops had been assigned, but they were not adequate. On August 13,

The 196th Pennsylvania Infantry outside Camp Douglas. *Chicago History Museum.*

1864, 802 troops of the 196th Pennsylvania Infantry arrived at the camp to supplement the guards. They were untrained, one-hundred-day troops with no military experience. They were totally unprepared for their assignment, and prisoners took advantage of the "puny boys," including a September 7 charge of the stockade fence resulting in the escape of twelve. One escapee was shot and expected to die.[234] Sweet was further concerned when he found that guards from the 196th were removing the percussion caps from their rifles when they went off shifts. Furthermore, guard units from the 8th and 15th Veteran Reserve Corps never loaded their weapons.[235]

While inspection reports were positive, the health of prisoners was deteriorating. Smallpox was, in mid- to late 1864, of epidemic proportions. Lieutenant Briggs's inspection report of September 4, 1864, stated, "The hospital for prisoners of war is not large enough. There are at least 200 prisoners sick in quarters that should be in hospital. Out of twelve deaths among the prisoners during the past week three of them died in quarters. I am informed by the surgeons that the supply of medicine is insufficient for the actual wants of the prisoners."[236] On October 8, Sweet reported 984 prisoners sick in barracks. He also indicated the increase in scurvy and questioned Colonel Hoffman's order to prohibit the sutlers from selling vegetables to the prisoners. Colonel Hoffman, in his October 14 response, authorized the sutlers to resume selling vegetables.[237] It is curious that Colonel Sweet, who knew of the existence of scurvy among the prisoners and who knew that available vegetables were an effective prevention of the disease, did not take action with either commissary providers or use money from the prison fund to acquire them.

Beginning in the summer of 1864 and until the end of the year, Colonel Sweet was preoccupied by the grand Conspiracy of 1864, which will be discussed in detail in Chapter 11. Colonel Sweet continued to manage the camp with an iron hand. Finally, on May 8, 1865, he received the long-awaited order from Colonel Hoffman. General Order 85.5 read: "Ordered, That all prisoners of war, except officers above the rank of colonel, who before the capture of Richmond signified their desire to take the oath of allegiance to the United States and their unwillingness to be exchanged be forthwith released upon their taking the said oath, and transportation furnished them to their respective homes."[238] Those not taking the oath were ultimately released and provided no assistance in returning home.

Colonel Sweet did the best he could with the resources provided to him. While his demands for discipline and cleanliness were considered harsh by some, these practices likely saved a number of lives. Sweet was the most professional of commanders at Camp Douglas.

Colonel Sweet left the army to reside near Wheaton, Illinois, with his wife and family, including his daughter, Ada, who was with him at Camp Douglas. Ada went on to be a significant factor in women's suffrage in Chicago. Sweet was a founder of Lombard, Illinois. One of his proudest moments was when he removed the word "male" from provisions in the Lombard charter that provided that "all citizens above the age of twenty-one shall be entitled to vote at any corporation selection."[239]

Prisoner Organization

Prisoners were organized into squads that often represented the population of a barracks or multiple barracks. Prisoners selected their own leadership. The senior leader was designated sergeant major. These sergeant majors organized the squads, coordinated the drawing of rations and clothing, often acted as an advocate for prisoners to camp management and generally managed the squads. Frequently, these leaders were members of the most represented Confederate military units in the squad. This organization structure was unofficial and could be changed by the guard force or camp management.

Chapter 7

Prisoner Exchanges Under the Dix-Hill Cartel and Oath of Allegiance

Exchange and the oath of allegiance were frequently topics of conversation and concern by Confederate prisoners at Camp Douglas. Diaries and journals of prisoners, especially those who were incarcerated for long periods of time, contained frequent comments about rumors of exchange and a discussion of the oath offered to or taken by prisoners. As the war dragged on and the idea of exchange became more unlikely, the oath was a common topic. When the end of the war was in sight, the topic of exchange and going home reentered the thoughts and writings of the prisoners.[240]

The exchange of prisoners was based on the Dix-Hill Cartel.[241] Negotiations for the cartel began in June 1862 and ended with the signing of the document on July 22, 1862. The document was negotiated and named for Major General John A. Dix for the Union and Major General D.H. Hill for the Confederates. The mere existence of the negotiations and the ultimate cartel was difficult for both parties. The Confederates wanted to be considered a sovereign nation, while President Lincoln refused to acknowledge the Confederacy as anything but an insurrection. As a result, the preamble to the cartel read: "The undersigned having been commissioned by the authorities they respectively represent."

The Dix-Hill Cartel consisted of six articles.

Article 1 stated:

> *Prisoners to be exchanged man for man and officer for officer; privateers to be placed upon the footing of officers and men of the Navy. Men and officers of lower grades may be exchanged for officers of a higher grade, and men and officers of different services may be exchanged according to the following scale of equivalents.*

The scale of equivalents ranged from one to one for officers and soldiers of equal rank to a general commanding in chief or admiral, who was exchanged for sixty privates. A lieutenant or noncommissioned officer was exchanged for two privates.

Articles 2 and 3 related to noncombatants and captured civilians.

Article 4 stated:

> *All prisoners of war to be discharged on parole in ten days after their capture, and the prisoners now held and those hereafter taken to be transported to the points mutually agreed upon at the expense of the capturing party. The surplus prisoners not exchanged shall not be permitted to take up arms again, nor to serve as military police or constabulary force in any fort, garrison, or field-work held by either of the respective parties, nor as guards of prisons, depots or stores, nor to discharge any duty usually performed by soldiers, until exchanged under the provisions of this cartel. The exchange is not to be considered complete until the officer or soldier exchanged for has been actually restored to the lines to which he belongs.*

This article was overly optimistic when it called for parole within ten days of being captured. While this parole was possible in a field situation such as Vicksburg or Harpers Ferry, it was unrealistic in situations where captives were sent to prison camps. The provision prohibiting conducting military operations caused difficulties in maintaining discipline and order, as reflected by the paroled Union soldiers sent to Camp Douglas.

Article 5 stated:

> *Each party upon the discharge of prisoners of the other party is authorized to discharge an equal number of their own officers or men from parole,*

> *furnishing at the same time to the other party a list of the prisoners discharged and of their own officers and men relieved from parole, thus enabling each party to relieve from parole such of their own officers and men as the party may choose.*

This article specifically covered the exchange provisions from parole. General U.S. Grant asserted that Confederates were returning to active duty on the war front without being properly exchanged. This might, in part, have accounted for the suspension of parole.

Article 6 summarized the other five articles.

The Dix-Hill Cartel was patterned loosely after the War of 1812 Nova Scotia Cartel. However, conspicuously absent in Dix-Hill was any mention of the treatment of prisoners while in captivity. Not until General Order 100 was issued on April 24, 1863, did the Union army have specific guidelines for the treatment of prisoners. Confederate guidelines were never placed in one document, but they can be found in a variety of orders and directives during the war.

Prior to Dix-Hill, exchange was often accomplished by an agreement between officers in the field. For example, in December 1861, L.M. Goldsmith, commander of the North Atlantic Blockade, negotiated directly with Confederate brigadier general Benjamin Huger to exchange ten Confederate navy and marine officers for prisoners held by the Confederacy.[242]

On December 11, 1861, the U.S. House of Representatives offered the following joint resolution:

> *Whereas, the exchange of prisoners in the present rebellion has already been practiced indirectly, and as such exchange would not only increase the enlistment and vigor of our Army but subserve the highest interests of humanity and such exchange does not involve a recognition of the rebels as a government; therefore: Resolved, by the Senate and House of Representatives of the United States of America in Congress assembled, That the President of the United States be requested to inaugurate systematic measures for the exchange of prisoners in the present rebel.*[243]

At the time of the first exchange under Dix-Hill in mid-1862, eleven Union prisons held 20,500 prisoners. Camp Douglas, with 7,800 prisoners, was by far the largest. Camp Morton was second, with 4,000. Other Illinois prisons Camp Butler in Springfield and Alton prison held 2,000 and 500, respectively.[244]

Prisoner Exchanges at Camp Douglas and the Oath of Allegiance

Camp Douglas participated in the first exchange of prisoners beginning on July 31, 1862, when Colonel Hoffman ordered an extra set of prisoner roles. On August 28, 1862, Colonel Tucker received orders to move 1,000 prisoners to Cairo, Illinois, to be exchanged in Vicksburg, Mississippi. They were to be accompanied by a company of armed guards.[245] Those not wishing to be exchanged were permitted to take the oath of allegiance, remain in Camp Douglas or join the Union military. By late September, the exchange was completed, although about 150 prisoners too sick to be transported remained in Camp Douglas. Approximately 8,500 prisoners were exchanged.[246]

Camp Douglas was without prisoners from September 1862 until January 27, 1863, when prisoners captured at Fort Hindman, Arkansas, began arriving. Approximately 4,000 were expected to arrive by February 1. In all, 3,800 was the final number of new prisoners. On April 3, 2,534 prisoners departed Camp Douglas for exchange at City Point, Virginia, while 229 chose to take the oath of allegiance and 350 were too ill to move. Based on these numbers, apparently nearly 700 died between January and April. It was reported that 260 prisoners died in twenty-one days from January 27 to February 18.

On April 7, Secretary Stanton asked Colonel Hoffman about the status of twenty-five prisoners who had arrived with smallpox. Colonel Hoffman's investigation indicated that the prisoners were from Camp Douglas, thus accusing General Ammen of knowingly shipping prisoners with the disease. In the heated exchange with Stanton, Hoffman placed the blame on General Ammen and his medical officer. General Ammen responded, "I feel conscious that I performed my whole duty faithfully, carefully and with judgment."[247] After this communication ended on April 9, the matter seemed to be forgotten.

This would mark the end of general exchanges at Camp Douglas until near the end of the war. By mid-1863, the Union had suspended all exchanges on the order of President Lincoln. This decision was in response to the Confederate position that captured African American soldiers would not be accorded protection as prisoners of war but rather treated as escaped slaves. In addition, the Confederates threatened to execute any white officer who commanded African Americans.[248] On April 24, 1863, General Order 100, Article 57, was drafted for President Lincoln, in part, because of his concern over the reaction in the South to the Emancipation Proclamation. It stated:

> *So soon as a man is armed by a sovereign government and takes the soldier's oath of fidelity, he is a belligerent; his killing, wounding, or other warlike acts are not individual crimes or offenses. No belligerent has a right to declare that enemies of a certain class, color, or condition, when properly organized as soldiers, will not be treated by him as public enemies.*[249]

Curtis Burke expressed the opinion of many Confederate soldiers regarding exchange for African Americans:

> *Friday January 8th 1864. We have had rumors for several days that all prisoners of war were ordered to Point Lookout, under Gen. Butler's jurisdiction to be kept till the Confederate Government will consent to recognize Butler and exchange negro soldiers captured. As far as I can learn most of the prisoners would rather remain prisoners a year longer than be exchanged through Beast Butler (as we call him) for negro troops.*[250]

The termination of the exchange of prisoners left the options of death, escape or signing the oath of allegiance as the only routes out of Union prisons. The oath presented a moral quandary to many Confederate prisoners. Robert Bagby, in his diary on February 27, 1864, offered an excellent description of this moral dilemma:

> *There was some recruitment in the camp about taking the oath. A good many were taking it. I disagree myself taking the oath was a disgrace alone. Although I was doing* [al]*right, taking the oath was more than I could stand. I was much sorry to see Muller, Ronnie, George, West, William, Melt and Amos taking the oath but would not question them. I felt lonesome having been left alone. I could not take the oath for I thought more of my honor than I did my case. How could I stay at home after taking the oath? How could they have confidence in a man who would take the oath? Honestly they could not. And yet it might be possible that I might take it someday but thought I would have to change a great deal. I could not think bad of the boys taking it and leaving here for they truly thought they were doing what was best. But I could not see the way they did it looks to desert a clause.*[251]

In spite of the fact that many shared these feelings, a significant number of Camp Douglas prisoners took the oath. Following is the postwar oath signed by Curtis Burke on May 27, 1865:

> *United States of America*
> *State of Tennessee*
> *Office of Provost Marshal*
> *District of West Tennessee*
>
> *I do solemnly swear, in the presence of Almighty God, that I will bear true allegiance to the United States of America and will obey and maintain the Constitution and Laws of the same, and, will defend and support the said United States of America against all enemies, foreign and domestic, and especially against the Rebellious League known as the Confederate States of America. So help me God.*[252]

The oath signed by J.M. Copley on June 20, 1865, is more typical of the postwar oaths taken. Direct reference to the Confederate States of America was omitted. It read:

> *United States of America*
>
> *I, J.M. Copley, of the county of Dickson, State of Tennessee, do solemnly swear that I will support, protect and defend the Constitution and Government of the United States against all enemies, whether domestic or foreign; that I will bear true faith, allegiance and loyalty to the same, any ordinance, resolution or laws of any State, convention or legislature to the contrary notwithstanding, and further, that I will faithfully perform all duties which may be required of me by the laws of the United States; and I take this oath freely, without any mental reservation or evasion whatever.*[253]

Those taking the oath before the end of the war became "Galvanized Yankees." Considered pariahs by other Confederate prisoners, they were quickly moved to separate barracks and given improved rations and other benefits. Bagby reflected this conflict in his diary on January 17, 1865: "The guards in the square had serious difficulty throughout the day as prisoners were divided into two parties on termed oath takers and the others opposing it. The anti-oath takers got the best of the fight. They fought with knives and a good many men were hurt."[254]

Many entered the service of the Union military. Some were offered enlistment in army units in the Western Territories protecting settlers from the Indians. Others chose to join the U.S. Navy, as this service was the least likely to come in contact with Confederate forces. Others, particularly those from the border states, were allowed to simply go home. Still others remained in camps as non-military workers such as clerks and carpenters. Burke recounts one of these offers:

> *Wednesday September 14th, 1864. At roll call two orders were read to all the prisoners, 1st. That all prisoners of war who wish to join a regiment of United States Cavalry to fight the Indians can do so by reporting at the express office. That all prisoners of war who are mechanics and workmen who have applied for the oath or will apply and who desire to work can do so by reporting at the express office. There was a large crowd around the express office all day.*[255]

Not all prisoners at Camp Douglas who expressed a desire to take the oath completed the process. On January 28, 1864, J.P. Tipton of Springfield, Illinois, wrote to prisoner Moses P. Davis. Tipton, who apparently negotiated the approval for Davis to take the oath, expressed his disapproval of Davis refusing to take the oath. The letter included the following:

> *Since you were in Camp Douglas you have written me three letters: have written your father's agent at Nashville, Ill.: and to all your uncles in St. Clair County, Ill. to use their utmost efforts in your behalf, stating to them your desire to take the oath. They all failed and then applied to me.*
>
> *I procured an order for your release, upon your taking the oath of allegiance and renunciation. I received a letter today from Brig. Gen. Orme stating that you refused to take the oath required by the government.*
>
> *I have made considerable sacrifice of time and money to procure your release. I have been twice to Chicago and all to no avail. You cannot take an oath to support the Government of the United States—because you are too much a rebel for that.*
>
> *I now sincerely hope that you may be kept a prisoner until the end of the war and then you will be compelled to take the very same oath that is offered you now or swing at the end of hemp. You have deceived your relatives as to your loyalty and passed the point of enjoying your liberty.*
>
> *The commanding officer I suppose has by this time reported your refusal to take the oath to the Secretary of War. If so, this will close*

> *the correspondence between us now and forever. I have no sympathy with rebels.*[256]

The number of prisoners at Camp Douglas who took the oath before the end of the war is unknown, but it certainly numbered in the thousands. The *Tribune* reported that "about a thousand" agreed to take the oath on March 21, 1862, and 3,500 on March 25. In August, when the first exchange was reported, 500 agreed to sign the oath.[257] James Mackey, on the eve of the general exchange, noted in his diary that former Tennessee governor William B. Campbell visited the Tennessee prisoners and was authorized to administer the oath to "all who wished to take it. 368 took the oath. Not all Tennesseans."[258]

Copley identified the Galvanizes Yankees as "loyal men" and drew parallels with Tories in the Revolutionary War. He noted that other prisoners considered those who took the oath dishonest and disgraceful and indicated that in late 1864 and early 1865, some two hundred oath takers were in barracks number fifty-three. In his opinion, "Honorable Federal soldiers looked upon and regarded this class of men with rather a suspicious eye, and who could not be trusted very far in anything."[259] Burke characterized taking the oath as "swallow[ing] the dog."[260]

At the end of the war, all Confederate prisoners were expected to sign the oath. By doing so, they received rations and transportation home. Those who refused to sign the oath would be released from prison and expected to find their own way home.[261]

Chapter 8

Prison Life: Stories and Treatment from the Prisoners' Perspectives

Up to this point, we have looked at Camp Douglas from the outside and examined the views of the developers of the camp, senior U.S. prison management, camp commanders and senior military and civilian officials whose job it was to prosecute the war. While we have seen some prisoners' reactions to their first looks at the camp and their reactions to exchange and the oath of allegiance, an important part of the Camp Douglas story lies in the feel for the life of the prisoner.

The camp, originally designed as a reception center rather than prison, was changed as it evolved. The location of the camp made sanitation and health issues a constant concern. Frequent changes in command undoubtedly resulted in equally frequent changes of tone in the camp.

This chapter consists almost exclusively of the reflections of five men, all of whom have already been quoted:

Robert Anderson Bagby, thirty-three at the time of his imprisonment, served with the First Northeast Missouri Cavalry. He was a prisoner from January 1863 until March 1865 and a "nurse" in the prisoners' hospital. After the war, Bagby returned to farming in Knox County, Missouri, where he remained until his death in 1900.

Curtis R. Burke, twenty-one years old, was a member of Morgan's Raiders, Fourteenth Kentucky Cavalry. He was imprisoned in Camp Douglas from August 1863 until March 1865. Burke had worked in his father's marble

Camp Douglas prisoners in winter. *Chicago History Museum.*

business in Lexington, Kentucky. His journal was dictated in 1915 at age seventy-three.

John M. Copley, Forty-ninth Tennessee Infantry, was held at Camp Douglas from December 1864 until June 1865. Copley wrote his journal in 1893. He would have come to Camp Douglas with the Fort Donelson prisoners, had he not been ill and in the hospital in Nashville when Fort Donelson surrendered.

William D. Huff, Thirteenth Louisiana Infantry, was captured at Chickamauga, Georgia, on September 2, 1863, and imprisoned at Camp Douglas from October 1863 until May 1865, when he was given transportation to New Orleans.

James Taswell Mackey, corporal, Forty-eighth Tennessee Infantry, was twenty years old when captured at Fort Donelson. He was a prisoner from February 22, 1862, until his exchange on September 7, 1862. Mackey was from Columbia, Tennessee, where his father was a successful tanner, farmer and businessman. His three brothers also served in the Confederate army.

His brother William died of illness shortly after enlisting. The other two survived the war.

The experience of these inmates from February 1862 until June 1865 covers the entire period of time the prison camp was in operation.

When examining the prisoners, some clear distinctions can be made. Several of the prisoners' homes and families were located in border states and states that were under Union control during most of the war. While contested, Tennessee and Kentucky were mostly in Union hands. Arkansas and Missouri saw guerilla warfare during much of the conflict, but most of the area was controlled by the Union. This offered prisoners with families living in these areas the luxury of receiving mail and visits. Not only did this offer them the comfort of contact with home, but packages with food, clothing and money provided them with goods and supplies not available to others. These "haves," such as Curtis Burke, were rarely hungry and offer the perspective of those prisoners not experiencing the deprivation suffered by others. Also in this group was James Mackey, who received letters from home, had over twenty dollars in sutler credit and spent the least amount of time (seven months) in Camp Douglas.

Some prisoners, who did not have access to family or friends, could depend on comrades from their unit to share resources with them. Members of Morgan's Raiders were the best example of these prisoners who benefitted from the support of members of their unit.

Yet another group was the "Galvanized Yankees." With special privileges, including improved living conditions, duties and food, this group was isolated from the general prison population. Few of these men maintained diaries or journals. Henry Morton Stanley, who later utter the famous phrase, "Doctor Livingston, I presume," was one "loyal man," as Copley called them. Records show that Stanley was a prisoner at Camp Douglas as a member of Company A, Sixth Arkansas Infantry, and joined "the Irish Brigade."[262] There is no mention of Henry Stanley—or John Rowlands, his real name—in the Irish Brigade records in the Illinois State Archives. Reportedly captured at Shiloh, Stanley arrived at Camp Douglas in April 1862 and wrote graphic descriptions of Camp Douglas in his book, published nearly forty years after his capture. Most of the very tall tales he wrote have no basis in fact and might have been written to justify his "galvanization." His fanciful story adds little to the experience of the soldiers who signed the oath and gives an unreliable account of conditions at Camp Douglas.

Prisoners with little contact outside the camp or little opportunity to receive packages could improve their lot with jobs in the prison. Robert Bagby and William Huff had no direct contact with their families and apparently received no mail while at Camp Douglas. Bagby's job as a nurse in the prison hospital gave him extra resources. Interestingly, his diary before coming to Camp Douglas was written in pencil. After arrival and his assignment as a nurse, his diary was written in ink. He never wrote of living in a general barracks or offered any information on the lack or quality of food. Huff obtained money from the sale of his artwork and can be considered a part of this group. Other jobs such as cooks, clerks and orderlies offered special privileges. The Freemasons are also included in this group. Both Curtis Burke and John Copley reported that the Freemasons had a separate barracks with unspecified advantages.[263]

The final group of prisoners was composed of those who had none of the advantages of other prisoners. Alone, with no contact with their home and family, these soldiers received only what was left. Unless the "haves" shared with these "have-nots," life at Camp Douglas was exceptionally bleak. The probability of illness due to a lack of proper food and exposure to wretched conditions was highest among this group.

Prisoners from each of these groups have different perspectives of prison life and present those perspectives differently. Burke, for example, spoke frequently of the lack of food yet also spoke of sumptuous meals available to him and his comrades. Bagby, a nurse, wrote of the condition of the ill prisoners differently than those observing illness from the barracks. At times, Copley's flowing narratives give the reader the impression that the words he wrote were more important than the events he observed. Mackey more frequently wrote very short passages, such as "March 17, 1862 Sun shone feebly. Mr. Jackson visited me," rather than lengthy entries. Huff's diary included detailed and meaningful drawings of camp life yet often skipped comments for weeks or months during his imprisonment.

The different circumstances of these groups and the idiosyncrasies of the individuals therein make a comprehensive understanding of camp life difficult. An accumulation of observations by prisoners offers a patchwork quilt of the Camp Douglas experience.

Daily Routine

As in many prison camps, days were often anything but routine in Camp Douglas. Frequent surprise inspections for weapons and contraband, work details and boredom and monotony were daily occurrences. One major factor that affected daily life in the camp was the weather. Nearly every diary and journal written by a prisoner contains daily comments on the weather. Temperatures, cloudiness, rain and snow were usually included in entries.

Official weather records in Chicago were not maintained until the 1880s; therefore, temperatures reported by prisoners are difficult to confirm. The *Chicago Tribune* reported ranges of temperatures weekly, recorded at E.L. O'Hara, Druggists, at 30 West Randolph Street in downtown Chicago.[264] In February 1862, temperatures ranged from 0 to 40 degrees above zero, while those in February 1863 ranged from 10 degrees to 50 degrees. Extremely cold temperatures were reported in December 1864, when the range was -14 to 48 degrees above zero. The coldest low recorded was -25 in February 1865. None of the temperature reports support the large number of -25-degree days reported by prisoners. The winters during the existence of Camp Douglas were most likely typical of Chicago winters.

On March 7, 1864, Burke recorded in his diary that the daily routine was ordered as:

> *1st to rise at the sound of bugle at sunrise*
> *2d roll call at sound of the bugle one hour after*
> *3d dismissal at sound of the bugle and breakfast*
> *4th fatigue detail at 8 o'clock A.M.*
> *5th recall of detail at 12 o' clock M.*
> *6th dinner at 12½ o'clock P.M.*
> *7th fatigue detail at 1 o'clock P.M.*
> *8th recall of detail 5 o'clock P.M.*
> *9th supper detail at 5½ o'clock P.M.*
> *10th lights out at 7 o'clock P.M.*[265]

Those not subject to fatigue detail or other duties had nearly eight hours of free time. Other than cooks, clerks and hospital personnel, such as Robert Bagby, a significant number of the prisoners had no routine duties.

John Copley recalled the camp routine by the bugler, who was second only to the guards in importance:

> *The next person of importance was the bugler. This personage is generally designated and called "the little bugler," but I shall simply call him "the bugler." He made his appearance inside the prison square, at the headquarters of the prison guard, twice each day, at 6:30 a.m. and at 6 p.m., for the purpose of giving the signals for roll call and to retire to bunk. At 6:30 a.m., when he sounded that bugle, we had to fall into line, fronting our barrack, and remain in line until the roll was called; and at 6 p.m. when we heard its shrill blast, every living prisoner within the prison square had to immediately retire to bunk. I only knew the bugler from the sound of his instrument—that is, I knew there was one on hand, as we rarely ever saw him, for his bugle would ring out before we thought of his presence at headquarters, then we had no time to look at him, our bunks being of much more importance. This was the only duty we knew of his having to perform on the inside of the prison square.*[266]

Roll Call, Inspections and Daily Details

In his diary, Burke indicated, "At role call every morning six men are detailed for the day. Two to bring water and cut wood for the kitchen, two to keep the barracks and street in front well swept, two to carry off the slop water."[267] Roll call was frequently a time-consuming matter. Often held outdoors in inclement weather, these long roll call formations often contributed to illness in the camps. Bagby reported arriving prisoners standing outdoors in January 1865 from daylight until late in the day. Similarly, Copley stood "several hours facing an icy breeze of mist" upon his arrival at Camp Douglas in January 1864.[268]

Bagby wrote of the results of this treatment of prisoners:

> *We had a good many that were badly frosted. One poor fellow had all his fingers frosted so they had to be taken off leaving nothing but what would be called club hands. Samuel had all his toes taken off. Those that were so frosted came with the last squad of prisoners. The weather was so cold as they came into camp at daylight and were kept standing in the square until late in the day to give time to search them and not been fit for several days before. A good deal of their clothing had been taken from them before they were led into Prisoners Square. Consequently a great many were badly frozen.*[269]

Bagby reported one death from this treatment of prisoners: "Calvin Harrison of Mississippi died of his battle with frost bite. All of his fingers had been taken off of each hand. Sometime before he died he was knocking around some logs of sausage. The boys always fed him but he finally began to decline and never got up again."[270]

Routine roll calls became less routine when the commander required a special count of prisoners. These special roll calls were often initiated by U.S. Army prison authorities.[271] Other extremely long roll calls would be held immediately after escapes or when prisoners were missing. Frequently, prisoners would be required to stand until the missing prisoners were found.[272]

One inspection reported by Burke was especially extensive:

> *We were all marched to the main square in front of headquarters where we found all of the prisoners from the other square also in line. All of the Yankee Lieuts. and Sergeants were set to work searching us. Some took our knives, money, etc. and put it on paper, but others kept no account. Like was done at Camp Morton. Then they came around again and took every good coat in the crowd, and distributed some thin cottonade pepper and salt jackets, and some thin black rediculous* [sic] *looking tight spade tail Yankee coats in the place of their warm coats received from home. Some photographs were even taken from our men. In the meantime a squad of Yankees and work hands searched our quarters and took all the good clothing they found, and the work hands stole some of the men's rations. All of the axes, wood saws, and spades were taken away, depriving us of the means of cutting up our wood and cleaning up our quarters. They left a few rakes I believe and said that we could comb our heads with them.*[273]

In the spring of 1864, Burke recounted an unusually cruel search by prison guards:

> *After the roll was called and we were expecting every minute to hear the bugle sound for dismissal, the Yankee sergeant and corporals commenced searching our barracks. In about half an hour they came out with a hand full of money nearly all Confederate that they found and had taken from the sick men in the barracks. Then they commenced at the head of the regiment searching men separately by running their hands into the men's pockets, feeling over their clothing, and turning them over to a private who made them sit on a barrel and pull off their boots. Then shaking the boots and*

> *feeling around their feet the men then put on their boots and formed a new line of two ranks as fast as they passed through the mill.*
>
> *The search was so unexpected that the men had but little time to prepare for it, but most of them succeeded in hiding their money, some about their clothes and others in the mud at their feet. Every cent of every description that was found except sutler's checks was taken. As soon as they finished searching our regiment we were dismissed. After standing out about four hours with orders to stay in our barracks till all of the regiments were searched. It was about an hour and a half before all of the regiments were dismissed, then the men went out and dug up their money. I understand that the Yanks got twenty-three thousand five hundred and forty dollars in all from the prisoners. No one appears to know what this indiscriminate robbery is for. This is the second time it has occurred to us in this camp.*[274]

On another occasion, Burke encountered an irresponsible guard officer, Captain Webb (or Wells) Sponable, who kept prisoners on roll call for over an hour because a blue jacket had been stolen from the workshop.[275]

Special inspections were called when commanders had a concern that weapons or other contraband was being held by prisoners. These inspections, conducted by guards and, at times, Chicago police, included the ransacking of barracks and removal of property from prisoners. Items taken by guards often included clothing, weapons, money, tobacco, daguerreotypes and extra cooking utensils.[276]

Many of these inspections and raids were contrary to Article 72 of General Order 100, issued in April 1863, which expressly stated, "Money and other valuables on the person of a prisoner, such as watches or jewelry, as well as extra clothing, are regarded by the American Army as the private property of the prisoner, and the appropriation of such valuables or money is considered dishonorable, and is prohibited."[277]

Free Time Entertainment

Prisoners' free time could be filled with a variety of activities. Burke reported that the *Chicago Tribune* and *Chicago Post* newspapers were available to prisoners.[278] He also wrote of artisans who produced "gutta-percha rings, breastplates, etc. ornamenting them with fancy sets of gold, silver, and pearl. There were about thirty ring makers in camp."[279] Burke

A locket made by a prisoner in December 1864 and purchased by Chester Durfee of the First Minnesota Infantry and Fifteenth Veteran Reserve Corps. The woman in the photo is presumably Durfee's wife. *Paul Russinoff.*

also spoke of artisans, as gold and silver were very much in demand by Union officers and soldiers. John Copley wrote of shoe cobblers, watch "tinkers" and tailors who plied their trades at Camp Douglas.[280] Burke noted an example of this handiwork: "I saw two toys out on end of a barrack below here that were worked by the wind, representing a negro and a white man striking at each other with paddles, and the harder the wind blows the faster they strike."[281]

William Huff spent much of his time as an artist or playing his guitar. He complained, "It is hard to get strings so I use my pencil more than my music. Engraving is almost played out so it is rather difficult to keep in tobacco."[282] Huff also recounted, "One of the features of Camp Douglas is the brokers who deal in almost everything. They buy and sell Confederate money, greenbacks, sutler's tickets. Gambling of every description is carried on here."[283] In Prisoners Square, a faro bank was reported in "full operation" on which the banker had amassed a fortune of $150,000 in Confederated currency.[284] In April 1864, Burke commented on gamblers at the camp: "The Yanks made the gamblers at the sutler store scatter and piled up their home-made tables in the center of the square at the lumber pile. The gamblers seem to have been effectually scattered as there is no tables in operation today."[285]

Haynie noted that "others revived games of childhood, and could be seen busily engaged in playing leap frog, or marbles, with an earnestness worthy of the happiest ten-year-old."[286] Burke recounted, "The prisoners amuse themselves out of doors running, jumping, flying kites and playing ball."[287] Other diary entries also mention the prisoners engaging in board games, cards, checkers, sporting events and other athletic activities in the camp.[288] There appears to have been little interference with these activities by the prison authorities.

Burke also recounted the prisoners' version of football: "Eleck Edgar raised subscription of three dollars and sent to the city by our Yankee roll call sergeant and bought a gum foot ball. It is now going the rounds in a crowd of some three or four hundred men in the center of this square and many a skinned and bruised shin will be the result of it."[289]

John Copley longed for books but found them in short supply. Other than books on arithmetic and algebra, he could find very few. His favorite pastime was playing euchre with three fellow prisoners. He and his partner Jake Pool played their opponents to see who would carry water from the hydrant for the whole mess. He wrote, "We were mere novices at playing, as compared to them, but experts in counting points, especially when not entitled to them."[290]

In the fall of 1863, Burke reported on a literary society established by Chaplin James Orr:

> *There was a meeting at the Chapel and I went. Religious papers were distributed to the congregation and parson James Orr had a lot of books which he wished to put in a library to be drawn out by members of a religious society that he was about to form. The object of this society is to improve the morals of the camp. No one but a member could draw books from the library. After service the congregation was notified that all that wished to join the society could remain and give in their names. About thirty of us gave in our names and drew a book each.*[291]

In March 1862, James Mackey reported, "I woke this morning to find the ground covered with snow to a depth of eleven inches; the snow has been falling to-day also. Cold as it has been, it has been a day of merriment among our fellow-prisoners who have kept up an unceasing warfare of snow-balls during the day."[292]

A broadside announcing a "Grand Concert" by Morgan's Raiders. *Tennessee State Library and Archives.*

Organized entertainment by prisoners was not unusual.[293] Fifteen-cent Yankee or three-dollar Confederate tickets to Jack Curd's Negro Minstrels would often result in three or four hundred prisoners crowding into a barracks for the show. Even though these shows could be authorized by the camp commander, guards often would break them up because they believed such large crowds were dangerous.[294] Flyers advertising concerts were often produced and distributed. For example, a "grand concert" by Morgan's Men was advertised for October 5, 1863, with "Old Robert Ridley" performing.[295] Impromptu dances could often be heard after supper, with music provided by a fiddle or two and "men with their hats off representing the women."[296]

Morgan's Raiders had begun publishing a newspaper, the *Prisoner Vidette*, in August 1862. After their capture and imprisonment at Camp Douglas, they published the paper there in March 1864. The *Vidette*, handwritten on "a sheet of foolscap," contained camp stories and rumors, as well as war news. Editorial comments were included along with speculation of the political future. There were also original poetry, songs, jokes and advertisements. One could buy the products of the camp artisans by going to a designated barracks whose address was printed in the paper.[297] Abraham Lappin placed an advertisement in the *Vidette* for handmade smoking pipes, which were sold "wholesale and retail at Lappin's factory, Block 17 three doors west of the south east corner. Give him a call you will not be otherwise than satisfied."[298]

The only known copy of the *Prisoner Vidette* can be found in the archives of the Chicago Public Library.

Civilian Visits

Authorized by prison authorities or not, civilian visits to Camp Douglas were common events throughout its existence. The horse trolley on Cottage Grove offered easy access to the curious to visit both Union soldiers and Confederate prisoners. The observation towers just outside the main gate were frequently filled with the curious, who could also visit the beer garden in the nearby hotel. Once inside the camp, visitors were accompanied by escort officers. Burke observed on a Sunday in April 1864:

> *Two ladies escorted by an officer passed through the principal part of our camp, and as usual created some excitement among the rebs. One of the*

> *ladies actually of her own free will and accord deliberately kissed a reb. My stars how the rest of us envied him. When they came to the crowd near the gate to go out, some reb cried out, "Give way to the right and left, let the artillery pass."*[299]

At the 1864 Fourth of July celebration, Burke noted, "A lady on the parapet yesterday took a fancy to a prisoner by the name of Derbis and sent him a basket of provisions and a bouquet today."[300]

Upon Copley's arrival at Camp Douglas in late 1864, he noted:

> *While occupying this barrack we had but little to occupy our time and attention, except to look at and study the people who came in from the city in great crowds to take a view of the last arrival of Confederate prisoners. These crowds were generally composed of women, who were sometimes escorted by plug hats and swallow-tail coats. Some few of the women greeted us with such epithets as "vile rebels, who should have been hung instead of being brought there, and they were sorry we were not all killed at Franklin." They generally spent an hour or two promenading the prison square. After entering the inclosure* [sic], *an officer would sometimes accompany them over the prison grounds. These inquisitive and silly visitors would look at us with as much amazement as the average country people do at a first class menagerie when it enters a town. A few of the women would take up handfuls of snow, and ask the prisoners "if they had ever seen anything like that down South." We were not subject to such close scrutiny every day, as the better class sometimes visited the prison, and from them we never had to reply to any such unkind or disrespectful expressions.*[301]

There were other frequent visitors, including politicians, military leaders, clergy and relatives of prisoners. Prison management, while not officially approving of these visits, did not interfere unless they disrupted daily prison life.

Religion

Religion and religious activities were a part of the prisoners' lives. The camp had several chapels, one of which, built in 1861, was converted to a hospital. The largest permanent chapel was built in 1864. Religious services were also held in barracks and in outdoor venues. Reverend Edmund B. Tuttle,

Church services at Camp Douglas. *Chicago History Museum.*

rector of Saint Ausgarius Catholic Church in Chicago, served as the post chaplain through the existence of Camp Douglas and was chairman of the Relief Committee. Dwight L. Moody, founder of the Moody Church, was a frequent visitor to the camp, often preaching in the chapel that the YMCA had built in Garrison Square in 1861. A number of other visiting chaplains and ministers visited the camp and performed religious services for the prisoners.

Reverend Tuttle frequently distributed religious newspapers and pamphlets. Burke noted of this material, "Some of the reading we respected, but most of it, the abolition articles, we read with utmost contempt."[302] Mackey wrote about an evening Bible class, "We had quite an interesting class; the 6th chapter of Luke was our lesson. The question of prayer to Christ was discussed, but not settled."[303]

Mail and Packages

Sending and receiving mail was permitted for the prisoners. In June 1862, Colonel Hoffman ordered, "Prisoners will not be permitted to write letters of more than one page of common letter paper, the matter to be strictly of a private nature or the letter must be destroyed."[304] From time to time, mail privileges were suspended by camp commanders. These suspensions lasted only a few days. In March 1864, Colonel Hoffman reinstituted package privileges for prisoners with the following instructions to prison camp commanders: "By authority of the Secretary of War I have respectfully to inform you that boxes containing nothing hurtful or contraband, sent to prisoners of war by their families or friends, may be delivered. Any uniform clothing or equipments [*sic*] of any kind for military service, weapons of all kinds and intoxicating liquors are among contraband articles. Any excess of clothing over what is required for immediate use is contraband."[305]

While receiving mail and packages was permitted, there was no guarantee that the prisoner would receive the goods sent to him. Copley noted that prisoners whose homes were inside Federal main lines could obtain mail, packages and money from home. He also indicated that writing a letter was permitted every ten days or two weeks and that these letters were examined by headquarters.[306] Mackey frequently mentioned receiving mail in his diary entries. Bagby reported a method of receiving postage and writing material: "In the evening I received some postage stamps from Mrs. Morris, though the express office. I got a line from John T. Shanks who was acting for the express office informing me of paper, envelopes and writing material."[307]

Prisoner Winnie W. Paul, in letters sent to his wife, who was living in Nashville, Tennessee, in October 1864 and January 1865 acknowledged receipt of letters and packages. He requested she send him "a pair of coarse heavy janes [jeans] pants and line them, and a bed ticking of something course and heavy to hold straw, one pair of yard socks." He also wrote, "I want Sue Kimbro to knit me a pair of gloves like she made Thos. Chilcutt 3 years ago and & I will send her a nice ring."[308]

The ability to get mail was a significant advantage for some prisoners. Not only could goods be provided but also money. Any money received was retained by the camp, and prisoners were given chits or checks to be used at the sutler store.[309] If money could be smuggled in to the prisoners or if review of mail and packages was lax, it could be used to bribe guards for escape or commissary personnel to obtain additional or special food. Periodic surprise inspections were aimed at preventing cash in the camp. Prisoners became very creative in hiding their money in their barracks or on themselves or burying it in the campgrounds. Because of the devaluation of Confederate currency, greenbacks were the currency of choice and the only currency of value to bribe guards or use in an escape.

Sutler Stores

Other than receipt from home, the only source for many items was the sutler store. Sutlers were privately owned civilian purveyors of important sundries for soldiers and prisoners. Sutlers were common in prisons, garrisons and with units in the field during the Civil War. While the only option for many items, the sutler was a constant source of complaint for soldiers and prisoners alike.

Copley effectively expressed the disdain in which the sutler was held when he wrote:

> *A sutler is one who follows the army, but keeps himself far in the rear whenever there is a prospect of battle. He never shows himself near the front unless the enemy is known to be two or three hundred miles off. He sells provisions and various flashy and trashy articles of merchandise, which will generally catch all the small change soldiers carry in their pockets. Whenever he can do so on the sly, he will slip a soldier a little bust-head whiskey, and at the same time swear it is a genuine article of old rye or bourbon, and charge one dollar for about two teaspoonfuls* [sic]. *Here he was far in the rear, and had no fears of the enemy on the front. He sold us some provisions and various articles of clothing, but no whiskey or intoxicating drinks of any kind; at least, I never knew of him doing it.*[310]

Sutlers were appointed by the Camp Douglas commander and paid a fee for the privilege of providing their services. The fees, ranging from $50 to $100 per month, depending on the whim of the commanders, were to be used for the prisoners' benefit.[311] Camp Douglas had separate sutlers for the prisoners and the garrison. Regimental commanders appointed garrison sutlers, who sold a variety of items, including pies, cakes, candies and cider. In 1864, there were no fewer than four sutlers for the guard regiments and the garrison.[312]

The sutler's line of products that could be sold was restricted by order of Colonel Hoffman and could also be restricted by the commander. The official list of authorized goods included tobacco, cigars, pipes, snuff, steel pens, paper, envelopes, lead pencils, pen knives, stamps, buttons, tape, thread, sewing cotton, pins and needles, handkerchiefs, suspenders, socks, underclothes, caps, shoes, towels, looking glasses, brushes, combs, clothes brushes, pocket knives and scissors. Grocery items included crushed sugar syrup, soap, butter, lard, smoked beef, beef tongues, bologna, sausage, cornmeal, nutmeg, pepper, mustard, table salt, salt, fish, crackers, cheese, pickles, sauces, meat and fish in cans, vegetables, syrups, lemons, nuts, apples, matches and yeast powder. They were also permitted to sell crockery, glassware and tinware.[313] In August 1864, for some unknown reason, Colonel Hoffman prohibited the sale of vegetables by the sutler. Colonel Sweet, in October 1864, requested approval for the sutlers to sell vegetables and other groceries at no expense to the government. This request was denied by Colonel Hoffman.[314]

The relationship of the sutlers to prison management was, at best, tenuous. Sutlers frequently used prisoner help to stock and sell their products. As a result, they were subject to criticism for preferential treatment and even accused of participating in escape attempts. Colonel DeLand believed that three sutlers assisted in the escape of prisoners in 1862. These problems between commanders and sutlers continued even though inspector James Hardie, in 1864, found "no irregular transactions by sutlers and no transactions between regimental sutlers and prisoners."[315]

Burke described the process for purchasing from the sutler. In September 1863, he wrote:

> *Pa* [Burke's father was also a prisoner at Camp Douglas] *got a letter from home dated the seventh inst. with one dollar marked on the envelope as taken out at headquarters. I took the envelope to Postmaster Shanks and he wrote me an order on the sutler for the amount in sutler checks. I took the order to the sutler and he sent it to headquarters to be approved before I was allowed to have the checks. In this way the prisoners did not get the money that came to headquarters for them, but it was taken out and the amount marked on the envelope. Then we had to take sutler's checks for it and pay whatever the sutlers choose to ask for his goods, which made the profit very large.*[316]

Prisoners also felt abused by sutlers. Many prisoners, especially after the war, complained of price gouging and poor-quality goods. Yet the prices and quality were the same for Union soldiers as for prisoners. There was no evidence in Camp Douglas records of black marketing or other serious irregularities.[317] Burke wrote often of buying goods from the sutlers and reported a raid by prisoners on a sutler in March 1864.[318] On March 25, 1864, he indicated that "the new sutler sells his goods very high."

In a letter to his wife, Confederate prisoner William Paul, Fifteenth Tennessee Cavalry Regiment, wrote, "The money sent by you and father has been received but is such small sums as not to be of much benefit as the prices of such as I need are very high and the sutler charges his own prices of such articles. Tobacco I have none at present & suffer more for want of it than rations."[319]

Near the end of the war, in early 1865, Burke provided a list of sutler prices:

> *January 3: flour, $20 per barrel; butter, 80c per pound; lard, 60c per pound; cheese, 50c per pound; smoking tobacco, 60c to $1.50 per pound; chewing tobacco, $3 per pound; envelopes and Paper, 3 for 5c; stamped envelope, 5c; black tea, $2.50 per pound; coffee, $1 per pound; sugar, 60c per pound; molasses, 75c per pound; black pepper, 20c per Paper; bottle of ink, 25c; black thread, 20c per skein; crackers, 25c per pound; one ginger cake, 30c; one apple, 5c; soda, 25c per paper.*[320]

Other Civilian Services

These services included a grocery store (a ten-dollar-per-month tax was paid to the prison fund at Camp Douglas), a photographer (five-dollar-per-month tax), a shoemaker (five-dollar-per-month tax), a milk and butter cart (five-dollar-per-month tax), a newspaper depot (one-dollar-per-month tax) and a vegetable peddler (no fee). The tax for the photographer, D.F. Brandon, was raised to ten dollars per month, and Brandon was later ordered removed from Prisoners Square by Colonel Hoffman.[321] Private laundry facilities were available for those with money. Officers were charged more since their clothing required ironing.

PRISONER RATIONS

Prison food was one of the most controversial subjects relating to Camp Douglas and all prison camps. The basic policy of both the Union and Confederate authorities was that prisoners should receive rations equal to those provided to the respective armies. Article 72 of General Order 100 stated, "Prisoners of war shall be fed upon plain and wholesome food, whenever practicable, and treated with humanity." Likewise, Article 56 stipulated that depriving prisoners of food could not be used as punishment: "A prisoner of war is subject to no punishment for being a public enemy, nor is any revenge wreaked upon him by the intentional infliction of any suffering, or disgrace, by cruel imprisonment, want of food, by mutilation, death, or any other barbarity."

Notwithstanding these provisions, rations were cut, partially in retaliation for observed treatment of Union prisoners and for disciplinary reasons. Candles were reduced from rations, as they were often used for escaping by tunneling, and hominy was eliminated by Colonel Sweet because it was being "entirely wasted."[322] In May 1864, Colonel Hoffman reduced rations because he believed "rations issued to prisoners of war is too large, as they waste a large percentage of them."

Rations to be provided to prisoners were determined by Colonel Hoffman and General Meigs. Local commanders were expected to acquire the provisions through local quartermasters and private contractors selected by the quartermaster. Any savings in the purchase of food was to be accounted for in the prisoners' fund to be used for the benefit of prisoners.

Colonel Hoffman circulated the rations allowed for prisoners in April 1864. Prior to this, there had been no specific instructions regarding the quantity of rations to be issued. The reduction in rations was at the direction of Secretary Stanton in retaliation for the Confederate government releasing sick and injured prisoners without exchange. This gesture of "goodwill" backfired when Secretary of War Stanton accused the Confederacy of allowing "savage and barbarous treatment and starvation."[323] Much of Stanton's position was based on a November 1863 report by S.J. Radcliffe, assistant surgeon of the U.S. Army, after his inspection of Union prisoners released from Belle Isle. Radcliffe stated, "To express fully the condition of this number language is almost inadequate, and none but those who saw them can have any appreciable idea of their condition. I do not pretend to particularize, for every case presented evidences of ill-treatment."[324]

The table below reflects Colonel Hoffman's allocations:

RATIONS PER PRISONER*	APRIL 20, 1864	JUNE 1, 1864	JANUARY 13, 1865	1861 CONFEDERATE DAILY RATION
pork or bacon (or) fresh or salt beef	10 ounces 14 ounces	10 ounces 14 ounces	10 ounces 14 ounces	12 ounces 20 ounces
flour or soft bread (or) hard bread (or) corn meal	18 ounces 14 ounces 18 ounces	18 ounces 14 ounces 18 ounces	16 ounces 10 ounces 16 ounces	18 ounces 12 ounces 20 ounces
Rations per 100 Prisoners				
beans or peas (or) rice or hominy	6 quarts 8 pounds	12½ pounds 8 pounds	12½ pounds 8 pounds	8 quarts 10 pounds
coffee, green (or) coffee, roasted and ground (or) tea	7 pounds 5 pounds 18 pounds	** ** **	** ** **	6 pounds
sugar vinegar candles soap salt molasses potatoes	14 pounds — 5 4 pounds 2 quarts 1 quart 30 pounds	** 3 quarts — 4 pounds 3½ pounds — 15 pounds	** 2 quarts 1½ 2 pounds 2 pounds — —	12 pounds 4 quarts 2 quarts

*Prisoners in public works received slightly higher quantities of rations.

**On recommendation of the surgeon in charge, sugar, coffee or tea was issued every other day to the sick and wounded only at a rate of twelve pounds of sugar, five pounds of ground coffee or seven pounds of green coffee or one pound of tea to every one hundred rations.[325]

The allocation and quality of rations, as well as waste of rations, were inspected on numerous occasions throughout the camp. Here are a few examples:

March 1863: "The rations were found to be good, wholesome and of the first quality. The reduced ration is issued in accordance with your instructions."

October 1863: "Rations abundant and good. Cooking in camp hospital good."

December 1863: "The prisoners are well supplied with food, the ration actually issued being three-quarters of a pound of bacon (1 pound of fresh beef three times a week), good, well-baked wheat bread, hominy, coffee, tea, sugar, vinegar, candles, soap, salt, pepper, potatoes, and molasses. These articles are all of good quality. There is no good system for cooking, each man being left to arrange for himself. The result is a great waste of food and fuel."

April 1864: "Their health, food, and clothing is satisfactory."

November 1864: "As much corn-meal is issued to prisoners as can be baked into bread. The plan suggested of permitting the prisoners to bake their own bread has been thoroughly tried, and it has been found to be attended with waste and a very heavy expense for fuel."[326]

The overall quality and quantity of food was adversely affected by private commissary providers. Shortages of rations delivered were not unusual and led to the potential court-martial of Colonel DeLand.[327] The quality of beef had been questioned since early in the camp's existence. In November 1862, the *Chicago Tribune* complained that the beef provided to the Union troops at Camp Douglas was "nasty" and "completely spoiled."[328]

In May 1862, Colonel Hoffman ordered Colonel Mulligan to cease allowing prisoners to bake bread because of excessive fuel costs. He mandated that bread be provided by outside contractors or city bakeries.[329] In August 1862, the *Chicago Tribune* reported that bakeries in Chicago could not provide bread to Camp Douglas because of the rapid increase in the camp's prison population.[330] In October 1863, General DeLand reported that two bakeries at Camp Douglas had closed because of problems with ovens.[331] Colonel Hoffman, in November 1863, directed Colonel DeLand to engage outside vendors to provide bread under very specific specifications.[332] From this point on, after the onsite bakeries were repaired, baked goods were provided by a combination of vendors and products baked at Camp Douglas.

The distribution and preparation of rations was guided by Colonel Hoffman, yet this situation differed from prison to prison. At Camp Douglas, each barracks included cooking facilities. Prisoners drew rations for their individual barracks, prepared the food and distributed it to other prisoners. At other Union prisons, rations were prepared in mess halls for a large number of prisoners. Preparation ranged from cooking stoves and materials provided by the prison to heating food on barracks heating stoves at the risk of punishment if caught. John Copley noted in his journal:

> *Cooking on the stoves was prohibited, and cans were not allowed on them under any circumstances; if one was caught on a stove, the owner of it, if he could be found, was sure to be punished, his can with the contents destroyed, even if it contained the owner's entire rations. Many times the owner would disclaim all knowledge of ownership of the can, and of course the others would not give him away; but the can and contents would not escape destruction.*

In 1863, Colonel Hoffman ordered the use of "farmers' boilers," stating, "The Farmer boilers are in use in several camps under my charge and are found to be the most convenient mode of cooking, and if they have failed at Camp Douglas it is because those who used them did not want to succeed."[333] This is a good example of blaming the prisoners for their plight. These boilers proved unsuccessful, as described by Camp Douglas quartermaster Captain Shurley: "Quite a number of the Farmer boilers used for cooking are unfit for use." Likewise, Colonel DeLand reported to Colonel Hoffman, "We have tried the Farmer boilers and they are a failure."[334] Prisoners were not pleased with the quality of food cooked in the boilers. Copley described the results as "a little pittance of meat which had been boiled to shreds until it contained no more substance than an old dish-rag would."[335]

Following is Copley's colorful description of eating at the prison:

> *Rations were drawn in bulk according to the number of men in a barrack, that is to say, ours contained two hundred men, and the sergeant drew two hundred rations, which was one meal for each man. The loaves of bread were presumed to weigh about one pound each before they were cooked; after being cooked, of course they were not so heavy. One loaf of bread was issued to every three men for one meal. It was divided into three equal parts, and each part was called one-third of a loaf. Each man at each meal received one-third of a loaf, and two-thirds of a loaf per day. Only on very rare occasions we drew any crackers, which was called hard bread. Corn-meal was never issued to us. Our meat was green beef, except once a week on Sunday morning,* [when] *we drew a little bacon. The beef weighed about eight ounces raw, and the bacon about five. When our meat was cooked and passed through the crumb hole the beef would weigh from four to four and a half ounces, and the bacon from two to two and a half ounces—that is, per ration.*
>
> *I weighed my rations of meat upon the scales at the sutler's store, on several different occasions, and they never exceeded the amount stated. Soup*

> *was made from the beef or bacon water, and once in a great while this water or soup would be spiked with a few beans or a potato, just enough to let us know or believe that a bean or potato had made its appearance somewhere near the kitchen, and perhaps had entered it. This soup contained one eye of grease to every quart of water, in other words, to every oyster can full. Sunday was the long looked-for day of all days; with it came our little ration of bacon. We considered this day as the Feast of the Passover, for we had passed over a long week of hunger and starvation.*[336]

In comparison with prison food, Copley also commented on food and foraging with the Confederate army in Franklin, Tennessee, before his capture:

> *After drawing our rations, which consisted of small pieces of pork, which had never been salted, we soon had a large camp-kettle full of potatoes and pork on a blazing fire we had made out of fence rails, and by the time the wee small hours were drawing near, we were enjoying a delightful supper consisting of Irish potatoes and fat pork, independent of salt. The ground on which we were camping furnished the potatoes.*[337]

He also recounted his first meal in Union hands in Nashville, Tennessee: "The Federal authorities now issued rations of pickled pork and crackers to us, the first we had drawn since the night before we left Columbia [Tennessee]."[338] This would have been three or four days between meals.

Huff, in June 1864, wrote, "They [prison guards] have taken our cooking vessels from us and instituted kitchens and shortened our rations giving us nothing but pork and bread and not quite enough of that. I do not mean fresh pork oh, no, but salt pickled pork full of fat and not water enough to wash it down." In August, he wrote, "All the stoves are taken out of the kitchen, only one boiler is allowed. Rations meat, bread, and water, the latter very scarce."[339]

Mackey, shortly after arriving at Camp Douglas, reported on February 28, 1862, "Clear and cold. I cooked to-day for the first time in my life."[340] Upon his arrival, Robert Bagby noted, "The boys chose me as commissary of our room for some reason and I drawed [*sic*] rations in abundance. I had forgotten to draw rations on the evening before when we arrived at the camp. Most of our men were hungry and did not have enough to eat when we ate last. The soldiers were very generous in dividing their bread freely, giving away some of the piece they had. No human being could ask for more generosity." Food or rations did not appear again in his diary after this mention.[341]

Curtis Burke recorded his first meal at Camp Douglas:

> *We received rations of crackers, bread, bacon, pickelled* [sic] *pork, coffee, sugar, potatoes, hominy, salt, soap, and candles. Of course, a man only got a handful of each when it was divided, but we received better rations here than we did at Camp Morton, Ind. I got Sergeant* [William] *Miller's coffee pot and we made a little chip fire in the square, and we had some coffee, crackers and broiled bacon for supper.*[342]

Burke had access to supplemental rations either from the sutler or through bribery of commissary suppliers. He reported extravagant Christmas dinners in 1863 and 1864. In 1863, his Christmas dinner included "biscuits, tea, beans and bacon, buttered bakers bread, toasted, molasses, boiled onions laid in butter, cheese, peach pie, apple pie, onion pie, plain doughnuts, and sweet doughnuts. The tea cups, mugs and glasses were refilled."[343] At the dinner, the following toast was offered:

The Toast of Morgan's Men

Unclaimed by the land that bore us,
Lost in the land we find,
The brave have gone before us,
Cowards are left behind.
Then stand to your glasses, steady,
Here's a health to those we prize.
Here's a toast to the dead already,
And here's to the next that dies.

At Christmas 1864, his fare included "Boiled beef, Biscuit with shorting Molasses, Tea with sugar, Chip beef, Potatoes with butter, Cheese, Soft Bread, Salt, pepper & vinegar. Delicacies: Prune Pie, Apple Pie, Onion Pie, Potatoe [*sic*] Pie, Vinegar Pie, Tarts, Ginger cake, Spice cake, Apple cake."[344]

Burke acknowledged buying rations on March 29, 1864, when he wrote:

> *My mess is out of meat and sugar and we don't draw rations till first of April, so we have to buy five pounds of sugar and eight or ten pounds of fat meat every other draw day extra. We buy from infantry prisoners at the rate of ten cents per pound of sugar and from five to seven cents per pound for fat meat. The infantry from the extreme south*

> *needs a little cash to buy things they cannot draw, so they save up part of their rations and sell them.*

This statement implies that the prisoners were receiving sufficient rations to use some to obtain cash for special food and non-food items. This barter between prisoners is a clear example of the "haves" and "have-nots" in Camp Douglas.

Substitution and restriction of rations was described by Burke, who wrote, "We drew ten days' rations today. Our candles are cut off, and we received meal instead of the portion of flour we were in the habit of getting, and all pickled pork instead of beef, three times in the ten days."[345] Again, on May 30, 1864, he noted:

> *We drew rations for ten days. The following is what my mess of eight gets for the ten days: Meal 24 cups, pickle-pork 22 lbs, hominy 4 qts, fresh beef 18 lbs, light bread 24 loaves, parched coffee 4 pts, molasses 3 pts, sugar 5 qts, salt 1 qts, potatoes 1 peck. No soap, flour, candles, pepper, peas, beans, or vinegar were issued this time. Our beef and bread is not all issued at once, but we draw them in three different drawings during the ten days, so that we get them tolerable fresh.*

In September 1864, Burke reported a shortage of rations: "We had hash for dinner, but hardly enough to do any good. We are getting boiled beef for dinner and breakfast eight days out of ten, and as we draw beef at dinner for breakfast also, we eat it all up for dinner without trouble and have bread and water for breakfast."[346]

Burke commented in his journal several times in January 1864 about prisoners catching and eating rats. This section of Burke's journal is often used as justification for the contention that prisoners at Camp Douglas were starving and eating rats out of necessity. These statements are open to interpretation. Was the consumption of rats a necessity, or was it more for entertainment? Consuming rats was reported in other prisons, including Camp Chase and Elmira. Lonnie Spear quotes a prisoner at Camp Chase, who wrote, "A 'rat killing' was about the only real entertainment we had."[347] In Michael Gray's *The Business of Captivity*, he quoted a prisoner who reported that "they [the rats] smelled very good while frying" and that "a boiled rat was superb." Rats were considered "Chinese delicacies" at Elmira.[348] Private W.G. Whitaker, Fourth Georgia Infantry, also a prisoner at Elmira, wrote, "Rats were great luxuries there.

It was a common thing to see someone carrying rats around to sell, at five cents a piece."[349]

The following entries are from Burke's journal:

> *Friday, January 19, 1864. The kitchen to number six barracks near ours was torn down and a lot of rats killed. Two men gather them up and clean them up to eat. I understand that rat eating is very extensively carried on in other squares, but my curiosity has never made me taste any rats yet.*
>
> *Wednesday, January 20, 1864. I saw Jack Curd with a large bunch of rats, which he said he intended to eat.*

(Jack Curd was a close friend of Burke. Burke, before being captured, wrote the following of Curd, "Jack (John) Curd was my partner. He was the life of the first section and in fact the whole company. I was generally sleepy and Curd would always wake me up with his nonsence [*sic*]." Curd was the leader of the minstrels that performed at Camp Douglas, a barber and a sheriff at trials held by prisoners against other prisoners and frequently participated in work details at the camp. All of these activities resulted in payment of some kind that allowed him to purchase food or other items. Based on his activities in the camp, and his relationship with Burke, it is unlikely that he ate rats out of necessity. Curd was so infamous among prisoners at Camp Douglas that the nickname of a particularly brutal guard was "Jack Curd in Disguise.")

> *Thursday, January 21, 1864. Our kitchen was torn down and some of the men had a great time catching rats. They even have traps set every night for rats. All of which they clean and eat. They clean them like squirrels and let them soak well in salt water.*[350]

It is unlikely that eating rats had the same stigma as today. Southern soldiers were accustomed to eating squirrels, raccoons, possums and nutria, which today is often found repugnant. Except for the cotton rat, Confederate soldiers were not accustomed to the appearance of the Norway (or brown) rat that began populating northern cities during the late 1700s.

In December 1863, Captain Levant Runes, commissary of prisoners, conducted a survey of sergeant majors of twenty-three Confederate units at Camp Douglas who were responsible for individual barracks and units. This survey represented 4,977 of approximately 5,800 prisoners in the camp and included questions on the quantity and quality of food.

Men catching rats at Point Lookout Prison. *Maryland Historical Society.*

Responses to food questions ranged from "very good" to "third rate," with a majority indicating the food was acceptable except for the inferior beef. Consistently, the sergeant majors reported that the quantity of rations was as required by camp orders, except that beef rations were often inferior and less than required.[351]

The recommended diet, both in the North and South, was 2,325 calories, 75.5 grams of protein and 77.5 grams of fat for garrison troops per day. Authorized prisoner rations provided a range from 1,400 to 3,000 calories, 30.0 to 245.0 grams of fat and 40.0 to 165.0 grams of protein, depending on the alternatives provided. The authorized diet failed to provide an adequate amount vitamins and minerals, except for niacin. These deficiencies, principally the lack of fruits and vegetables, contributed to incidents of disease in the camp. The diets and its deficiencies were similar to those of non-prisoners. Diet-related diseases such as dysentery and diarrhea were the leading killers in the Civil War.[352]

One disease that could have been avoided was scurvy. While only thirty-nine deaths resulted from the 3,745 cases treated at the Camp Douglas hospital,[353] some of those treated and released undoubtedly died of other causes as a result of the effects of scurvy. In August 1864, Colonel Sweet requested approval for the sutlers to sell vegetables because of the increase in scurvy cases. That October, Colonel Hoffman refused to reverse his decision that sutlers were prohibited to sell vegetables and suggested to Colonel Sweet that he reduce the meat ration to pay for vegetables or use the prison fund for that purpose.[354] Records lack any justification for the position taken by Colonel Hoffman, as vegetables were readily available in Chicago.

While ration quality and quantity varied greatly at Camp Douglas, prisoners usually received food that met the "plain and wholesome food, whenever practicable" standards of General Order 100.

Prisoner Clothing

In addition to the quality and quantity of food, inadequate clothing and bedding were major issues for prisoners at Camp Douglas. The butternut uniforms issued by the Confederacy were not designed to protect prisoners from the Chicago winter. Like all soldiers before and after the Civil War, heavy and unwanted equipment, from overcoats to shelter gear, was often abandoned in the march to and during the conduct of battles. Confederate soldiers at Fort Donelson and Nashville typically shared this "travel light" attitude. Even before the battle at Franklin, Tennessee, in November 1864, Copley observed, "Many soldiers were barefoot, and their clothing very ragged." In Nashville, after being captured, he noted, "But few of this little crowd wore shoes or boots, the majority of them being barefooted, and had been for some time previous, and not many of us wore anything except outside clothing. In the warm climate of the South, some two years prior to this, the Army of Tennessee had dispensed with such unnecessary luxuries, for the reason that the Confederate States Government was financially unable to furnish that class of clothing to its soldiers."[355]

The first prisoners arriving from Fort Donelson were described thusly: "Many of them have no overcoats at all and supply their place with horse blankets, hearth rugs, coverlids, pieces of carpet, coffee sacks, etc. etc. Many looked pale and actually had attacks of ague chills as they stood awaiting the preparation of their barracks."[356]

While there is little evidence regarding the issue of clothing in early 1862, prisoner Robert Thomas Williams, Fourth Texas Militia, recorded the following in his diary on August 26, 1862, "Drew our coats today." The well-known photograph on page 69 shows five prisoners wearing Union army overcoats. The question remains whether these were issued to these men or given to them for the photograph and then taken back.

Early in the camp's existence, clothing and bedding provided by women's and church groups in Chicago supplemented the limited amount of goods provided by the Union. The support of local women continued throughout the war. In February 1863, requests for as many as 2,000 shirts, 2,000 drawers and 1,200 pairs of shoes were made to local organizations by Confederate surgeons. These requests were filled as funds could be collected.[357] The Sanitary Commission also provided similar supplies to the camp. The supply of clothing from prisoners' family and friends was a significant source for the camp.

In October 1863, Colonel DeLand reported to Colonel Hoffman, "For outer clothing I have thus far supplied from a lot of gray pepper-and-salt clothing in possession of Capt. J.A. Potter, U.S. quartermaster, turned over to him by the Government some time since, originally intended for the State troops of Illinois and Wisconsin. Underclothes and blankets forwarded by you have been used, and I shall want more as the season advances." It is clear that neither the U.S. prison officials nor the camp commander had anticipated the need for clothing.

M. Clark's inspection report in October 1863 included the following: "Quality of clothing hospital good. Quantity of clothing hospital deficient, very deficient for prisoners; some clothing sent to prisoners by friends. Blankets and bedding hospital bedding is very deficient; about 1,200 prisoners are without blankets."[358]

The survey of Sergeant Majors, mentioned earlier in relation to rations, also included questions on clothing and blankets. In December 1863, seven of twenty-three surveyed indicated insufficient blankets for the men assigned. In response to a question of clothing received since arrival at Camp Douglas, most had received some clothing from the camp and from packages from home. None indicated that the replacement clothing was sufficient for the number of men assigned to the units.[359]

Captain Levant Runes, commissary of prisoners, reported to General Orme in December 1863 that he had issued nearly 1,000 jackets, a variety of other clothing and 1,280 blankets since September 1863. Runes stated further:

> *A considerable amount of clothing must still be distributed among those prisoners from the more southern states. The bedding consists of prairie hay, of which I have ordered each month but this from twelve to fourteen pounds for two men. The bunks are intended to accommodate two men each, and*

> *the amount furnished I regard as sufficient. In the early part of this month I received orders from Colonel DeLand, not to order any more straw until a new contractor could be procured. The prisoners have received no new straw this month; more ought to be furnished at once.*[360]

Burke described the clothing provided to prisoners who were leaving the smallpox hospital and returning to their barracks:

> *We then had to throw away our old, but warm cloths and put on our new suits of blue, consisting of thin shoes without socks, unlined pants without drawers, a good gray shirt and a thin frock coat with the tail trimmed with scissors or a knife into a clawhammer or spade tail, looking very odd. Every other button was also cut off. All kept their old hats. Our toilet at last completed by tieing* [sic] *our cravats (if we had one) A La Brummel.*[361]

The straw bedding, delivered to the camp by private vendors, was noted in Burke's September 16, 1864 entry: "I saw several wagon loads of straw ticks taken to barrack 41, the convalescent hospital." William Huff observed a near riot when bedding was delivered:

> *At intervals of about a month a load of hay is brought to supply the place with mattresses. The scene then takes place* [that] *would beggar description. The wagon drives in but before it* [reaches] *the center of the square the Rebs fall out with the cry "Hay." They charge and stop it where it is met. The driver is nowhere. One fellow gets an arm full and starts to the barracks but before he gets clear of the crowd his arm full is reduced to a mere handful. Three or four more enterprising than the rest climb on top of the load. By this time the driver with a whip and pitch fork gets through the crowd and someone pushes off. One fellow required a menus* [sic] *with the fork before he would leave. The driver now commenced to throw off the hay with scores of hands raised to catch the lot that falls.*[362]

For those with greenbacks, clothing could also be obtained from sutlers.

A late source of clothing and blankets for prisoners at Camp Douglas and other Northern prisons was the Confederate government. Confederate brigadier general William Nelson Rector Beall, an 1844 graduate of the U.S. Military Academy, was sent to the officers' prison at Johnson's Island, Ohio, after he surrendered on July 9, 1863, at Port Hudson, Arkansas.[363] In November 1864, General U.S. Grant and Judge Robert Ould, Confederate

Hay Battle, Camp Douglas. *Lieutenant Colonel W.W. Williams Jr.* American Heritage, Picture History of the Civil War, *Bruce Canton.*

agent of exchange, reached an agreement that would allow General Beall, named "C.S. Army Agent to Supply Prisoners of War," to sell Southern cotton through the Union blockade. The one thousand bales of cotton were held in Northern prisons. None of the proceeds from the sale was to benefit anyone in the Confederacy except the prisoners. Upon the sale of the cotton, after taxes and expenses, General Beall had $332,789.66 to spend on over 13,000 pairs of pants, 13,200 blankets, 11,175 pairs of shoes and other items of clothing.[364]

Contained in the Eleanor S. Brokenbrough Library at the Museum of the Confederacy in Richmond, Virginia, are records of the delivery of a variety of clothing, shoes and blankets to Camp Douglas by General Beall. In February and March 1865, he sent 2,760 jackets, 1,984 blankets and 3,650 pair of boots, along with other clothing items. At the time, there were between nine thousand and eleven thousand prisoners at the camp. Curtis Burke noted a "great sensation in camp" when a notice from General Beall was posted promising "clothing, blankets, etc."[365]

Even with these supplements, clothing continued to be a problem at Camp Douglas through the end of the war.

Sanitary Conditions

Sanitary conditions, or lack thereof, were a constant problem at Camp Douglas. From the time Judge Fuller selected the site, its proximity to the lake, poor drainage and swampy, sandy soil plagued Union soldiers and Confederate prisoners alike. Diseases relating to sanitation, including dysentery and smallpox, accounted for over half the prisoners treated in the hospital, as well as numerous deaths.

Even before the camp leadership began to take action, on May 1, 1862, the *Chicago Tribune* reported the need for a survey to arrange for "the

A wet day at Camp Douglas. *From* Photographic History of Civil War, *Vol. 7.*

complete drainage of the grounds." It repeated the reports on inadequate drainage on October 10, 1862. Mud and slush were common any time it rained at Camp Douglas.

These problems were well known to camp management from the very beginning, and they became the source of many comments by inspectors and representatives of the Sanitary Commission. In June 1862, Henry Bellows, president of the Sanitary Commission, reported, "The place is as desperately circumstanced as any camp ever was, and nothing but a special providence or some peculiar efficacy of the lake winds can prevent it from becoming a source of pestilence before another month has gone over our heads." He commented on standing water and poor policing of the camp. After an inspection in February 1863, Dr. Humphrey recommended the camp be abandoned.[366] In May 1863, comments included "deplorable conditions," "filth" and "little drainage," as well as recommendations for improved sewage facilities.[367] In October 1863, medical inspector M. Clark found drainage inadequate, policing neglected, sinks with "no management" and the prison generally filthy. He did note that sewers were being installed.[368]

Colonel DeLand informed Colonel Hoffman in October 1863 that sewers were being installed to allow latrines to be flushed by water into the sewers. He also noted that soil boxes were being used. These soil boxes added an additional risk to prisoners and guards since they needed to be cleaned daily. Old latrines were reported closed and covered. Offal, which was being disposed of in large barrels, continued to be a problem.[369] In 1864, Burke reported that offal was being handled by a civilian contractor:

> *The slop or soap grease man drives a two-horse team around every day or two. He is paid by the government (that is, the federal government) to pick up and haul off all the offals* [sic] *in camp, and to save trouble he pays the men* [in] *smoking tobacco, which is nothing more than tobacco stems ground up to save the soap grease, etc. separate in barrels till he calls for it. A man that takes him a bucket full of soap grease gets a hand full of tobacco, and a man that takes him a barrel full of soap grease only gets about twice as much.*[370]

John Copley commented on the improvements made by Colonel DeLand:

> *At the north end of the streets, the water closets, more familiarly known to soldiers by the name of sinks, were located. The water was conveyed within the prison square by pipes leading from the lake to the reservoir, and from*

> *that to the prison. A sewer conveyed the filth from the sinks to the outside of the prison walls, the water being conveyed by hydrants into the sewers to wash off the filth from the prison.*[371]

Burke wrote of prison details being used to remove standing water: "Friday September 11th, 1863. On rising I felt as stiff as if I had been beaten all over with a stick, from sleeping on the bare plank. A detail from the regiment made drains to drain the standing water off."

Even with attempts to solve the water and mud problems, they persisted. Burke noted on February 27, 1864, "The whole camp ground was nearly covered with standing water, looking almost like a large pond. The Yankee roll call sergeant had some trouble to get our regiment out in line in the mud." On March 11, 1864, he wrote, "The mud on the way to and from the sutler store and sink is about eight or ten inches deep and no prospects of its drying up soon. This may encourage the spread of the smallpox."[372]

Prisoners were detailed to reduce the water by digging ditches. Burke reported in his journal:

> *Monday March 14th, 1864. Our Yankee sergeant brought six spades, one rake and two wheelbarrows and called for a detail of nine men to dig a ditch in front of the barracks. The detail was taken from company A in alphabetical order. They dug sixty feet of ditch by twelve o'clock, and were dismissed.*

> *Wednesday June 22d, 1864. At roll call thirty men were detailed from our regiment to grade the street in front of our barrack, commencing at the head of the roll all the A's, B's, and part of the C's were taken. At eight o'clock we fell in line and marched to the tool house where we were supplied with picks, spades, shovels, rakes, and wheelbarrows. I chose a shovel. Then we marched back and went to work. We dug a ditch or drain on each side of the street close to the barracks, and threw the dirt into the center of the street, which was then raked so as to make it in an oval shape to throw the rain off into the drains on each side of the street.*[373]

In his April 1864 inspection, General Orme continued the criticism of drainage and general policing of the camp.[374] The inadequacy of the three-inch water pipes was noted early and brought up again in mid-1864. Approval was finally received to increase the size to six inches in September 1864.[375]

Huff noted problems with water in October 1863 ("October 4, 1863—Water is supplied by hydrants which are scarcely enough. Often a Yankee comes to make the rebels wait until he has drawn water and then we can get ours") and again in the summer of 1864: "July 31, 1864—Hydrants have been stopped since morning. It is intolerably hot and we are almost dying of thirst…August 1, 1864—Still no water, hydrants stopped. It is too hot to stay anywhere or any place in comfort."[376]

The improvement made after General Orme's inspection and the completion of the sewer system resulted in five privies and five hydrants in Prisoners Square by September 1864, according to a September 8, 1864 "Plan of Camp Douglas Showing Present Arrangements of Sewers and Water Pipes." Adjutant General Haynie's report at the end of the war indicated that there were 3,600 feet of water pipe and 6,000 feet of sewer in the camp.[377]

Under Colonel Sweet, the cleanliness of the prisoners and their clothing and proper area policing were emphasized. His actions resulted in significant improvements in sanitation. Copley reported on the effect of Colonel Sweet's efforts:

> *The sanitary regulations were very strict, and the authorities had them rigidly enforced. They required us to keep the streets clear of all trash of every description. We were prohibited from emptying any vessel containing dirty water on the streets. They made it our duty to scour the floors of the barracks once a week, or twice each month, anyhow, and to sweep them clean once each day. The barrack sergeant (who was a prisoner) made an alphabetical list of the names of all the members of his barrack, and as their names came on the list, were detailed accordingly, until all had scoured the barrack.*
>
> *Spitting on the floors or inside the barracks was strictly prohibited. If the police guard discovered any filth or spittle on the floor, it would insure* [sic] *all the members of a barrack a two hours ride on Morgan's Mule. The most important regulation was in regard to cleanliness of the person and clothing of the prisoners. The great majority of us were only two* [sic] *glad to avail ourselves of the means placed at our command for preserving cleanliness of our person and clothing; but there were those with us who were very careless and indifferent concerning their person and clothing, and sometimes such persons paid very dearly for their neglect.*
>
> *Friday of each week was the regular wash day, in order that our clothing would be in good shape for inspection at roll call on the following Sunday*

> *morning; but we were at liberty to do any extra washing on any other day we might see proper. There were a few of the prisoners who followed washing for others as a regular business, and for which they charged a small compensation—that is, from two and a half cents to five cents per garment. Those who were financially able to hire their washing did so, but the great majority of us were unable to hire anything done; hence, we had to wash our own clothing, and wear it without starch or ironing. But very few of the prisoners had an extra change of clothing, and when wash day came we washed our shirts during the forenoon, and in case our pants required washing, we did that in the afternoon. We allowed no filthy person to remain in his filth, and when we discovered one, he would be immediately taken charge of by the others and forced to wash himself and clothing up in good shape. If anyone failed to wash his clothes, or have it done, we at once organized a court, composed of a judge, clerk, lawyers, sheriff, and jury, then tried the prisoner for uncleanliness and uncleanly habits. He was sure to meet with a conviction, but never an acquittal.*
>
> *The penalty was generally very severe, especially if he was a stout and healthy man. The sentence of the court, after the jury found him guilty as charged, would be that he be taken by the sheriff to the wash house, there stripped, and two men thoroughly scrub him with soap and rags, until the skin was red. One dose of this was sufficient; it never had to be repeated upon the same person. He was then compelled to wash his clothing. Scarcity of clothing shielded no one from the pains and penalties of the wash house. The accused had to pay the court costs, all of which could be settled up and paid with "thirds of bread" or "chews of tobacco." If the party was too poor to pay the costs, the court would remit all except the penalty. All the property a man owned was on record in his own name, and not hid behind his wife; hence, we all knew the exact amount of property owned by each man in a barrack.*[378]

The addition of washhouses in Prisoners Square supported Colonel Sweet's cleanliness edict. These houses were one-story, box-like buildings supplied with a water hydrant, with tubs, buckets and soap provided by the camp.[379]

While attempts were made to make improvements in the camp and to require prisoners to improve hygiene, sanitation was a problem throughout the existence of the camp. General conditions and a lack of appreciation for sanitation contributed greatly to illness and disease at Camp Douglas.

GUARDS

This section examines the individual guards who interacted with the prisoners. As mentioned before, the stability of the guard force began to be achieved in mid-1863, when Invalid Corps (later designated the Veterans Reserve Corps) soldiers were assigned. A majority of these soldiers had combat experience and should have had an appreciation and some compassion for their enemy. Yet the attitude of the guards toward the prisoners varied greatly depending on individual personalities and experience.

None of the guards at Camp Douglas had any formal training as prison guards. Guard instructions were limited and frequently changed as circumstances in the prison changed. Needless to say, none of the guards were properly prepared for their assignment.

Unlike prisoners who arrived in late 1863 and 1864, Robert Bagby found the guards most accommodating. On the second day of his incarceration at Camp Douglas, he wrote, "The soldiers were very generous in dividing their bread freely, giving away some of the piece they had. No human being could ask for more generosity."[380] Bagby's attitude toward guards likely changed as he experienced them becoming less friendly as time wore on.

In December 1863, with General Orme in command of Camp Douglas, Colonel James Strong was assigned command of the prison. His organization of the guard force consisted of two separate and distinct units. The stockade or parapet guards provided security for the perimeter of the camp and acted outside Camp Douglas to capture escapees. They also acted as provost-guards of the city and handled any other problems off the camp's grounds. The camp police or camp patrol was the second unit and operated inside Camp Douglas. This group had the most day-to-day contact with prisoners, as they conducted roll calls and barracks inspections and administered discipline within the camp.

Stockade guards were armed with rifled muskets and later with revolvers, since the muskets issued were of very poor quality. In June 1864, Colonel Sweet reported to Colonel Hoffman, "These guns have all been condemned, and the inspection and report condemning them forwarded properly, with requests on the part of the commanding officer to the Ordnance Office for new arms and blank requisitions on which to draw them. This was done in February last, since yet nothing has been heard from them." He further stated in his dispatch that the stockade guards would be armed with revolvers.[381]

Much of the stockade guards' time was spent manning guard posts on the stockade fence. Guards were stationed at intervals of fifty to one hundred feet apart and surrounded the entire prison compound. They were responsible for the "dead line" and enforcing limits placed on prisoners' movements and communications after lights out. They were to stop escapes when prisoners attempted to breech the stockade fences. With limited training and poor equipment, these guards often failed in their responsibilities. Stockade guards were the primary bribery targets for prison escapes.

Copley described the stockade guards as follows:

> *One set of guards, composing the entire chain-guard upon the parapet, were kept on guard duty eight hours out of twenty-four. Their orders and instructions were to shoot every prisoner who attempted an escape from the prison, or crossed the dead line; to shoot out all lights which might be seen in the barracks at night; to fire upon all squads of three or four prisoners who might congregate on the streets in a group during the day. At least, the parapet guards claimed to have such instructions, and the manner in which they acted, indicated it. They rarely, if ever, entered the prison square on guard duty, as their duties were confined more particularly to the parapet and on the outside of the prison walls.*[382]

Even with poor muskets, shootings were not uncommon. Bagby wrote in his diary:

> *January 13, 1865. A man in one of the wards of the 3rd Division, a guard shot at someone out in the square, and the ball entered the leg of this man in the hospital. The other man* [in the square] *was said just before day*[light] *that morning went to the privy to make water but because of debility could not reach the privy and it broke. He took hold with his hands to check the flow when a police guard saw him. He thought the young man getting his pants to make water in the street. The ball entered the leg below the knee, breaking the first bone and lodging in the left foot just below the ankle joint. After supper the doctor came in and amputated the right leg. The young man bore the operation well. They failed to reach the privy and I could see they were drawing the reins tighter every day.*[383]

The camp police were organized into units with two sergeants, two corporals and five privates, commanded by one officer. A unit was responsible for at least one row of four barracks in Prisoners Square, or up to eight hundred prisoners.

The camp police were frequently unarmed or armed with revolvers. One of their primary officers from late 1863 was Lieutenant Joel A. Fife, who had an office in Prisoners Square. Lieutenant Fife was also responsible for mail and packages to the prisoners. Nearly everything that took place within the prisoners' area was under the jurisdiction of Lieutenant Fife and the camp police. Punishment was almost always administered by the police. This unit could—and often did—enter prisoners' barracks at any time day or night. Copley also described these guards:

> *The police guards within the inclosure* [sic] *of the prison were armed with large army pistols, loaded. The authority of each was absolute, and from it there was no appeal—at least, an appeal made by any of us would not have been heard by higher authority. Their duties were to patrol the prison grounds and barracks at all hours during the day and night; to see that all the rules and regulations of the prison were strictly carried out; that no plots or conspiracies were planned or organized among the prisoners to escape; and that the sanitary rules and regulations were rigidly executed. Quite a number of them were within the inclosure* [sic] *of the prison walls day and night.*[384]

Prisoners referred to four of the most infamous police as the "Big Four." Both Curtis Burke and John Copley identified these four as the cruelest police and those who administered the most brutal punishments. Copley, in his usual colorful writing, described each of these men:[385]

"Old Red" O'Hara

> *The first of them was nicknamed "Old Red." His proper name was O'Hara. From his name and dialect he would be pronounced a native of and an inhabitant of the Emerald Isle. He derived the name "Old Red" from being red-headed, the hair being a fiery red. In stature he was larger than the average man, and possessed an enormous parallelogram-shaped head, which presented a low forehead, and which indicated the opposite of all culture and refinement. This oblong head was surmounted with a forest of coarse red and bushy hair; a nose fashioned more for use than ornament, and the centre* [sic] *of attraction between two prominent cheek bones; across this and below the nose nature had placed a tremendous horizontal aperture, which his two large ears prevented from making the entire tour of the head, and contained a score*

or more of ugly, ill-shaped teeth, which must have been very useful in devouring large quantities of pickled beef and hard-tack.

His body, arms, legs and feet were large, though his general make-up and form were by no means symmetrical. His complexion was red, face ornamented with large red pimples or bumps to such an extent that it constantly reminded one of the chicken-pox or big red measles; in fact, his entire oily skin appeared to be infected with vermin. His rough, brawny hands were better fitted for the plow-handles than for anything else, and certainly an artist would never have selected his long bony fingers for models of beauty.

The large, ill-shaped nose, the two dull gray eyes placed in the midst of a pair of unsightly cheeks, gave to his countenance a most hideous and semi-comic appearance and expression. Two ponderous ears stood out in bold relief, one on each side of his head, somewhat resembling the side lamps of a carriage. In addition to all this came the comical arrangement of his hair, which stood out in bold defiance of all efforts of discipline of the hand or comb; every hair stood out straight, separate and alone, and seemed to be afraid each of the other. I am confident that this head of hair never succumbed to the arts of civilization.

He wore a number twelve shoe or boot, and sometimes wore socks; whenever he wore shoes, which was most of the time, he could often be seen without socks on those monstrous feet. The legs of his pants were large and always too short, lacking about an inch of reaching to and making close connection with the top of his socks—that is, whenever he wore socks. It appeared to the boys in prison that when his measure was taken for clothing, he certainly stood in the water ankle deep at least. The skin of his ankles very much, in color, resembled the rind of a pumpkin at ripening time. The pale blue pants and his skin, as shown on his ankles, presented quite a contrast. His address was repulsive in the extreme.

When in his presence, one would know it without seeing him, for the cold chills would at once run up and down the back. One would feel that he was in the presence of or near some monstrous, hideous and slimy serpent. Such were the feelings the atmosphere would inspire one with when he was near at hand. His sense was that of the meanest type, and his composition contained nothing save that of the blackest and worst character. In appearance, he resembled one of those terrible and frightful beings whom Pollock describes that he saw writhing in the Lake of Fire, while he stood near the brink of the abyss of eternity sketching its inmates.

"Little Red"

The second specimen of these was called "Little Red." I had his full name but cannot at present recall it, although time can never erase his personal description from memory's tablet. He differed materially in his personal physique from the former I have described. In stature he was smaller, head a little above medium size, very irregular in shape and covered with sandy-colored hair, and many of the prisoners called him red-headed; hence, the origin of the name "Little Red." His eyes were of a steel-gray color, giving to his countenance a cold and hard expression; the nose, of medium size and a little inclined to be sharp at the point, was almost hid from view by two round and bloated cheeks; the mouth large and filled with a set of unsightly and disgusting teeth; it was a perfect harbinger of filth, the stench emitted there from when it opened, would permeate the atmosphere for a distance of several feet.

The most striking attribute of his chin was length. He was stoutly built and possessed large feet, which were minus an instep, the heels of which were straight like those of a negro. His countenance and expression sadly lacked all which indicates anything amiable or intelligent. He somewhat resembled the "Fool's Pope," described by Victor Hugo. He appeared to occupy about the same relation to the others which a general roustabout on a steamboat does to the officers who command it.

"Old Billy Hell" McDermott

A third prominent personage and important factor was in the shape and person of Billy McDermott. He was better and more familiarly known to the prisoners as "Old Billy Hell." Old Billy was rather small in stature, as well as in everything else. An oval-shaped, rough, hard and knotty cornfield cymling would make a fine photograph and an excellent representation of his head, which was covered with thick, dark hair; shaggy eyebrows hung over two small, squint eyes, which resembled those of a hog; the nose was small and long, the end always pointing to the left; his mouth large, but kept somewhat in the background by a pair of large, thick lips; a short neck, which appeared to be swallowed up by the shoulders; the knees were perfect strangers to each other, and no sort of enticement could bring them together; the feet were large and flat; his expression was anything to look upon but pleasant.

"Prairie Bull"

> *The finishing touch and crowning capstone of this quartette* [sic] *presented itself in the person of "Prairie Bull." He was indebted to the Texas troops for this beautiful sobriquet. His head was straight from the back of the neck to the crown, and covered with very thick, dark hair, which he parted in the middle at the back of the head, and in front, like a woman parts hers; the ears were large and thin, but not the kind which indicate generosity; his eyes were small and of a cold lead color, and shaded with heavy eye-brows, which embraced each other above the bridge of the nose; the nose was large, and the nostrils always expanded; his big mouth contained a set of long teeth very much resembling the incisors; the lips were thick, and continually kept in such a strain of fear and terror of each other that they could never be induced to touch; his jaws were those of a monster in size; the neck short and thick; his arms, legs and feet were patterned after those of a gorilla more than from any other animal; the skin was the color of that often seen when yellow jaundice makes its first appearance—that is, when in its first stage; he was tall, and a little hump-shouldered, and possessed the frame of a giant, and generally went in a stooping posture, and very fast, so much so that the tail of his blue blouse was constantly trying to play leap-frog with the back of his neck.*
>
> *Nature, it seems, had stamped the atrocity of his character on his countenance. His hideous features, coupled with a demoniacal expression, revolted every living thing near him. He carried the expression of a demon wherever he went, and the photographed impressions made upon one's brain will forever stand out on memory's wall in bold relief.*

Copley recounted one exchange between a prisoner and Prairie Bull:

> *A prisoner in our barrack was sick and hardly able to walk, but started to the hydrant for water; on the steps of the barrack he met old Prairie Bull, who, without a word, drew his pistol and shot the prisoner down, breaking his thigh near the groin. The wounded man had to remain where he fell, from the early part of the night until the following morning, when he was taken out and died during the day. This inhuman wretch, this fiendish slimy serpent who would have made any one sick to have touched him, refused all aid and assistance to the wounded man; but promptly informed us that if we touched the wounded prisoner, he would shoot us all down like dogs.*[386]

Copley went on to write, "The majority of the others, if not all, were much better men in every respect than these favorites. We never had to avoid and shun the presence of the others, like we did these; in fact, when these four were on the inside of the prison square, we felt like we were in the midst of and at the mercy of a lot of wild animals which had just made their escape from some menagerie."[387]

Burke, in his journal, also identified these four police:

> *We have a mean set of guards with one exception, a little corporal by the name of Norton. We nicknamed the four privates, viz: Old Red, Jack Curd in Disguise, Hessian Dutchman, and the Wild Irishman. Old Red, alias O'Hara, is the most vindictive. He is always on the alert, watching for a chance to shoot somebody. I often hear it whispered through the ranks, look out, here come Old Red. He bayoneted several of the men, and we have no particular love for him.*[388]

Copley gave the following examples of the arbitrary and unusually cruel punishment administered by the "Big Four":

> *These different punishments would be administered for the most frivolous and insignificant offenses which could be imagined, and the prisoners would hardly ever know, or have any idea what offense had been committed. Most of these different punishments would be inflicted after night, in the barracks, and sometimes during the day. Old Red, Prairie Bull, Little Red and Old Bill McDermott were the prime executioners.*
>
> *Who were these men? Probably night could tell more about them than day. They were the unsightly, hideous, midnight ghouls in human shape, who prowled over the prison square after night for no other purpose save to find some frivolous excuse to exercise their assumed authority. They were the ghastly and hungry hyenas digging into the prison barracks for little, trivial violations of some foolish and insignificant rule of their own manufacture, and of which the prisoners knew nothing until marched out for punishment; then these guards would hardly ever let them know what rule or regulation had been violated, or the offense which had been committed.*
>
> *The water-closets were several feet from the barracks, and the rules and regulations in regard to going to and returning from them were very strict and severe. No excuse for failing to go to them when a prisoner was sick, would be accepted, but men with a scorching fever were compelled to go out of the barrack in cold, freezing wind and blinding snow at any and all*

> *times, either day or night. When necessity forced any one to visit the water-closets, he had to go directly there and return without stopping between them and his barrack, no matter how sick and weak he might be; if he stopped on the way and any of the police guards of the "big four" saw him, he was sure to receive a severe flogging with a leather belt. Their belts all had a large brass buckle on them, and frequently the buckle would be used in administering a flogging.*
>
> *Just outside the kitchens, slop barrels were always kept for the purpose of depositing beef bones, and such other scraps and refuse as came from the kitchens; these would often remain until late in the afternoon without being removed and emptied. The hungry prisoners often resorted to these barrels in search of a beef bone from which to make soup, or bake by the heating stoves in order to obtain the grease.*
>
> *Whenever either or all of the "big four" caught any of the prisoners near the barrels, or would see any prisoner with a bone, they would make him take it in his mouth, get down on his hands and feet, go up and down the street from one end to the other, and bark like a dog, or imitate it as near as possible, the guard all the time laughing at the prisoner and keeping a pistol cocked at his head ready to fire. The "big four" called this the dog performance, or barking like a dog. Sometimes the "big four" would allow the prisoner to stand up and walk erect from one end of the street to the other, carrying the bone in his mouth; at the same time they would take their stand at some convenient place within range of the prisoner, in the event that an army pistol became necessary to be used as a persuasive means to enforce this method of punishment.*[389]

In addition to Lieutenant Fife, who was described by Copley as one who was "very distant and reserved, and avoided all familiarity with the prisoners,"[390] Captain Webb (or Wells) Sponable, Camp Douglas inspector of prisons, was well known to the prisoners and often accompanied the "Big Four" on their rounds in the prison.

Copley described Captain Sponable thusly:

> *There was a third officer* [others mentioned were Colonel Sweet and Lieutenant Fife], *who formed the keystone to the arch of this trio, one so-called Captain Webb Sponable, Inspector of Prisons, but more particularly Inspector of Rations, especially when he became a little short of cash. His name really should not be associated with the former officers whom I have described, but it cannot well be avoided.*

> *He was of medium stature: figure grotesque and ugly in the extreme; features coarse; face resembling a well-grown artichoke, covered over as it was with large bumps; hair stood straight up, when not kept saturated with grease or oil; forehead very low, with the eye-brows joined together above the bridge of the nose; eyes set far back in the head; nose very large and always carried upon it a strawberry hue; ears of ordinary size, very thin and lay close to the head; jaws and chin very large and unsightly; neck short and bullish; teeth stood out prominently and never presented a neat or clean appearance and seemed to be coated with a yellow substance of some kind; his expression and countenance appeared to be dark and cloudy most of the time; the legs were so frightened at each other that no amount of persuasion could induce them to come close together; suspended at the extremities of the legs were a pair of large feet, like those of a negro.*
>
> *The swift and irregular step, the unmeasured and harsh cadence of his accentuation, the wandering and far away look which took about ten times as long as another's to arrive at its object; all this was in admirable keeping with his unsightly person, big nose, ugly chin and knotty skin, which betrayed not the slightest symptoms that any principles inclined to be humane and generous circulated or passed through or beneath its cellular texture; these gave him quite a ludicrous appearance, whenever he perambulated the prison square, trying to favorably impress every one with his peacock looks. This Captain Webb Sponable will be long remembered by all the inmates of Camp Douglas.*[391]

Rarely would anyone, including officers, attempt to stop a guard from administering punishment.

While the brutal activities of the "Big Four" were infrequently stopped, "Old Red," on one occasion, was dissuaded from attacking a prisoner by an officer of the guard. Copley recorded the following event:

> *Old Red was a most consummate coward, as was fully demonstrated one day. He happened to come up our street alone, but armed to the teeth with two large army pistols; he attempted to assail one of the prisoners who chanced to be standing near one of the kitchen slop-barrels. The prisoner seized a piece of plank near by, and with it made a lunge at the old villain, who at once turned and fled for life. It was for dear life that he ran, followed by the prisoner close at his heels, striking at his head with the plank at every bound.*
>
> *He ran into the officers of the guard's quarters to save himself and for protection, the prisoner following him to the door. We expected nothing more*

nor less than for the prisoner to be riddled with bullets, but we intended that a few more of us would take a hand at the game, regardless of consequences; but it appeared that the officers and other guards were not disposed to interfere; they only stopped the prisoner at the door and would not allow him to enter. Old Red wanted the officers to give him permission to take two or three and go up to the prisoner's barrack and give him a flogging; they refused to do so, but gave him permission to go alone and flog him to his heart's content, provided he would leave his arms at the quarters.

He postponed the thrashing, and to my knowledge, the prisoner had failed to receive it up to the time we left the prison, and I am confident that the flogging has never been administered. That same afternoon we learned that the officers witnessed the beginning of the row, and seeing what they did, accounted for their non-interference. It was well for him that he failed to come to the barrack, for we all determined to so completely dissect him, that not a piece of him could be recognized or found by the authorities to bury.[392]

The authority of the guards was unquestioned by the prisoners, and there were no appeals against any actions taken by the guards.[393] Not even approval from the camp commander was effective in stopping guards from acting. Burke recorded one occasion when guards stopped the presentation of prison minstrels:

The show [w]*as about half over when the Lieutenant of the guard with a few guards came in at the side door on the stage in the midst of the contrabands and said, "What does all of this noise here mean at this time a night. You want to get out of here everyone of you. I've received no orders to let this thing go on."*

Jack Curd then pulled out his permit from Col. DeLand to show it to the Lieutenant, but the Lieutenant would not look at it, but said, "Get out of here you black ruffle shirted s____." So each one of the band grabbed something and left before myself and others in the back part of the room hardly knew what was the matter, and we all went back to our quarters glad to get out of the crowd.[394]

Even when officers had issued no authority to the police, they were unwilling to stop police action. Burke wrote in his journal:

Friday September 16th, 1864. Old Red, alias O'Hara, broke up religious meetings in barracks 13 and 25, and said that if he caught any more

> *singing and praying in the barracks he would put them in irons. Some of the men then saw Capt. Sponable about it, and he told them that the guard had no orders to break up such meetings, but that he left such things to the guards and if they choose to break them up he would not interfere.*[395]

Guards also provided important service to the prisoners. In the winters, they were responsible for keeping fires burning in stoves through the night. During an extremely cold period in January 1864, Burke wrote, "The night was very cold, but the guards kept the coal stoves red hot all night, which kept the barracks warm, and we selpt [*sic*] well."[396]

Burke reported one semi-compassionate act by guards:

> *In the night a crazy prisoner in Barrack No. 15 got up and walked up and down the barrack saying "I see Jesus, I see Jesus!" He then bolted out into the street and saw the lamp on the fence and said "There's Jesus. I see his light," and making for the lamp at the same time he tore it from the fence and run with it saying "Glory! Glory! I have got Jesus." A guard fired at him. The ball smashed the lamp and knocked it out of his hand. He then run* [sic] *down to the gate where the guards caught him and took him back to his barrack.*[397]

While prisoners had little or no redress against punishment or ill treatment by guards, they did have opportunities to harass the guards. Copley wrote of one such humorous act:

> *We could also boast of one ventriloquist, who could perform many tricks which at the time were considered marvelous, but now very common. The only name by which he was ever known among the boys was that of "Pig." We suppose that he obtained this name on account of being so diminutive in stature. This little "Pig" belonged to the Forty-second regiment of Tennessee Infantry. We had been familiar with him and his tricks from the beginning of the war, and had never grown tired of him, as he was such a jolly little fellow. He was captured with us at Franklin, Tennessee. For some time his ventriloquism was a great annoyance to some few of the guard at Camp Douglas. "Pig" would watch for them on the street, and the first thing they knew or heard would be a lot of chickens squalling in their pockets, or some unusual noise under their caps.*
>
> *They would grab their pockets or snatch off their caps in utter amazement and confusion, and finding nothing, together with the uproarious laughter*

> *of the prisoners, caused them to become more confused then* [sic] *ever, but generally they would laugh it off. When they definitely learned the originator of these jokes, he was compelled to desist.*[398]

Copley related another story that was told to him by other prisoners. This story was passed from prisoner to prisoner, yet no single group of prisoners took credit for the act:

> *Lieutenant Fife owned and kept a beautiful black terrier dog with him on the inside of the prison. This dog was a great favorite and pet with the prisoners, but one day the cooks in one of the barracks enticed the dog into their kitchen, killed and dressed it nicely, and cooked it; then invited quite a number of the other prisoners to dine with them, as they had a rare dish for dinner—they ate the dog and drank the soup. Soon after this Fife wanted to find his dog, but could learn nothing of it whatever. He posted a notice on the bulletin board, offering ten dollars for the return of his dog. The prisoners read this notice, and someone wrote under Fife's notice the following lines:*
>
> *For lack of bread the dog is dead,*
> *For want of meat the dog was eat.*[399]

William Huff wrote in his diary of a sutler's dog being eaten by prisoners. This might have been Lieutenant Fife's dog.[400]

Simply stated, prisoners did not like the guards, who ranged from those who acted in a military manner to those brutal guards recounted in this section.

Prisoner Punishment

Much of the punishment administered at Camp Douglas was similar to that applied in both the Confederate and Union armies. The most cruel and brutal punishment was frequently administered by the most sinister guards, the "Big Four." Copley wrote in his journal, "There were many of the guards and non-commissioned officers who were disposed to treat us as strictly prisoners of war, and as humane as their instructions and orders from their superiors would permit. I cannot call to mind an instance wherein we were personally ill-treated either by an officer or guard, except by those whom I have particularly named and designated."[401]

Those he named and designated were the Big Four: "Old Red" O'Hara, "Little Red," "Old Bill Hell" McDermott and "Prairie Bull." Burke had given these same four guards the following names: "Old Red," "Jack Curd in Disguise," "Hessian Dutchman" and "Wild Irishman."[402]

Colonel Sweet's Morgan's Mule was the punishment of choice by the Union guards for even the most minor infractions. Failure to properly police the area or dirty clothing could get the prisoner two hours on the mule. Particularly egregious infractions would add sandbags or cannonballs attached to the legs. John Copley provides a colorful description of the Mule:

> *After the signal given at 6 p.m. for the prisoners to retire, we had to do so without delay, and were not allowed to speak or whisper to each other under any circumstances, but had to go to sleep, and then be very careful as to how loud we slept. When any of the prisoners were heard by the guard to whisper or talk, he would call for the one who did the whispering or talking, and if the right one could not be definitely located, all the prisoners occupying the barrack would be marched out to Morgan's Mule, forced to mount and ride from two hours to half a night, barefooted, and with no covering on them save their thin and ragged clothing. Many of the prisoners were so thinly clad they could scarcely hide their nakedness. The latter part of the winter of 1864 and first part of 1865 were extremely cold, and the Federals complained of its severity, and stated that the weather was the coldest which had been known for several years.*
>
> *Often the guards would tie, or cause to be tied, a heavy weight of some kind to each ankle of the prisoners. The weights would weigh from twenty to one hundred pounds, and generally consisted of bags of sand, but if these were not convenient some other heavy substance would be substituted. The cords which held these weights often cut through the skin of the ankle. After being mounted on the Mule, the "big four" would turn the prisoners over to the sentinel on the parapet, at the same time instructing him for what length of time to keep them, and when the time expired to allow the prisoners to return to their barrack, but to shoot anyone who attempted to dismount before the time was out.*
>
> *Several of the prisoners were badly frostbitten, and were nearly frozen to death while on this frame.*[403]

Mackey also commented on the horse: "March 30, 1862—Cloudy and cold, strong wind from the west. In the evening a large crowd gathered around Col.

Riding Morgan's Mule. *Chicago History Museum.*

[James A.] Mulligan's quarters to witness the spectacle of two men sitting astride a wooden horse for intoxication, and a Tennessean bound to a tree awaiting his trial for murder."[404]

As Copley noted, even minor infractions could result in a ride on the Mule:

> *His* [prisoner Polk Goodrich] *first experience with them occurred with* [guard] *Old Billy, within three or four days after our admittance inside the prison, and in the shape of a two hours ride on Morgan's Mule during a real cold night. Polk had an idea that he could get up and warm by the stove, but Old Billy came in the barracks at once, and marched him off to the Mule. He never could be induced after night to make another attempt to warm.*[405]

Escaped prisoners returned to Camp Douglas might be forced to march around the compound wearing a sign announcing their infraction or be required to wear a barrel. In 1864, Mackey described this punishment: "May 23, 1862—Clear and beautiful. To-day eight prisoners were compelled to carry a long board lashed to their backs on which was inscribed the words 'Escaped prisoners recaptured.' Their crime was an attempt to escape. The guard who betrayed them was promoted."[406] In large letters, "Thief," "For disobeying orders," "For washing in barracks," "Lousy," "For meddling with other people's business" and "For going to the other square" was on the card fastened to a prisoner's back in 1863.[407]

Burke described standing on a barrel as punishment: "Three or four rebs are standing on barrel heads at the gate as a punishment for various offences. One of them for being caught with several canteens of the over joyful that he had bought secretly from some guard."[408]

Wearing a ball and chain was also common for those caught attempting to escape. Burke described this punishment:

> *John Shackelford returned to the barrack from the dungeon (Duce of Diamonds) with his ball and chain still on. The ball weighs 64 lbs and*

> *a chain about 3 ft. long attached. Three of Chinault's men were caught trying to make their escape last night. Today they and another for some other offence were balled and chained and put to work at the dirt pile in the center of the square filling the carts that are hauling off the dirt.*
>
> *The chain to each iron ball or block is four or five feet long and very stout, with a clasp to lock and unlock to fit around the ankle at one end. The ball looks as if it will weight* [sic] *about fifty-six pounds. The men have leather straps tied to their balls to enable them to carry them about when they have to move more than the length of the chain. The men call their balls and chains their time pieces. One of them takes his off on the sly by means of a fiddle string which he doubles and twists in the key hole of the clasp, and unlocks it whenever the Yanks are not about.*[409]

Kneeling in the snow was also a common punishment, and one of the most painful punishments was to be hanged by the thumbs. Copley described both:

> *Another favorite method of punishment was this: Every man in a barrack would be marched out on the snow in front of the barrack, formed in a line of one rank, and then told by the guards that under the snow and ice could be found plenty of corn for them to parch and eat, that they must reach for it, which was done in the following manner: The guards would point their pistols, cocked, at the heads of the prisoners, make them bend their bodies over in a stooping posture, until the tips of their fingers would touch the ground under the snow and ice, the knees having to remain perfectly stiff and straight and not bend in any manner. They would be compelled to stand in this position from half an hour to four hours, and never for a shorter time than half an hour, the snow and ice being very deep all winter, often twenty inches. This was called, by the guards, "reaching for corn" or "reaching for grub." Frequently many of those who were being punished in this way would become so exhausted and fatigued they would fall over in the snow in an almost insensible condition; these were apt to receive a flogging with a pistol belt, administered by the guard, or receive several severe kicks and blows. Often these men would stand in that position until the blood would run from the nose and mouth; the guard would stand by and laugh at it.*
>
> *Another mode was to make the prisoners sit down on the snow and remain sitting for two hours, without rising or changing positions. On one occasion, for some little, trivial and frivolous offense, all the prisoners occupying barrack No. 1 were marched out in front of their barrack, formed in a line of one rank, and made to sit down on the*

> *snow and ice for two hours. I visited that barrack soon after the men had been released, and the indentures made by them in the snow told what they had been doing all that time, as their shapes were plainly impressed in the snow. P.E. Lively and Dick Litsey, of Texas, were two of the crowd who had to sit on the snow.*
>
> *There was still another method of punishment, bordering on and a little akin to the former I have named. The guards would make all the men in a barrack march out and stand erect on the snow from two to four hours, and not allow them to stir or move their feet to keep warm. The guards would leave them in that position and go off to other parts of the prison, but in a short time return, and examine the snow to see if it had been displaced by the movement of any of their feet. If there were any, it would be fortunate for the prisoner if he escaped with only a flogging with a pistol belt on the naked back, which would amount to all the way from forty to one hundred lashes. Sometimes the prisoner would be beaten over the head with the butt end of a large army pistol, or a piece of plank.*
>
> *Another favorite method of punishment was to tie prisoners up by the thumbs. This was accomplished by tying a strong cord around each thumb, then throwing one end over a scantling or beam above the head, drawing the cord until the arms and body were stretched until the toes would just touch the ground or floor. Prisoners tied up in this manner frequently had to remain suspended until life was almost extinct, before the guards would cut them down. I have seen the blood run from the nose and mouth of some who were thus punished. This punishment often compelled those upon whom it was inflicted to lie in bed for several days, unable to walk.*[410]

Colonel DeLand once ordered five men hanged by their thumbs for threatening to hang a prisoner named Stovall for informing the Union guards of some men who were planning to escape.[411]

Punishment was limited only by the imagination of the guards. Especially harsh punishment was described by Copley:

> *There was still another favorite mode of gratifying their insatiate thirst for punishment. They would procure half of a barrel or large box, have a hole made in it large enough for the prisoner's head to slip through, and so as to let the barrel or box rest on the shoulders; when this ornament was placed over the prisoner's head he was forced to walk from one end of the street to the other, from half a day to a whole week every day continually. This was very severe punishment. The barrel or box was very heavy, and all the*

> *time pressed on the shoulders with nothing to protect them, which made the carrying of either very painful and annoying.*
>
> *Still there was another mode, differing from all the others, but fully as harsh and severe, if not worse. The guards would procure a ladder long enough to reach from the ground to the top of the plank wall which inclosed* [sic] *the prison grounds, the upper end of the ladder resting against the side of the parapet and the lower end on the ground just over the dead line. The prisoner would be compelled to climb up and down the ladder from morning till night, every day for a whole week, and sometimes longer; he was not allowed to stop and rest at all. One prisoner had to climb and descend this ladder for nearly a whole month. The only time that any rest could be obtained would be during meal time and at night. He was in charge of the sentinel on the parapet, and if he stopped to rest would have been shot. This tried men's souls, as well as their constitutions.*
>
> *Often if only one man was taken out to be punished, he would be stripped naked to the waist and given from fifty to one hundred lashes with a broad pistol belt on the naked back, so severe that the blood would trickle down the back to the heels. If a barrel was convenient, the prisoner would be stretched across it; if not convenient, then he would be stretched across the foot of a bottom bunk and whipped.*[412]

In January 1865, Burke reported some rather unusual and creative punishment:

> *About midnight two patrol guards came in our barrack and caught one of the men sitting by one of the stoves smoking, and made him climb up on one of the rafters and act circus. He was sitting astraddle* [sic] *of the rafter to blow. After performing numerous feats, when I gave Henry a punch in the short ribs to wake him up to see the performance. I pointed to the actor and whispered to him to look and keep quiet. He looked rubbed his eyes and looked again and said "That is nothing but some body's old cloths hanging there." But he soon discovered his mistake as the guard ordered the performance to go on. Just then someone woke up and not knowing that a guard was in the house spit on the floor. The guard immediately ordered him out of his bunk and made him take the place of the man on the rafter, who was glad enough to get off. The second actor performed about half an hour and was dismissed.*

On another occasion, he reported, "Several men in the same barrack [Number 5] were caught sitting at the stove. They were made to put their feet in the second bunk and their hands on the floor, and in this position they were whipped with belts by the guards just as a negro would be whipped or worse."[413]

Robert Bagby noted in his diary special punishment for standing too near a barracks stove: "Police caught two men standing by too close to the hot stove a few nights before and they stripped their clothes off and stuck the poor fellows so close to the stoves and burned them until they could not sit down. He was so sore. All such punishment they were inflicting upon them, such as making them stand in the cold and strapping their mouths with straps of leather and slapping them with straps of leather for petty offences."[414]

Confinement in the White Oak Dungeon, or Four Diamonds, in Prisoners Square was often used as punishment. Burke reported:

> *Tuesday November 3d, 1863. Some men of Cluke's and Johnson's regiments in another square dug some underground passages for the purpose of escapeing* [sic], *and came near finishing them* [the tunnels] *when some traitor told on them, and the Yanks marched them all out in the public square in front of headquarters and put a guard around them with orders to shoot any person that sit down. Some fifteen or twenty finally stept* [sic] *out and acknowledged being the principal diggers and were sent to the dungeon.*

Again, on July 4, 1864, Burke wrote:

> *A man from my regiment and two others had their heads through a hole in the roof of an empty barrack hugely enjoying the races,* [Chicago Driving Park, a race track, was located west of the camp near what is now Indiana Avenue] *when a Yankee caught them, and put them in the dungeon till morning. A prisoner was put in the four of diamonds today for selling several suits of clothes that were sent to other persons, in his care by some benevolent person or persons in Kentucky.*[415]

In 1862, the *Chicago Tribune* reported on White Oak Dungeon, "This institution, which is an important part of Camp Douglas, is now doing a brisk business, numbering about one hundred inmates. It may be readily understood that this place is not an attractive one, especially when occupied by over one hundred, with but barely standing room. Nothing so readily takes the starch out of these 'rampageons' secesh as does of 'White Oak.'"[416]

Punishment was a routine in Camp Douglas. However, except for insidious punishment created by evil guards, corporal punishment was common in all

Union military camps. The Mule, wearing signs or barrels, hanging by the thumbs and the use of dungeons were common punishment for Union soldiers.[417]

Escapes

Escaping from Camp Douglas was a common occurrence. Its distance from the South and Canada, however, made successfully returning to friendly hands unlikely. Frequently, prisoners would escape and ride the Cottage Grove trolley to downtown Chicago, only to get drunk and then be identified as a prisoner, arrested and returned to camp. Prisoners, unfamiliar with the North and Chicago, might have believed that Southern sympathizers were available to assist in their escape.

Mackey acknowledged that prisoners were aware of Confederate sympathizers in Chicago: "July 21, 1862. The Democrats and abolitionists of Chicago had a riot in the city to-day. Success to the former."[418] Perhaps prisoners were intent simply to get out of Camp Douglas, only worrying about further movement later. Nonetheless, the levee district of Chicago was attractive for the debauchery it offered.

One enterprising, if not intelligent, escapee was apprehended at the recruiting office of the Irish Brigade when he tried to enlist in Company I, Light Artillery. The recruiting officer discovered he had "secesh" buttons on his clothing. He confessed to being a prisoner but said he was anxious and willing to serve in the Federal army. He was returned to Camp Douglas.[419]

Most escapees planned to return to the South either directly through downstate Illinois or Indiana or to Canada and then to the Confederacy. Prisoners were often captured in central and southern Illinois. Two escapees attempting to go to Canada were Clayton Everett and James G. Blanchard. They had booked passage in Chicago on the schooner *Grace Murray* for Buffalo, New York. The *Murray* was intercepted and Everett and Blanchard captured by Deputy U.S. Marshall James Henry, who was assisting Captain Fitzgerald, dispatched from Camp Douglas by Colonel Mulligan, when the schooner arrived in Detroit.[420]

One successful escape was made by Morgan's Raider Sergeant Henry Stone of the Ninth Kentucky Cavalry:

> *On the night of October 16, 1863, having been confined in prison three months, accompanied by one of my messmates, William L. Clay, I tied my*

> *boots around my neck and in my sock feet climbed the prison fence, twelve feet high, between two guards and made my escape. My brother Dr. R. French Stone, who afterwards practiced his profession in Indianapolis until his death, five years ago* [1914], *was then attending Rush Medical College at Chicago. We found him next morning after making my escape as he was entering the college building. He showed us over the city, and during the day we dined at the Adams House, an excellent hotel. It was the first "square meal" Clay and I had eaten in several months, and I have often thought since that it was the best dinner I ate during the war.*
>
> *My comrade and I left the city by the Illinois Central going to Mattoon* [Illinois], *thence to Terre Haute* [Indiana], *where we tarried at a German hotel two days, most of the time playing pool, having written home to some of my family to meet me there. After seeing two of my brothers and obtaining some additional funds, we came by rail to Cincinnati, thence by boat to Foster's Landing, Ky., and from there footed it through Bracken, Nicholas and Bourbon counties.*[421]

Stone was captured several days later at his boyhood home in Bath County, Kentucky, and imprisoned in Mount Sterling, Kentucky. He escaped near Winchester, Kentucky, while being transferred by wagon and made his way to Canada by train from Paris, Kentucky, via Cincinnati, Toledo and Detroit, where he remained until April 1864. During his stay in Canada, he reported meeting "a lot of Confederates who had gotten out of Camp Douglas." He returned to Kentucky and later reentered the Confederate army in Virginia. He surrendered in Washington, Georgia, and was paroled on May 9, 1865.[422]

Early in the camp's existence, Chicago police and soldiers from Colonel Mulligan's Irish Brigade were poorly prepared to guard the Confederate prisoners. Inadequate stockade fencing, poor night lighting and indifference on the part of guards created an environment that invited escape attempts. Technically, taking a walk outside the gate might have been considered an escape attempt; many prisoners merely returned to their quarters after an outing. The fact that guards and prisoners shared space in White Oak Square provided many opportunities for fraternization and bribery. In early 1862, Colonel Tucker, the first commander of Camp Douglas, acknowledged the need to improve security, especially the stockade fencing suggested by Colonel Hoffman. He also indicated the likelihood of guards accepting bribes.[423]

The escape that led to Colonel Tucker's urgent request for the approval of the stockade fence took place on July 23, 1862. Prisoners, using ladders made from their bunks, breeched the western stockade fence; twenty-one escaped, with four recaptured almost immediately. It was reported that they had probably received outside help from Southern sympathizers. Union guard Private Charles White, Company C, Sixty-seventh Illinois Volunteer Regiment, joined the escapees, leaving his uniform behind.[424]

In May 1862, the *Chicago Tribune* reported the arrest of Union lieutenant Patrick Higgins for assisting prisoners in an escape. The paper noted, "One man, it is said, agreed to pay him $150; others were to pay smaller sums—the price of liberty having no fixed rate." At the time, Lieutenant Higgins was being cashiered from the army.[425] Colonel Hoffman complained to Secretary of War Stanton that charges against Lieutenant Higgins had been ignored.[426] Higgins's fate is unknown.

Reports of escapes were of concern to the citizens of Chicago. In July 1862, the *Chicago Tribune* reported that a large number of escaped prisoners were marching toward the city, adding that "thirty to forty were killed by guards." The article ended by suggesting that Chicago establish a Home Guard to protect the city. The next day, the newspaper admitted the story was entirely false.[427]

Early in Camp Douglas's existence, the use of paroled Union soldiers or any available unit to guard prisoners created a confused environment that encouraged escape attempts. Changes in command further complicated control of escape attempts. Not until Colonel DeLand took command in August 1863 was a significant effort made to increase security at Camp Douglas. The addition of Colonel James Strong, in early 1864, provided continuity in the guard force using Invalid Corps personnel.

In 1864, William Huff commented on the effect of increased physical security at Camp Douglas: "Lamps have been put up all around the fences and are kept burning all night that a guard may see a prisoner before he gets to the fence and fire at him. Fairly difficult to escape but now and then one fellow is lucky enough to do so."[428]

Morgan's Raiders, who arrived in Camp Douglas in mid-1863, were frequently involved in escape attempts and were a source of difficulty for the guard force. In September 1863, the *Chicago Tribune* reported, "The Union suffers wherever Morgan's desperados have been."[429] The suspension of the Dix-Hill Cartel exchanges increased the number of escape attempts, as did the increased population in the camp.

Escapes continued, in spite of security improvements. In February 1863, guard Charles Sprague intercepted three individuals dressed in Union uniforms who asked to be permitted to leave the camp at Sprague's guard post. Sprague refused, detained the men and called for the officer of the guard. Upon investigation, two of the men were determined to be Texas prisoners and the other Union private W.G. Porter, 106th Illinois Infantry. Porter had stolen uniforms from his comrades and agreed to assist in the escape. He was arrested and confined pending trial. The Texas Confederates were returned to their barracks.[430]

Not all bribery attempts were successful. On September 3, 1864, a bribe involving a ten-dollar gold piece resulted in the arrest of those attempting the bribe. The guard was permitted to keep the ten dollars as a reward. On September 6, six prisoners attempted to scale the stockade fence to reach a carriage that had arrived on Cottage Grove Avenue. One was shot and killed by guards and the other five captured.[431]

The *Chicago Tribune* reported escapes throughout the war. Frequently, these reports had incorrect information. It appears that the *Tribune* received little cooperation from Camp Douglas relating to information on escapes. On November 13, 1863, the paper published a statement given to Provost Marshall James by escaped prisoner Samuel Force. Force recounted being approached by a Union guard when they were both at a sutler's store. For a bribe of twenty dollars, the guard would facilitate his escape. Force purchased civilian clothes from the sutler and escaped. He remained in Chicago and found employment. He was found out when he asked about taking the oath of allegiance. Force was arrested and returned to Camp Douglas.[432]

Diary and journal entries about escape attempts were often based on rumors unless the escapes were from the writer's barracks. Prisoners also reported the recapture of escapees. Early in his time at Camp Douglas, in September 1863, Curtis Burke noted, "James Pratt and Thomas Ballard put on citizens cloths after dark and by bribing the guards or otherwise escaped. They had tried to escape three or four times before. The escape of prisoners from this prison had become a common nightly occurrence."[433]

Colonel DeLand reported to Colonel Hoffman a significant escape on December 3, 1863, when one hundred prisoners tunneled out of the barracks in White Oak Square. He reported that fifty were apprehended by troops from the camp and local police with the hopes that additional prisoners would be captured in the near future. He also reported that he was removing the floors of the barracks to deter further escapes and acknowledged, "This will undoubtedly increase the sickness and mortality, but it will save much trouble and add security."[434]

Burke reported several escapes in 1864. On March 23 of that year, he wrote, "Twelve men escaped from the [White Oak] dungeon last night by means of a tunnel. Three of them passed out after day light, and but for day light coming too soon for them everybody in the dungeon would have escaped. The hole was soon discovered after day light and filled up."

Later in March, he wrote:

> *Sunday March 27th, 1864. A tunnel was discovered by some treacherous rebel and reported to the Yanks. It is in the other square by the side of the fire place* [in] *a kitchen near the fence. The rebs were busy cooking over the covered hole when an officer came in and said, "What are you cooking over that hole for? Ain't you afraid your things will fall in?" "There is no hole here," said the rebs. "Yes there is take the pots off, and I'll show you." The rebs moved their things off and the officer removed the fire and ashes and raised a trap door disclosing the hole, much to the feigned astonishment of the rebs.*
>
> *The officer was angry and told the men that he would find every hole that they dug, and it was no use to dig them. The hole was filled up by pressing the rebs standing around into service. The men that dug it say that it would have been through on the outside of the fence in one night more. They had been detained a couple of nights on account of water rising in the hole. The ground being still very wet from the recent rains. There was only a few rebs that knew where the hole was, but there was a good many that suspicioned that there was one somewhere in that neighborhood and so put on their best cloths for two or three nights past, in the hope of finding it, and escaping. The diggers were afraid of traitorous-spies and worked secretly.*
>
> *Many true men were not posted. They were out slipping around as soon as it was well dark to learn something, and whenever they heard a noise or saw a Yankee patrol they would dodge into the nearest barracks like scared rats. Some rascally fellow played what would have been a severe joke on one Robert Lowery of Company A. of this regiment, had he succeeded in escaping.*

Burke continued, "Wednesday September 7th, 1864. Six men reported to have escaped last night. They charged the fence with two axes and one striking right handed and the other left handed soon broke a plank in two large enough to get out. I only saw two shots that were within three feet of the hole. Bad shots for fifty yards."

Following is Burke's last writing of escape:

> *Tuesday December 6th, 1864. Henry Allen of Co. B was staying at the sutler store and escaped rather mysteriously. The other clerks five in number*

> *were arrested and locked up in the express office to make them tell how Allen escaped, and how much money he took. Report says that he was hauled out in a barrel and that he took two or three hundred dollars from old* [prisoner] *Nightingale, who believes it all, and also that the other clerks have been robbing him too. The store is closed.*

Robert Bagby wrote of the same escape in his diary: "December 7, 1864. A young man by the name of Henry Allen made his escape the night before. It was supposed he went out in a load of barrels from the sutler store in the square. They had all of the other clerks arrested at the sutler's store."[435]

Huff also wrote about escapes in 1864: "Many of the prisoners have escaped lately by tunneling but that is about 'played out' now for they are raising all the barracks four feet above the ground…My friend and mess mate John D. Murtah was shot in attempting to escape from here. The ball penetrated the hip, making its exit at the groin. I do not think the wound dangerous."[436]

Using ladders to scale the stockade fence was common and sometimes mortal for prisoners. John Cecil, Eighth Kentucky Infantry, was shot and mortally wounded by guards when he and two others attempted to scale the wall. The other two succeeded.[437]

There was a certain honor about escaping. Prisoners supported the escape attempts by their fellow inmates. However, escaping at the expense of others was not received well by prisoners. Bagby reported of one such instance in October 1863:

> *Mr. Stewart, warden of Ward C, had borrowed a watch from a patient in order to have the time in the ward. And in a few nights the watch was stolen. Mr. Stewart and I suspected a patient from Ward C by the name of Samuel Guess for being guilty and had a search but the watch could not be found. We still believed Guess guilty and kept an eye on him.*
>
> *In the morning Guess, in writing, acknowledged his guilt to Mr. Stewart. The reason he did so* [took the watch] *was that Guess and two others were about to escape but had a falling out. Guess had stolen the watch for the three to make an escape by giving the watch to a guard on a bribe. I talked to Guess for long time. I thought he was the meanest man I had ever seen. I gave him a good lecture. He cried like a child and said he would never do the like again.*[438]

The attitude of camp commander Colonel Sweet regarding escape was expressed in Camp Douglas General Order Number 96, issued on September 28, 1864:

> *Captivity is one of the incidents of War, and a prisoner has the right to escape if he can, taking the risks and consequences. The Col. Commanding blames no man for a desire to go from his custody, and in reversed positions would, beyond all doubt, be actuated by the same motive. It is your right to escape, my business and duty to keep you, and as you are eight thousand men, whose lives and fortunes, in the event of your attempt to escape, must be largely affected by my temper and disposition. It is but fair that you should know exactly what may be expected, both for individuals and the whole body of Prisoners.*
>
> *If a single prisoner makes an effort to escape, he will be punished either by being shot by the guard in the act, or by a subsequent order of mine. He alone being responsible should alone be punished, but the whole body of prisoners of war will be held responsible that no organization or combination is made to attack the guard in force. And if such an attack is made, from the very nature of the case, the necessary means to repel it and restore order will endanger the lives of all in the prison square, those who are in the plot, as well as those who are not, and the Col. Commanding feels that humanity and a regard for the lives of the prisoners under his charge, requires that he should remind them of the risks incurred by an insurrection.*[439]

The exact number of escapes from Camp Douglas is unknown. Estimates from the *Official Records* place the number at slightly less than four hundred in the second half of 1863 and 1864 (the number of escapes mostly likely peaked in late 1863). It is likely that a total of between 450 and 500 prisoners escaped from Camp Douglas. Probably more than half of the escapees were recaptured. Those who escaped and were captured shortly afterward were probably not accounted for in these numbers.

The number of prisoners killed by guards while attempting to escape is also impossible to determine. George Levy, in *To Die in Chicago*, estimates that twenty-five prisoners were killed in escape attempts.[440] Illinois adjutant general Haynie, in his report after the war, stated that there was "only one [prisoner] shot by guard."[441] This is a completely nonsensical statement with no basis in fact.

War News

Prisoners received news of the war from a number of sources. They had access to newspapers, except the Southern-sympathizing *Chicago Times*. Letters from home and newly arrived prisoners also provided information on the war. The most often-mentioned sources in diaries and journals were rumors from prisoners and guards. Prisoners such as Curtis Burke and Robert Bagby wrote often of war news. Bagby's writing was based almost exclusively on rumors, while Burke commented on both newspaper articles and rumors. Other journals, such as that of James Mackey, made almost no mention of war news. While John Copley gave a graphic description of camp life, he never mentioned any war news.

Many of the rumors documented by prisoners were incorrect. Their comments emphasized information that demonstrated that the South was winning the war. Bagby wrote that prisoners from the battle at Nashville reported, "[Confederate general] Hood had whipped [Union major general] Thomas." He added, "They [Confederate prisoners] told quite a different story to what has been published." Fourteen days later, he noted that "Thomas had whipped Hood."[442]

Likewise, Burke wrote often of Confederate military successes and little of Confederate failures. During the early days of the Battle of the Wilderness, May 7–20, 1864, Burke wrote, "We are all very eager to hear the news of the great battle between Gens. Grant and Lee in front of Richmond, Virginia. We are confident of Lee's successes and the impregnability of Richmond."[443] On July 18, 1864, Burke wrote, "Rumors that Washington City is in the hands of the Confederates." He also wrote exaggerated reports of Confederate action at Petersburg, Virginia, and during Sherman's Atlanta Campaign. It is clear that information on the war was available to Confederate prisoners through Northern newspapers. There is no evidence of Southern newspapers being available to the prisoners at Camp Douglas. Additional war news was certainly available from letters from family members. It remains a mystery why some prisoners wrote frequently on the war and others did not.

Chapter 9

Prisoner Health and Medical Care

Faced with the knowledge that death from disease was more likely than death from an enemy's bullets, prison health and medical care were of constant concern to the commanders of the camp and U.S. army prison management. Even before becoming a prison camp, the health of Union soldiers was a problem at Camp Douglas. The *Chicago Tribune* reported a serious outbreak of measles in late 1861—over one hundred soldiers were ill, with the disease spreading rapidly. Poor sanitary conditions and inadequate hospital facilities were also noted in the article.[444]

Frequent inspections were conducted by the U.S. Army and the Sanitary Commission, with comments and recommendations referred to Colonel Hoffman and the camp commander. Many of these inspections resulted in improvements in medical care. However, changes were frequently deferred by General Meigs and Colonel Hoffman based on financial and operational dictates.

The overall health of the prisoners was the result of several factors. Many prisoners were in poor health upon their arrival at Camp Douglas as a result of the rigors of battle and weather conditions at the battle sites and during transportation to the camp. Severe weather at Camp Douglas, coupled with prisoner clothing not suited to cold winter temperatures, also contributed. Treatment of prisoners upon arrival at the camp added to their already poor health. They were required to stand for extended periods in inclement weather while they were being processed. This procedure was unexplained and inexcusable. For the entirety of Camp

Douglas's existence, poor sanitary conditions persisted, adding to disease among prisoners.

While medical facilities were available to prisoners, these facilities were inadequate. Furthermore, the primitive nature of Victorian-era medicine did not offer care that properly addressed prisoners' needs. As reported in 1864, over 30,000 total prisoners and over 12,000 prisoners at one time were supported by, at most, three hundred hospital beds.[145] Ill prisoners were treated in the barracks, where contagious diseases could easily be transmitted to others. In *To Die in Chicago*, George Levy noted that a medical study in 1864 found 577 patients in all Camp Douglas hospitals and 1,547 sick in barracks.

Prisoner diseases treated and deaths in Camp Douglas hospitals are shown in the following table:

Cases of Disease and Death at Camp Douglas, February 1862–June 1865

Cause	Cases	Deaths
Fevers, such as smallpox and malaria	15,938	1,407
Diarrhea and dysentery	13,455	698
Anemia	585	4
Consumption (Tuberculosis)	259	113
Rheumatism	3,212	37
Scurvy	3,745	39
Bronchitis	1,628	27
Pneumonia and pleurisy	4,655	1,296
Wounds, injuries and unspecified diseases	1,279	80
Other diseases	25,332	308
Total	70,088	4,009

Source: *The Medical and Surgical History of the War of the Rebellion*, Vol. I.

Camp Douglas Medical Inspections

In May 1863, a report from the U.S. Sanitary Commission concluded:

> *By recent reports under date of April 5 ultimo from two eminent members of the medical profession, Drs. Thomas Hun and Mason F. Cogswell, of Albany, N.Y., employed by the Sanitary Commission as special inspectors of hospitals, it is evident that the improvements promised by Colonel*

> *Hoffman have not been made and that the state of the hospitals in question is many degrees worse than when his attention was called to the condition of its inmates.*[446]

In October 1863, an inspection was conducted by A.M. Clark, acting medical inspector of prisoners of war. In addition to comments on the sanitation and physical facilities of the camp, Clark noted:

> *Hospital discipline not as strict as it should be. Hospital diet and cooking good, but cooking arrangements not carefully inspected. Hospital, heat and ventilation well heated by stoves; ventilation utterly lost sight of. Hospital, capacity very deficient; present capacity, for guard, 50; prisoners, 120; the chapel will increase this to 180. State of hospital records in most respects well kept. Medical attendance deficient; two more medical officers should be detailed to this post. Additional accommodation should be at once provided for at least 600 patients. There are now some 150 sick men lying in the barracks who should be in hospital and receiving attention.*[447]

Colonel DeLand responded four days after receiving Clark's report. He disagreed with many of Clark's conclusions, ending his response to Colonel Hoffman with, "I assure you, colonel, we are all doing all that can be done, with a reasonable regard for economy, to improve the condition of this camp and to benefit its inmates. But it takes time. Already there have been about $20,000 of improvements made, and there is room for much more. The calls of necessity and security were answered first; those of humanity come next."[448]

Camp Douglas surgeon Arvin F. Whelan reported to General Orme, camp commander, in December 1863:

> *There is not hospital capacity enough at present, but will soon be remedied, for there is now being erected a fine, commodious building for use of sick prisoners, capable of holding 200 patients, with ventilation, furnaces, hydrants, bath-room, & etc. The buildings now occupied as hospital* [by] *both Federals and prisoners were originally built for other purposes than which they are now used, and hence many inconveniences are experienced daily in treating the sick properly.*[449]

Surgeon O.T. Alexander, acting medical inspector for the U.S. Army, inspected Camp Douglas in July 1864 and reported a number of improvements from previous reports. He stated:

> *The hospital is a good two-story building, with four wards, mess-room, kitchen, etc., adjoining a two-story laundry. It is outside the prison inclosure* [sic], *distant about 200 yards, in a separate inclosure* [sic]. *Capacity, 200 to 225 beds. Built last winter and spring at a cost near $*[illegible]. *Occupied in April. As it is not large enough to accommodate all the sick prisoners, two of the old abandoned buildings are being moved into the hospital inclosure* [sic], *which will give the hospital an additional capacity of seventy beds. This will accommodate all sick prisoners, except smallpox cases. They are treated outside the camp in part of a building that was used as cavalry stables. It has, however, been converted into a comfortable ward; is well ventilated and policed.*[450]

Delivery of Medical Services for Prisoners

Union soldiers and prisoners received medical treatment in separate facilities. Both principal hospitals were in South (or Hospital) Square. Additional facilities for Union soldiers were located in White Oak Square, and two barracks in Prisoners Square were converted to hospitals for prisoners. The smallpox hospital, located away from the main camp, provided treatment for both Union and Confederate soldiers.

John Copley wrote about the prison hospital:

> *The prison hospital was located just outside of the prison square, in what we called the Federal square,—that is, this square was fenced in with a plank wall similar to ours, and the troops who were stationed there for guards had their quarters within this inclosure* [sic]. *The prison hospital was a large building sufficient to contain all the sick who were assigned to it. It was supplied with bunks, cots and stretchers, mattresses, blankets, sheets, and cotton pillows, all of which were kept ordinarily clean,—in fact, everything was about as good as could have been expected under the circumstances.*[451]

Delivery of medical services was provided by Union surgeons, contract civilian doctors and Confederate surgeons. In December 1863, Dr. Clark reported that treatment was delivered by three Union surgeons and two contract physicians.[452] Camp surgeon Arvin F. Whelan, in December 1863, reported, "There are four contract surgeons, on duty with prisoners, and five acting surgeons, who volunteered their services, and were detailed from among the prisoners, being graduates of medical colleges, and so far have shown themselves to be men of fine medical talent anxious to do their duty and conform to the rules of the camp and hospital."[453]

Prescription drugs, when available, could be obtained from either the hospital or the drugstore located in the camp. In October 1863, Curtis Burke wrote about purchasing medicine: "I took two powders and went to the drug store and got six more on Doctor Flag's prescription. No prisoner can get medicine at the drug store unless he had a prescription from the doctor of his square. Pettis and Flag are the doctors for White Oak Square."[454] Later, Burke noted, "Medicines of the right kind could not be procured…This barrack raised $14 by subscription and got a small basket of medicines from the city with it. Several other barracks have bought medicines for their own use, to be kept in their barracks."[455]

Confederate Surgeons

Captured Confederate surgeons provided medical treatment to prisoners with mixed success. The *Chicago Tribune* reported that Confederate surgeons were "derelict in the performance of this office, and the prisoners are sadly neglected by them."[456] Three days later, the paper noted, "These gentlemen appear to have been gentlemen of infinite leisure in Dixie; at any rate, they are contumacious and refuse to obey orders of the Post Surgeon."[457]

Post surgeon Dr. William D. Winer was forced to relieve several Confederate doctors in May 1862 and replace them with civilian surgeons. Two doctors submitted their resignations to Dr. Winer, who replied that prisoners could not resign. After threats of punishment, including confinement to the dungeon, hard labor and wearing a ball and chain, the Confederates relented and grudgingly accepted orders from Winer.[458]

Curtis Burke also commented on Confederate surgeons, writing, "All our doctors deserve censure for their neglect of duty for some time past."[459]

Prisoner Comments on Health

Prisoner health was often mentioned in diaries and journals. Burke noted in August 1864 that "everybody walks light and speaks in whispers on account of the sick. Medicines of the right kind could not be procured. The hospitals are crowded and that is the reason why the men are allowed to die in the barracks. There are a good many more sick but none dangerously."[460]

Robert Bagby, as a nurse in the prison hospital, had a close view of prisoner health and medical treatment. Every entry in his diary began with the general condition of patients. Common comments were "Boys doing very well" or "The others are managing very well." At the same time, he listed those who had died since he last indicated deaths by name.[461]

James Mackey commented infrequently about sickness among the prisoners but wrote in great detail about the death of his comrades.

John Copley simply stated, "Sickness of some kind prevailed all the time within the inclosure [*sic*] of the prison walls."[462] He was also proud that he was seldom sick. He wrote, "I was never sick in the slightest degree while there. I never missed a meal or roll-call, and I attribute my remarkable good health to my cleanly habits, together with my cold bath at the wash house, which I never failed to take every morning before breakfast."[463]

Smallpox

Several smallpox epidemics broke out during Camp Douglas's existence. Nearly every inspector commented on the disease and the need to avoid the spreading and treatment of the killer.

In March 1863, citizens were concerned about the spread of smallpox from Camp Douglas to the civilian population of Chicago. They asked for an evaluation of the significant increase in smallpox by the Chicago Board of Health. Dr. B. McVickar, D. Brainard and Dr. L. Chaney conducted an inspection of Camp Douglas and reported to the mayor that the patients were well cared for, that a program of vaccination had begun and that there was little concern of the disease spreading outside the camp. Their recommendations included isolating the patients, burying the dead at least six feet under ground and burning all the clothes of those infected. The statement from the post surgeon, Dr. George H. Park, that there would soon cease to be smallpox at Camp Douglas was wishful thinking.[464] These smallpox scares continued, including reports in January 1864 of the rise of the disease at the camp.[465]

Burke reported on an epidemic of smallpox on March 1864: "The smallpox is raging moderately. Only four cases were taken from this square today…I learn that about two thirds of the prisoners sent to the smallpox hospital have died, and that there is about forty cases in the hospital now."[466] This increase in smallpox cases was also reported in medical inspector John Marsh's April 16, 1864 report.[467]

While a smallpox vaccine was available, many prisoners and Union soldiers avoided it because of possible infection resulting from the treatment. Burke commented on the vaccination on three occasions. In February 1864, he wrote, "A case of smallpox was taken outside of the camp to the smallpox hospital, from the next barracks below us, and several other cases are reported, causing considerable uneasiness among the prisoners, and the Yanks themselves. Some Yankee surgeon came around and vaccinated nearly all of the Fifth and Fourteenth Ky. reg'ts. I concluded to put it off to see how it served others, not believing that the matter was pure."

In September 1864, he wrote, "Our regiment was vaccinated and I washed mine off and squeezed it to keep it from taking. For I would rather run the risk of the smallpox than have the sore that some of them have on their arms." That December, he wrote, "A doctor came in and vaccinated every man that has not been vaccinated lately or wanted to be vaccinated over again."[468] Burke continued to report additional smallpox cases on February 15 and 16, 1864.

Copley also commented on vaccinations and smallpox concerns:

> *Cases of varioloid, which is a light form of small-pox, were of frequent occurrence. The army surgeons came inside the prison and vaccinated all of us twice, while I was there. Those of the boys upon whom the vaccine matter took effect and caught cold with it, had very sore arms, which would inflame and be very painful for several days.*
>
> *I seemed to be proof against all the forms of this dreaded disease, as my bunkmate was sick with the loathsome affection two weeks before being removed to the hospital, and I was compelled to occupy the same bunk with him every night, and I was twice vaccinated, all of which failed to have any effect upon me.*[469]

Copley wrote of smallpox patients and how they were treated before reaching the hospital:

The diseases most prevalent were fevers and small-pox, the latter especially so. Those who were sick received very little attention until removed to the hospital, which sometimes was not done until the patient had grown very sick. The only assistance we could render was to hand them a drink of water, or some other little simple attention. Their fare was only the regular rations allowed to them while well; they suffered for nourishing food, as their appetites would refuse such as we could obtain for them. After being removed to the prison hospital they fared much better in every respect, and many recovered who would have died had they not been removed to it. Those who were so unfortunate as to take the small-pox, were removed to the small-pox hospital, which was located somewhere beyond the city limits.[470]

Curtis Burke Becomes a Smallpox Victim

In October 1864, Burke contracted smallpox. He wrote the following in his diary:

I feel a little better than I did yesterday, and picked up a basin with the intention of taking a wash, but I was stopped by several and after a little examination told that I was broken out with the smallpox, and must not wash, but go to bed immediately, which I did. I was not much surprised altho [sic] *I had not the least idea that I was taking the smallpox, as I had felt no pains in my back or head nor even a sore throat. Dr. Pettus came and examined me and pronounced it a light case of smallpox and gave an order for the (red) ambulance which soon drove up to the door.*

I put on my worst cloths, taking an extra check shirt, and jumped in with seven others, myself making the eighth. We moved off, stopping at the gate long enough to be counted. We stopped again at the Yankee Doctor's office near the Hospital in the Yankee square and were inspected by a Doctor a few minutes, and then moved through the south gate out of camp to the smallpox hospital which stands about four hundred yards from the fence on the south side of camp and near the Douglas Institute and monument. We jumped out and went in to the stove. The building is long but larger than our barracks.

I saw the patients had frightful looking faces and hands and some were very lightly broken out. I half recognized one of the Reb nurses and asked him to see that I got a go[o]*d clean cot. He said he would and started off. In five minutes another nurse told me a cot was ready and I followed him into the next ward, which also appeared to be crowded with patients on both sides. The nurse stopped at an empty cot and told me to take that. I thought it was the cot I had spoken to nurse No. 1 for, but on looking at it I could see old scabs sticking all over the blankets, and I began to wonder how I could lay under blankets full of scabs. I turned the cover back and the smell nearly staggered me, but I though*[t] *if I must, I must! So I undressed and got in. Just then nurse No. 1 (John Craig, Woodford Co. Ky.) passed with some blankets for a cot for me not knowing that I had been accomodated* [sic]. *I concluded as I was in bed I would try it where I was. Everything appeared to have a mean smell. I noticed the floor was still damp from being scoured. I felt damp sticky spots on my blankets. Most of them* [were] *sticky and felt disagreeable. The roof* [was] *very open and airy. There was two holes that I could crawl out, besides numerous large cracks near the center of the roof. There was two stoves and but one in use. Something was the matter with the pipe of the other. I saw no other prospect than to freeze if the October weather turned very cold. I had but two blankets to cover with and one between me and the cot with no tick.*

I heard a coffee mill in the next room which indicated that dinner time was near at hand, also that said room was the kitchen. I had a very bad case on each side of me and they smelled very bad. The flies annoyed them a great deal. My covering disgusted me so that I could not bear it as high as my chin, so I took my extra check shirt by the arms and turned it over and over till it made a roll and wound it around my neck to keep from catching a cold. I knew that I would have to get used to it and concluded to watch what was going on around me. I noticed that the patients, and especially the bad cases, called often for water, and the nurses did not like to give it, often telling them that they were killing themselves drinking water, so I made up my mind not to take a single drink of water during my sickness or so long as I kept my right mind. I resolved also to stay in my cot till the Doctor said I was well enough to get out.

A small table was set out in the middle of the floor and the nurses came in with a waiter of sliced bakersbread, several large coffee pots, a pitcher of milk and a tin cup of sugar, also a few soda crackers and roasted potatoes. The patients that were able sat up in their cots, and I followed suit, protecting myself the best I could. A plate with a slice of bread on it and a tin cup half or two thirds full of weak coffee was given to each. The worst cases got toast and a cracker or potatoe [sic]. *My appetite was good and I went through mine in a hurry. As soon as all were done the plates were gathered and the table and contents moved into the first ward.*

I could feel the cool air coming through the canvas in the bottom of my cot and noticing that all the other cots had mattress[es] *on them. I spoke to Mr. Jackson, one of the head nurses, about it and he raised one for me which made my cot feel much better. There are ten nurses in all and a Yankee stewart* [sic] *that they call "Napoleon." Supper came and we got the same as at dinner. At dusk an oil lamp swinging in the center of the room was lighted.*

My head felt very light and I was afraid that I might get out of my mind. When I looked at the lamp my fancy turned certain rays and shades into a lady dressed in black with a white handkerchief to her eyes. If I looked at the roof or wall the rain stains transformed themselves into something hideous, and if I shut my eyes I would instantly imagine I saw funeral processions, grave yards and other things that I did not wish to see. I was very restless and did not know what to do. I did not feel sick, but I could not sleep. I was very nervous. Several persons died during the night. I was glad when day light began to appear.

The next day, Burke wrote:

I feel better than I expected to feel. I have no pains or sore throat, but a very good appetite. Chas. M. Byrnes came out with a light case from my company. A milk woman comes within a few yards of the hospital every morning and evening and sells milk at 10 cents per quart and 10 per gallon for butter milk. The nurses go out and purchase for those patients that have the change. During the day apples and cakes come to the door for sale. I crave milk more than anything else and I am without a cent. I have been looking for Pa to send me some change from camp. Our breakfast and dinner and supper are the same. I passed another sleepless night though not so restless as the night before.[471]

As time progressed, Burke reported:

The bumps are coming out on my face, but not very thick. There is but few on my hands and on the rest of my body they are very scattering. I find it necessary to spit a great deal to keep my throat and head clear in which the spit box about two feet from my face on each side is very handy. The nurses appear very kind and often tell me that I have a very light case, but I must wait patiently and let it have its way. I take a couple of spoonfulls [sic] *of light looking fluid that has but little taste to it, two or three times a day.*

> *They call it No. 2. I am getting pretty well used to the ways of the place, and do not mind the nurses tramping back and forth with coffins.*
>
> *The bumps on my face are getting dark spots on them showing that they are drying up. The nurse says that in nine days they will all be dried up and scaled off and I will be well enough to return to camp. My medicine was changed to a dark looking fluid that tastes bitter. They call it No. 1. It is to make me dry up and to give a good appetite. I am as patient as could be expected. There was thirteen new cases arrived during the day. The nurses say it is more than ever came out in one day before. We are beginning to be crowded.*
>
> *The nurses told me that I was well enough to wash my hands and face and sit up. I had not been allowed to wash since I broke out with the smallpox and I was glad enough to avail myself of the opportunity to get the dirt off of my hands and face, which I did with warm water and felt a great deal better.*[472]

Burke left the smallpox hospital and returned to his barracks on October 19, 1864, twelve days after being diagnosed.

Robert Bagby's Encounters with Smallpox as a Nurse

As a nurse in the prison hospital, Bagby came in contact with cases of smallpox, the smallpox hospital and staff. Fear of the disease was reflected in a diary entry in February 1863:

> *I went with the undertaker to the dead house to load in some dead. What a site…there were nine fellows laying there. It looked so much like we were hermits. They may be more compelled to treat each other better. When I went in there I did not know one of the cases had died of small pox. I felt it my duty to assist. I took it in stride. I could die with a clear conscious knowing that I done my duty. I did not hear from the pox hospital. There was still a great deal of talk about the caring of the sick* [there], *they* [the nurses] *were making it out of the ward as fast as they could.*[473]

In November 1864, Bagby noted a serious problem in the smallpox hospital. This was only a month after Burke had been released. He wrote,

"There had been 35 new cases the day before increasing the number of patients to 255. From what I could learn it was distressing to take care of them. A great many had no blankets and no bed. They were compelled to lie about on the floor like hogs. I received no names and no papers."[474]

Finally, on December 18, 1864, he wrote, "Smallpox now on the decline."

Fear of the dreaded smallpox and concern over other possible diseases brought on by the poor conditions in camp, poor rations and severe winters kept good health on the minds of the prisoners at Camp Douglas. Their ultimate fear was dying in a hostile land without the support of their family and neighbors.

Chapter 10

Death in the Civil War and at Camp Douglas

More than 2.0 percent of the nation's population died as a direct result of the Civil War. These 620,000 men equaled the 1860 population of Maine, more than the entire population of Arkansas and Connecticut and more than the entire male population of Alabama and Georgia.[475] A total of 30,218 Union soldiers died in Confederate prisons, or 15.5 percent of those held, while 25,976 Confederate soldiers died in Union prisons, or 12.1 percent of those held.[476]

The total number of deaths at Camp Douglas is somewhere between the 4,243 names contained on the monument at the Confederate Mound in Oak Woods Cemetery and the 7,000 reported by some historians. Best estimates place the total at between 5,000 and 6,000. The exact number has never been established, thanks to poor record-keeping by both the Union and Confederate armies and the actions of those who cared for the bodies after death.

C.H. Jordan, a longtime and respected Chicago funeral director, had an oral agreement with Camp Douglas to remove and inter prisoners who died at Camp Douglas at a cost of $4.75 each. The bodies were to be buried in the City Cemetery, located at what is now the southern end of Chicago's Lincoln Park. The $4.75 included removing and interring the bodies and furnishing the coffin. Jordan's costs were about $1.00 to $1.50 for a burial plot, plus less than $1.00 for the coffin.[477]

In addition to the burials in City Cemetery, Jordan managed the shipment of nearly 150 bodies to relatives in the South. Establishing the exact number

Undertaker C.H. Jordan moved the Confederate dead from Camp Douglas to City Cemetery. *Chicago History Museum.*

of deaths becomes difficult when considering these shipments; grave-robbing for medical purposes, which was common at the time; and the movement of up to 655 bodies from graves at the smallpox hospital at Camp Douglas. One thing is certain, however—those from Camp Douglas were interred in City Cemetery's potter's field, which was subject to flooding and sand blowing over and covering or destroying the grave markers. A total of 3,384 bodies were said to have been interred in the potter's field. The *Chicago Tribune* reported on the poor burial procedures of prisoners interred there, noting that the bodies were left very close to the surface on low land near Lake Michigan.[478]

Based on inventories and documents of the time, up to 50 percent of the prisoners who had died by April 1863 vanished. It was reported that bodies were washed into Lake Michigan and often found at the water intake "cribs."

Prisoners' Bodies Moved to Oak Woods Cemetery

In January 1867, the army agreed to remove remains from City Cemetery. Most cemeteries in the city that accepted the bodies of Union soldiers, including Rosehill and Graceland, refused to accept Confederate remains. Oak Woods Cemetery (located at Sixty-seventh Street and Cottage Grove Avenue) agreed to bury the Confederate remains for $3.00—$2.00 for the grave site and $1.00 for the burial. This did not include disinterment. The contract for removing the bodies from City Cemetery was awarded to M.O. O'Sullivan for $1.98 each, including a coffin. City Cemetery reported that 3,384 bodies were removed, with only 40 bodies missing.[479]

Oak Woods Confederate monument, Chicago. *Linda Keller.*

The move to Oak Woods took place between April 13 and April 30, 1867. O'Sullivan was paid based on 3,384 bodies. Oak Woods never confirmed the number of coffins received. Ultimately, the Union quartermaster reported that 4,039 Confederates (3,384 from City Cemetery and 655 from the Camp Douglas smallpox hospital) and 12 Union soldiers were at Oak Woods. Reconciling these with the 4,243 names on the Confederate monument has never been done. The total number of bodies buried, shipped or lost in Chicago will probably never be known.

One example of confusion and poor record-keeping of deaths at Camp Douglas is the case of the two Confederate soldiers named Jonathan Bond. In January 1863, Jonathan Bond, Fourth Tennessee Cavalry, was captured at Stone River Tennessee and sent to Camp Douglas. Private Jonathan Bond, Seventeenth Texas Cavalry, was captured at Fort Hindman, Arkansas, and also sent to Camp Douglas in January 1863. Both Jonathan Bonds were ill in the camp's prison hospital in March 1863. The Texan Bond died of "congested lungs" on March 31, 1863, while the Tennessean Bond also died on March 31, of pneumonia. In April 1863, a clerk likely thought there was an error in reporting two soldiers of the same name on death rolls on the same day. Texan Jonathan Bond's name was removed from the death roll. Only "Jonathan Bond, Co. B 4th Tenn. Cav." appears on the bronze tablets of the Confederate monument in Oak Woods Cemetery. It is likely that Texan Jonathan Bond is also interred at Oak Woods.[480]

Of the thirteen names of dead mentioned in the Robert Bagby diary, seven were listed on the Confederate monument at Oak Woods Cemetery. Four of five names included in James Mackey's diary were listed on the Confederate monument.[481]

Even with the poor record-keeping, it is acknowledged that more Confederate soldiers are buried in Chicago than anywhere else north of the Mason-Dixon line.[482]

The Victorian Attitude Toward Death and Prisoners' Reactions

Drew Faust, in her comprehensive book about death in the Civil War, noted the following about the Victorian attitude toward death: "In the eyes of a modern reader, men often seem to have been trying too hard as they sought to present evidence of a dead comrade's ease at dying or readiness for salvation. But their apparent struggle provides perhaps the most eloquent testimony of how important it was for them to try to maintain the comforting assumptions about death and its meaning with which they had begun the war."[483]

The attitude that the soldier took into the Civil War and this need to comfort in death were well outlined in James Mackey's comments on the death of his comrade:

> *Mr. George D. Armstrong, a man loved by his friends and respected by his enemies, to-day closed his eyes upon the pleasures and pain of the world. In him we lose one of the most loved and most useful members of our company. And his wife, too, will have to mourn the loss of that noble, tender-hearted husband; two bright children will also look in vain for a kind father's caresses. This is a changing world & many are the shadows that must fall upon our pathway while we sojourn here; friends, however dear, the Lord in his wisdom may remove. Many will be the tears shed for him, but those who mourn for him must remember that it is God who took him. Desolate must be the home he once blessed with his presence, and desolate to the heart of the wife he so dearly loved. Whither he has gone we cannot go now, but the final judgment we shall see him.*

Two days later, he concluded, "To-day I took the last glance at my friend Armstrong as he lay calm and still in death."[484]

Faust points out that the importance of family and God's will was central in the Victorian attitude toward death. The good death included the concept of accepting dying for God and country. How one died was a reflection on how one lived and the quality of his afterlife.

Victorian-era people believed it necessary to die among family, with their support at one's bedside. This was key to the family observing death and assessing the dying person's soul and to accepting and understanding the chances for the family reuniting in the afterlife.

Robert Bagby showed his disdain for a brother failing to support his brother's death: "Soon after I got up one man died by the name of Royal Jennings, a Tennessee conscript. He seemed to be a man of no energy. His brother was in there complaining some. We thought he did not pay the respect to his brother he might after days of sorrow."[485]

Mackey recounted a sudden death with clarity but without the compassion of his previous chronicling of death:

> *This afternoon about two o'clock Mark Pugh of CO. E. came to sudden death. He had just taken some medicine which made him sicken at the stomach. He went to the door to vomit, but was soon brought back by his comrades in a dying state. His death was instantaneous. He bursted* [sic] *open when being put in the coffin. It is supposed that he was poisoned. He was of good standing among his comrades.*[486]

Prisoners were forced to compensate for the lack of family and failure of death to meet the acceptable standards of the good death. Frequently, Civil War soldiers retained remembrances of home in the form of pictures, lockets and hair cuttings. Prisoners took great effort to protect these personal items when guards conducted inspections. The loss of these items would represent the loss of contact with home and loved ones.

Bagby wrote of fellow prisoners supporting their comrades: "Three deaths to report and one in the barracks. W.B. Geang, NC Reserves, of the fever, James Cox, 15 Tenn., also of fever some of his friends sent him word from his mother that she would be sending him some money and clothes that he wanted. As soon as he learned this he said he would never need them for he was going to die. Then very restless soon became irrational and died in six or eight hours."[487]

Fellow prisoners offered support for dying prisoners as well as a surrogate family on which to depend and to accept their death. This, coupled with diary and journal entries and letters home eulogizing the dead, provided the prisoners with as much comfort as possible when facing death. While most of the diaries and journals would not be seen by the families of those whose death was mentioned, they provided the writer with the comfort of knowing that a good death occurred for his comrades.

Accepting death or the prospect of death as God's will was a common form of creating a good death out of the chaos of the prison camp environment. Just as important as acceptance of death was one's behavior in life. Virtuous behavior was necessary to be received by God. A description of these virtues was carefully recounted by Mackey in the death of George Armstrong.

There are other examples of the testimonials to the dead that reflected the good death. Mackey wrote:

> *Another one* [Thomas Johnson] *of our company breathed his last to-day. The King of Day just commenced his course across the azure sky when his gentle spirit took its flight to Him who gave it. His pilgrimage on the earth was terminated ere he arrived at the age of manhood, but not before he tasted of life's trials and disappointments. He met his trials and difficulties with Christian fortitude. Reason told him that his pathway through life must be fraught with disappointments and endured with patience. He was not a Christian by profession, but he tried hard to be one by practice. I knew him for five months as a soldier, and I never knew a young man try harder to discharge his duty. He was kind and affable to all, treated everyone with respect and tried to have everybody love him. Had he lived he would have*

> *made a loved and useful man, but alas! The Lord chose to take him to himself, and that, in his youth. As it is, we can only mourn his loss, and console ourselves with the hope that he is in a better world where sorrows are never known.*[488]

Mackey's short but to-the-point eulogy of David Bond was enough to qualify Bond's as a good death, although it lacked direct reference to God:

> *Last night David E. Bond, a member of our company, breathed this last. He was a gentleman in every sense of the word, and his death is lamented by all his comrades. In his dealing with his fellow-soldiers he was faultless, honest, sociable, and high-minded; he always treated others as he would have them treat him. He was sick for more than two months, his disease was typhoid pneumonia. Peace to his ashes.*[489]

An example of the death of a prisoner whose life was less than superior yet still redeemed in the end was also recorded by Mackey:

> *Mr. James M. Akin, I am sorry to say, breathed his last early this morning. His death, though not unexpected, cast gloom over the comrades he left behind. He was gentle and agreeable among his fellow-soldiers, seeking to give offence to no one. He was fair and honest in all his dealings with his fellow-men, and died, it is believed, owing no one. During his connection with our company his peculiarities in many instances excited the ire of many of its members; but nevertheless he never asked a favor of any one that was not granted. It was his misfortune to be very irascible, which occasioned him to speak insulting sometimes to his best friends; but with the disappearance of anger came sorrow for the offence, and he was as good a friend as ever. His differences with his comrades were soon forgotten by both parties, and never resulted in hatred. His death is bitterly lamented by all; and more sad tidings I know cannot be borne to his parents and friends at home than that he is no more. Peace to his ashes.*[490]

Suicide was not uncommon in prison camps. Methods ranged from charging the stockade fence when escape was impossible to merely giving up when ill. Bagby described the attempted suicide of a hospitalized prisoner:

> *Walter P. Reys Co A 55th Ga. He had gotten transferred from the smallpox hospital and was afflicted with raising* [vomiting?] *which should have*

> *perhaps caused his death eventually. In the evening he asked one of the nurses for a pin* [sic] *knife to trim his finger nails. On getting the knife he went to work on his nails. Nurses, not suspecting anything of the kind, paid no attention to him for some time. When someone noticed him bleeding freely they thought it was from the lungs. They were starting to get him some medicine when they noticed a knife in a spittoon near the bed side. On* [a nurse] *reaching for the knife, Reys grabbed it. On examination they found he had stuck the little blade in a main artery in several places, cutting it in one or two. On speaking of it he said he was going to die anyway and wanted the boys to let him have a better knife to finish the work. If they could not do this, they could cut his throat for him.*[491]

Bagby does not report the ultimate fate of Reys.

Bagby, who saw death daily in the prison hospital, remained positive on the subject:

> *The night before patients were doing very well. But there were a great many dying in the camp. Was as high as 35 bodies in the dead house at one time. That day this was enough to discourage any man. Yet I retained my high spirits thinking perhaps the time had not come yet, as the war was yet going on with all the horrors. Notwithstanding all of this…some things seemed to tell that all things might come right, for all thing were going so fast it seemed to me that I would live through it all and be great help to the sick and dying.*[492]

Early in the history of the camp, the *Chicago Tribune* reported prisoner deaths by name. After mid-1862, the paper stopped this reporting and rarely mentioned prisoner deaths. Prisoners saw their comrades become ill and die, hoping that they would not be next. Supporting fellow prisoners as they faced death and documenting the good death was an integral part of camp life.

Chapter 11

The Conspiracy of 1864

The story of Camp Douglas is not complete without considering the Conspiracy of 1864. While the conspiracy had little direct effect on Camp Douglas, it absorbed much of the time of camp commander Colonel Benjamin Sweet during the last half of 1864 and was a topic of wild rumors and colorful speculation in Chicago.

The climate for conspiracy began well before the August 1864 Democratic convention in Chicago. In November 1863, the Ohio Conspiracy was widely reported in Chicago. This plot, interrupted in Ohio, included plans to free Morgan's Raiders prisoners at Camp Chase, Ohio, and Camp Douglas. In addition, plans were to seize the U.S. steamer *Michigan* and ultimately take several states out of the Union. Dick Merrick and Samuel Thomas, both from Chicago, were implicated in the plot, thus bringing the conspiracy directly to Chicago.[493]

The stage was set for the Conspiracy of 1864. The Sons of Liberty, bushwhackers and guerillas reportedly led by Captain Thomas H. Hines, CSA, initiated a conspiracy to free the prisoners at Camp Douglas, raze Chicago and then move to release prisoners at the Rock Island prison during the August 1864 Democratic convention. Hines had been a Confederate agent in Canada after successfully directing the escape of General John Hunt Morgan from the Ohio State Penitentiary in Columbus in November 1863. Hines was in Chicago prior to the Democratic convention and again before the election of November 1864. Undoubtedly, he wanted to cause disruption of the election and perhaps even the attack on Camp Douglas and Chicago. He was skilled in operating outside the Confederacy with great flexibility.

Charles Walsh, alleged leader of the Sons of Liberty, was to provide "many thousands" of soldiers for the assault; however, he could muster only twenty-five. Additional support promised from local Copperheads and other conspirators never materialized. Captain Hines; John Castleman, his second in command; and British soldier of fortune Colonel George St. Leger Grenfell realized the assault was not possible. Hines and Castleman wisely returned to Canada. Grenfell remained in Chicago as an English gentleman interested mostly in hunting in Central Illinois.[494] The initial phase of the conspiracy was over before it began.

Colonel Sweet was not to be deterred by the inaction of the conspirators. The climate of conspiracy, the large number of Democrats in Chicago for the convention and Sweet's desire to improve his political résumé demanded that he address and perhaps embellish the ongoing threat of a conspiracy. Colonel Sweet continued warnings of the conspiracy through November 1864.

Conspiracy at the Election in November 1864

Sweet recruited a convicted felon and Confederate prisoner at Camp Douglas, John T. Shanks, to join the conspirators in Chicago while posing as an escaped prisoner. Shanks's task was to identify high-ranking conspirators and obtain evidence against them.[495] It is curious that Shanks was selected for this mission. Captured as one of Morgan's Raiders in July 1863, Shanks enjoyed special treatment at Camp Douglas, operating as a clerk in the express office. It was speculated that he had earlier saved the life of Colonel DeLand, Camp Douglas commander, when Shanks arrived at the camp.[496]

Known to both Captain Hines and Colonel Grenfell, "Shanks was considered a forger, thief, traitor, spy, liar, perjurer, and a coward; in Hines words, 'a blacker-hearted villain never lived.'"[497] It seems highly unlikely that the Confederate conspirators would take Shanks into their confidence.

Robert Bagby also had intimate knowledge of Shanks, whom he first mentioned in writing in October 1864:

> *In the evening I received some postage stamps from Mrs. Morris through the express office. I got a line from John T. Shanks, who was acting for the express office, informing me of paper, envelopes and writing material. I suppose he kept*

> *the paper and envelopes…I did not know how many stamps that he was good at* [he had taken]. *I concluded I would investigate the matter and if he had any right to this. All was sent in for charitable purposes. I was to distribute the material as the detainees needed it and I suppose Mrs. Morris had obtained permission to send such.*[498]

Bagby's diary shows that he clearly did not trust Shanks, and it seemed that Mrs. Morris, wife of former Chicago mayor Buckner Morris, who was a defendant in the subsequent trial of conspirators, knew Shanks. It is difficult to believe that the conspirators were unaware of the fact that Bagby and the other prisoners at Camp Douglas believed Shanks was a spy for Colonel Sweet. Bagby reported:

> *There was a great deal of excitement in the camp in consequence of a rumor afloat that John Shanks had made his escape from the prison on Thursday or Friday night before. And he with a squad of Copperheads and rebel officers were captured not far from the camp on the lake shore, where they had a good many guns and pistols. All hands of us thought Shanks had been sent out as a spy to see if there was any truth in the rumor of a plot going on through the state. We thought through the day to our satisfaction that Shanks had trapped the fellows who were there, if there was anyone.*[499]

Bagby's disdain for Shanks is evident in the following passage:

> *There was nothing more concerning the conspiracy and the release of the prisoners at Camp Douglas. But I learned how John Shanks had tricked Buckner and Morris. He went to the Morris house perhaps in company with some Federals in disguise, Shanks representing them as being escaped prisoners. They (Buckner & Morris) of course had seen Shanks and knew that he had undoubtedly been a prisoner. Shanks told others he was to get away and Morris giving him a hand and supper was prepared for them. They being so confident Shanks was sincere, they led him to the secrets of the organization, just about ready to act. Of course, Shanks reported this to the authorities. This made me sick. Question. What should properly be the fate of such a man? Mrs. Morris had been furnishing the prisoners with clothing. She had been instrumental in Shanks getting many things,* [and] *if not him, some of his friends. Then for him to show such meanness was the crowning act of this treachery.*[500]

Bagby's final comment on Shanks was:

> *I heard that John Shanks had taken the oath and obtained a situation from the authorities. He was calculating to marry in the city a young lady that was said to be very nice. What a pain that she could not be informed of what kind of man he was. It was considered he had a wife and three children in Texas and was reported he had one in Tennessee. But that was not all—the man told me that he confessed that he had been guilty of forgery and many other rascally tricks in Tennessee and he made the work to free prisoners at Camp Douglas as long as he had money and worked.*[501]

One of the components of the November conspiracy was a major breakout from Camp Douglas by Morgan's Raiders. In September, James Burke, who likely would have known of any major escape attempt, commented in his journal, "It seems the Yankees were badly scared last night thinking that there was a plot among a good many of the prisoners to break out. I see notice of it in the papers today." Burke also noted the possibility in November: "There are plenty of rumors about arms etc. being found near camp. At night we had unusually strict orders to keep quiet."[502]

On November 6, Colonel Sweet warned General John Cook, commander of the Military District of Illinois, in Springfield:

> *The city is filling up with suspicious characters, some of whom we know to be escaped prisoners, and others who were here from Canada during the Chicago convention, plotting to release the prisoners of war at Camp Douglas. I have every reason to believe that Colonel Marmaduke of the rebel army is in the city under an assumed name, and also Captain Hines of Morgan's command, also Col. St. Leger Grenfell, formerly Morgan's Adjutant-General, as well as other officers of the rebel army.*[503]

Arrests and Trial

Sweet then conducted a raid on November 6–7, 1864, in downtown Chicago, arresting Walsh, Grenfell and several other Shanks-identified conspirators, including Judge Buckner S. Morris and his wife.

The *Atlantic* magazine of July 1865 published a fanciful account of the conspiracy. The article reported the availability of 20,000 men in Illinois to initiate the attack on Camp Douglas and Chicago. The Chicago attack, it reported, would result in an army of 100,000 to continue the attack on the North. The unsubstantiated report also stated that 5,000 armed men were in Chicago in July 1864. The article asserted that the "American Knights," spread all over the West, numbered over 500,000 and that 350,000 of them were armed.[504] The *Atlantic* gave Colonel Sweet credit for thwarting the conspiracy with the help of an unnamed Confederate major, who reported to Sweet details of the conspiracy and John Shanks's involvement as an informer.[505]

William Bross, in his paper presented before the Chicago Historical Society in 1878, also gave Colonel Sweet and his "sleepless vigilance" credit for saving Chicago and the West from this major threat.[506] Bross reported a conversation with Sweet in which the colonel said, "Do you know there are ten thousand stand of arms secreted in cellars and basements within four block of us [the Tremont Hotel in downtown Chicago]?"[507] Interestingly, Bross's only mention of John Shanks was that he was arrested, as an escaped prisoner, along with the conspirators.[508]

The *Chicago Tribune* reported in detail on the conspiracy and the subsequent trial. These reports added to the intrigue of the conspiracy and offered additional opportunities for perpetuating rumors and exciting conversation in Chicago.[509] The trial was held in Cincinnati, where Grenfell was sentenced to death (he later escaped from prison); Morris was found not guilty, but his wife, Mary, was banished to Kentucky. Others convicted, including Walsh, received sentences up to five years.[510]

Colonel Sweet's Justification

Colonel Sweet wrote a detailed report to Brigadier General James B. Fry, provost in Washington, D.C., in November 1864 stating that he "thwarted the expedition" and caused the "large number of Sons of Liberty and other guerrillas," all armed, from four midwestern states to disperse to their homes. He further stated: "[On the] 6th day of November, late in the afternoon, it became evident that the city was filling up with suspicious characters, some of whom were escaped prisoners of war and soldiers of the rebel army; that Captain Hines, Colonel Grenfell, and Colonel Marmaduke were here to lead; and that Brigadier General Walsh of the Sons of Liberty had ordered large numbers of the members of that order from the southern portions of Illinois to co-operate with them."

He went on to report the arrest of the conspirators on November 7, along with "106 bushwhackers, guerrillas and rebel soldiers." On November 14, he arrested a number of additional conspirators and stated, "An examination of many of the persons so arrested shows, beyond all doubt, that the Sons of Liberty is a treasonable, widely extended, and powerful organization, branching into almost if not all the counties of the State."

In his offering congratulations to the troops under his command, he reported to Fry, "A garrison overworked for months, its officers and enlisted men met the demand for added and wearing duty necessary to hold harmless the great interests committed to their care, with a cheerful alacrity and steady zeal deserving the warmest commendation."[511] Most of Colonel Sweet's assertions of guilt were not confirmed by the subsequent trials.

The question remains: Was there ever a conspiracy? Many believe the conspiracy existed only in the mind of Colonel Benjamin Sweet and in the wishful thinking of the Confederacy. At any rate, the Conspiracy of 1864 is forever woven into the fabric of Camp Douglas.

Chapter 12

Reasons for Conditions and Death at Camp Douglas

Written analyses of conditions and death rates of Confederate prisoners in Union prisons have looked to blame rather than investigate or understand the reasons. Sanders, in *While in the Hands of the Enemy*, places blame on leadership of both the Union and the Confederacy for conditions, with little discussion of their reasons.[512] In his *Andersonvilles of the North*, James Gillispie implies over-exaggeration of Confederate reports, crediting this to the Lost Cause movement. Actions at Union prison camps were often mentioned without a discussion of the underlying reasons.[513] Peckenpaugh's *Captives in Grey* looks at the truth and fiction of Union prison camps, again without a study of underlying reasons.[514] Doyle, in *The Enemy in Our Hands*, offers a comprehensive history of the treatment of prisoners. His work gives us some idea of the historic basis for the treatment of Civil War prisoners.[515]

Each Civil War prison camp was unique, and this uniqueness required different decisions by commanders that guided treatment of prisoners. These command decisions and the idiosyncrasies of the men who made them caused circumstances for the prisoners to vary from prison to prison. Because of each camp's uniqueness, it is difficult to compare them. The severe weather at Camp Douglas makes it difficult to compare it with the Union prison camp Point Lookout in Maryland, while barracks at the Union prison in Elmira, New York, render an obvious but meaningless comparison to the Confederate prison at Andersonville. Rather, it is more productive to consider the reasons for the treatment of prisoners at all camps and the circumstances that made each prison unique.

Conditions at Camp Douglas were primitive at best and deplorable at worst. However, it must be said that conditions everywhere during the Civil War could be thus categorized. Clearly, under twenty-first-century standards and science, Civil War prison camp conditions and the resulting death toll were unacceptable and avoidable. But this was not necessarily so in the nineteenth century.

It is important to look at conditions and death under the circumstances, knowledge and attitudes of the 1860s. The Civil War, in and of itself, was unique. Neighbors, brothers and countrymen who had fought together for independence less than ninety years before filled the Civil War with personal and familial conflicts.

Prison conditions were a result of the knowledge and attitudes of the period, as well as errors of omission and commission by prison leadership.

Lack of a Strategic Plan for Treatment of Prisoners of War

The lack of experience in managing captives was a significant factor in both the Union and Confederate strategies. Both sides failed to plan for holding prisoners of war. Military leadership needed to address only the circumstances of their soldiers. Getting prisoners out of the way was of paramount importance; there was no need to develop a strategy for the incarceration of military prisoners, and thus no strategic or tactical requirements were considered in the housing of prisoners.

To a great extent, the die of prison camps had been cast before the Dix-Hill Cartel in 1862 and April 1863, when General Order 100 became effective.

The Confederacy provided no specific guidelines for the treatment of Union prisoners. Treatment of Union prisoners in Confederate prisons was mainly left up to the individual commanders. Places designated as prison camps by the U.S. Army received little notice of plans to ship prisoners to the camps. Camp Douglas received mere days' notice before receiving prisoners. The camp and Chicago were ill prepared to receive, feed, clothe and house prisoners.

Until the suspension of prisoner exchanges in mid-1863, incarceration was thought of short term. The lack of planning and naïve belief that prisoners would be quickly paroled allowed for the delay and deferment of much-needed improvements and additions to prisons. The suspension of exchange had a profound impact on prison conditions. After it became obvious that prisoners would be held for extended periods of time, it was a matter of playing catch-up.

Camp Douglas (as well as many other Union prisons) had been converted from a facility for receiving Union soldiers, and this further complicated responding to prison needs. Everything from a lack of basic security provisions, such as stockade fences, to the segregation of prisoners from guards needed to be addressed as the number of prisoners in a camp and the length of time they were likely to remain there grew.

Had there been any strategic focus on prisoners, many of the unacceptable conditions at Camp Douglas could have been avoided or at least minimized. With proper planning, it is very likely that Camp Douglas would not have been selected as a prison camp in the first place. There was ample space in and around Chicago to construct prison facilities that would have eliminated many of the problems experienced at Camp Douglas. These facilities could have been constructed at costs equal to or less than what was spent to convert Camp Douglas to a prison camp. Certainly, sanitary conditions could have been improved and opportunities for escape reduced in a facility built specifically for prisoners.

Lack of Training of Leadership, Guards and Prisoners

With the lack of strategic focus, no training was provided to the officers and soldiers responsible for securing prisoners of war. Officers selected to command prisoners were chosen based on military convenience with no regard for experience or ability to meet the needs of the command. These officers were field commanders who expected troops to respond to their rank and position. Finding that prisoners lacked respect for their captors, as well as respect for any form of military protocol, challenged the commanders, who had received no preparation for their sudden responsibility for balancing the needs of prisoners, garrison personnel and the community. No formal training existed for these officers, yet many took professional responsibility for their commands and commanded to the best of their limited ability. Only by trial and error did commanders find solutions to problems in the prisons.

Enlisted guards were likewise selected from those who were available at the time and those who could not be better used in combat or elsewhere in the army. Training was nonexistent. Instructions to guards were often little more than, "Watch them, and shoot if they don't do what you tell them to do." While many guards were responsible and handled their duties in a professional and compassionate manner, many took the lack of guidance as an opportunity to dole out brutal punishments. Perhaps the most significant lack of training was that of the common soldier subjected to captivity. Training of soldiers was tactical—how to move, how to shoot and little more. No training was offered on how to act as prisoners of war.

Military structure broke down. The common soldier held as a prisoner was faced with responding to the demands of guards, who were armed and willing to use their weapons, or imprisoned noncommissioned officers and fellow prisoners. More often, they responded to the guards, reducing the opportunity of their superiors to provide leadership to the prisoners. This led to a failure of the chain of command in prison camps and a lack of prisoners providing mutual support to their comrades. In Camp Douglas, the mutual support of men in units, such as Morgan's Raiders, was a rare example of how prisoners should have acted, if properly trained. The sharing of food and supplies and supporting the ill and injured could have significantly improved overall conditions for prisoners. The "haves"-versus-"have-nots" environment at Camp Douglas could have been reduced through proper training.

The most vivid example of the breakdown of military authority is the existence of the Raiders at Andersonville, where total anarchy rendered mutual support of soldiers nearly impossible. In fact, the survival-of-the-fittest attitude that prevailed at Andersonville contributed significantly to the death toll.

The subsequent training of American soldiers on how to act as prisoners in twentieth-century warfare, culminating in the creation of the Code of Conduct for U.S. Military in 1955, is testament to the importance of this training. Providing mutual support and maintaining the chain of command were just two important components of a soldier's conduct that were never realized in the Civil War. Article 7 of the Code of Conduct, which states, "I will never forget I am an American, fighting for freedom and responsible for my actions, and dedicated to the principles that made my country free," was never a consideration by the men in Union and Confederate prisons.

Actions expected of American soldiers in Articles III and IV of the Code of Conduct include using every means possible to resist, a responsibility to escape and assist in escapes, refusing to accept parole or special favors, keeping faith in fellow prisoners and respecting the chain of command. These behaviors were typical of the actions of many of Morgan's Raiders at Camp Douglas. These soldiers were captured in the summer and not immediately subjected to the severe Chicago weather, although they did endure two severe winters in Camp Douglas. The death rate of members of Morgan's Raiders at Camp Douglas was between 6 and 8 percent, as compared to 15 percent for other prisoners.[516] These soldiers were probably in better physical condition than other prisoners when they arrived at Camp Douglas and had more access to family and friends for money and goods. It is likely that their actions and support of one another, in keeping with the future Code of Conduct, contributed significantly to this lower death rate.

Lack of Preparation for Long-Term Incarceration

The unrealistic provision of the Dix Hill Cartel provided an excuse for deferring facility improvements of prison camps. The financially conservative attitudes of Union leadership, including those of General Meigs and Colonel Hoffman, were great contributors to the Union being late in responding to prisoner needs. Yet before the suspension of the exchanges, this financially conservativeness and deferral of improvements was understandable. Like their subordinates, General Meigs and Colonel Hoffman had no training and no experience in handling prisoners before being assigned to their roles in prison management.

Time and time again, the requests by Camp Douglas commanders for facility improvements were met with negative responses. Justification for this was the belief that the prisoners were there only temporarily. For example, improvements to the sewage removal system were not completed until October 1863, and an adequate water supply for the camp was deferred until late 1864. Additionally, separate prisoner barracks in Prisoners Square were not provided until late 1864. During this time, the prison population doubled from six thousand to more than twelve thousand. Hospital facilities, in spite of demands for increased capacity, never met the needs of prisoners. Projects that were too little too late continued to plague Camp Douglas during its existence and contributed directly to poor prison conditions and high death rate. Were these delays planned, or were they the result of a naïve lack of understanding of the long-term reality of Civil War prison camps? Evidence would indicate that since projects were eventually completed at likely greater costs at prisons marked by management difficulties and increased populations, delays were not nefarious.

High Leadership Turnover

With the possible exception of Colonel Sweet, commanders of Camp Douglas had no desire to hold their position. Colonel Tucker, General Tyler, General Ammen and Colonel DeLand each served as camp commander for four months only. Colonel Mulligan served for three months and General Orme five months. During General Orme's tenure, Colonel Strong was effectively the prison commander, although his headquarters were not located in the camp. The Orme/Strong relationship added to the confusion, as the two officers shared responsibility but often had conflicting motives. Colonel Sweet served for fourteen months, although for three of those at the beginning of his command, he and Colonel Strong were not quartered at Camp Douglas, reducing their effectiveness. This high turnover rate, plus the assignment of junior officers to command of the camp when there were few prisoners, resulted in setbacks for the long-term development and immediate repair of the camp. When there were few prisoners in camp, there were more opportunities to make repairs and improvements to the facility. Unfortunately, the young captains assigned to command had little authority and even less influence over U.S. Army prison management.

The priorities of each commander were different and changed when the officer was reassigned or left the service. New commanders started from scratch on implementing any improvements. Not only did they need to learn the needs of the camp, but they also needed to understand how to approach Colonel Hoffman.

The constant reordering of priorities led directly to the deferral and delay tactics of the U.S. government. The changes in command allowed General Meigs and Colonel Hoffman to further delay action until a new commander was in a position to recommend improvements. Undoubtedly, Meigs and Hoffman convinced themselves that the lack of demands by new commanders was a sign that there were no immediate needs.

Lack of Prisoner Immunity and Diet Change

A majority of the Confederate soldiers had been raised in a rural environment. The lack of contact with large numbers of men living in proximity provided these men with little natural immunity to disease. Crowded and unsanitary conditions in prison camps led to increased exposure to a variety of diseases to which the Southern soldier had never been exposed. Smallpox, measles, pneumonia and dysentery were diseases that found unwilling hosts in the Confederate prisoners.

The Confederate soldier found avoiding and fighting these maladies difficult. Without question, this condition contributed to the overall poor health of the prisoners. There was little in nineteenth-century medicine that would allow doctors treating patients to understand or address this condition.

While in the Confederate army, the diet of the Southern soldier consisted principally of pork and corn. Rations at Camp Douglas were mostly poor-quality beef and bread with some cornmeal. This dietary change made the adjustment to prison life even more difficult and caused significant instances of gastrointestinal problems. While this might have been correctable by prison management, it is unlikely that they understood the effects of this notable change in diet.

Condition of Prisoners on Arrival at Camp Douglas

Many prisoners coming to Camp Douglas were in poor physical condition before they arrived. There were a significant number of deaths within days or weeks of arrival. The first prisoners arriving at the camp were from Fort Donelson. These men had been in battle for four days in rain, snow and freezing temperatures. The garrison at Fort Donelson surrendered on February 16, 1862. After capture, prisoners were placed on unheated riverboats headed to Cairo, Illinois. Some prisoners continued up the Mississippi River to St. Louis. From Cairo or St. Louis, the men were transported on unheated rail cars, arriving in Chicago between February 20 and February 27 in below-freezing temperatures. Prior to their departure, General Grant had ordered that the prisoners receive two days' rations in preparation for their transport to Cairo and that they be allowed to keep clothing, blankets and private property that could be carried on their person.[517]

James Mackey reported very cold and wet weather en route to and at Fort Donelson from January 27 through February 16. His travel to Chicago began on February 16. He arrived in Cairo on February 18 and then traveled on to St. Louis, arriving February 20. He then went by rail to Chicago and marched four miles to Camp Douglas, arriving there on February 22.[518]

About 1,300 prisoners arrived at Camp Douglas from Arkansas's Fort Hindman on January 27, 1863. These prisoners, who had experienced freezing temperatures during and before capture and were subjected to extremely cold weather at Camp Douglas, contributed to the most deaths in a month (387) at Camp Douglas in February 1863.

The last large groups of prisoners were captured in Franklin and Nashville, Tennessee, in late 1864. John Copley was with the Army of Tennessee on the march from Atlanta in mid-October 1864. After resting in Florence, Alabama, from October 31 to November 19, 1864, he began the march to Franklin. At the pitched Battle of Franklin on November 30, Copley was captured. He and the other prisoners were marched to Nashville, where they arrived on December 1. During the march to Franklin and at Nashville, Copley reported that the troops had little to eat and were poorly clothed, many of them barefoot. Receiving their first food since November 29 in Nashville, the prisoners were transported by rail to Louisville. After a night in Louisville, they marched to a depot and were loaded "on board a train of box cars and were packed in like beef cattle for shipment." The prisoners arrived at Camp Douglas at daylight on December 5, 1864. The prisoners stood in snow for "several hours" while they were stripped-searched before being placed in barracks.[519]

Infantryman Edgar Jones, Eighteenth Alabama, wrote of conditions at Nashville: "The weather is bitter cold. Many men are bare-footed and more and more becoming so every day. There are no blankets except the ones we carried all summer. [I] had but one and that had eighteen bullet holes in it."[520]

Dressed in uniforms designed for mild temperatures and showing the wear of battle, these Confederate soldiers offer vivid examples of the rigors of war and the difficult conditions they faced while being transported to Camp Douglas. With their compromised physical condition, prisoners were almost guaranteed illness and possible death. Union guards did nothing to alleviate the conditions of the prisoners when they required them to strip and stand in the freezing weather. Once in barracks at Camp Douglas and given medical treatment, their physical circumstances improved—although for some it was too late.

The poor condition of prisoners arriving at Camp Douglas and the resulting increase in illness and death were the subjects of a number of reports and comments by commanders and inspectors.[521]

Inadequate and Primitive Medical Care

Medical care during the Civil War was representative of the dark ages of medicine. Well after the war, with the development of the germ theory by Louis Pasteur and its subsequent application to surgical sterility by Joseph Lister, surgeons were able to operate with a substantially reduced risk of infection. Lister began applying carbolic acid to compound fracture wounds, and the mortality rate from amputation plummeted from 45 percent to 15 percent. Had medical sterility been practiced during the Civil War, untold lives could have been saved. However, since these concepts were a quarter of a century away, it is difficult to blame Civil War surgeons for their unsanitary practices.

The smallpox vaccination was developed by Edward Jenner in 1796. Used widely in the Civil War, these vaccination programs were not always effective. As recounted earlier, fear on the part of all soldiers that infection from the vaccination was worse than the prevention of smallpox minimized the effectiveness of this preventive measure. However, it is likely that immunization programs at Camp Douglas were effective in protecting many prisoners and guards from the dreaded disease.

Medical treatment at Camp Douglas and elsewhere in the Civil War was rudimentary at best. This inadequate and primitive medical care at Camp Douglas was exacerbated by inadequate facilities. The lack of and questionable value of drugs during the war further contributed to medical care that proved unreliable. Poor administration of preventive measures—such as requiring smallpox patients to share filthy bed clothing, having those with smallpox remain in barracks with unaffected soldiers and failing to provide vegetables for the prevention of scurvy—clearly contributed to illness and death. All of these factors and the general overtaxing of limited medical facilities made Camp Douglas a hotbed for disease.

Conclusion

These reasons and contributing factors for conditions and death at Camp Douglas offer a look at the camp and the Civil War with nineteenth-century reality. This is not intended to excuse poor treatment of prisoners. Rather, these factors explain some of the actions of prisoners and prison administration. Ignorance and perhaps indifference from military command in both armies contributed to the prison problems.

Camp Douglas was a dreadful place for prisoners, just as the Civil War was a dreadful experience for both Union and Confederate soldiers. A war fought with modern weapons and antiquated tactics found a nation ill prepared to face the death and destruction that followed. Prisoners, both Union and Confederate, are equal victims of this War Between the States.

There are many anecdotal incidents of mistreatment in prisons on both sides. These are, for the most part, the byproducts of overzealous guards and commanders who failed to stop such actions. There is not sufficient evidence to support the existence of any broad conspiracy to murder or grossly mistreat prisoners at Camp Douglas or any other Civil War prison camp.

Chapter 13

Other Union and Confederate Prison Camps

A comparative study of Camp Douglas with basic information on other Civil War prison camps is informative. Over 150 facilities were used as prisons during the Civil War. Most of these facilities in both the Union and Confederacy were not originally built as prisons.

Like Camp Douglas, a majority of Union prisons were originally constructed as reception and training facilities for Union soldiers and therefore included wooden barracks and other military facilities. Adding a taller stockade fence with guard stands was about all that was necessary to convert these facilities to prisons. Based on prison population, tents were used from time to time to supplement the barracks.

Confederate prisons were usually buildings that had been converted to serve that purpose. Many were tobacco warehouses or similar, mostly open facilities. Conversion was more difficult in these facilities than in the barracks environment, especially adding toilet facilities and adequate water. Barren stockades such as Andersonville and Camp Ford offered little or no shelter and inadequate sanitary facilities. Confederate prisons were centralized in and around Richmond, Virginia, until later in the war, when facilities were developed in states such as Texas, North Carolina and Georgia.

The following tables provide a summary of major Union and Confederate prison camps.

MAJOR UNION PRISONS

PRISON	TYPE	YEARS OPEn	MOST PRISONERS HELD	DEATHS
Point Lookout, Maryland	Tents with high fence	1863–65	22,000	3,584
Fort Delaware, Delaware	Coastal fortification	1861–65	12,600	2,416
Camp Douglas, Illinois	Barracks with high fence	1862–65	12,082	4,454
Elmira, New York	Barracks with high fence	1864–65	9,441	2,933
Camp Chase, Ohio	Barracks with high fence	1861–65	9,423	2,260
Rock Island, Illinois	Barracks with high fence	1863–65	8,670	1,960
Camp Morton, Indiana	Converted buildings/ fairgrounds	1862–65	5,000	1,763
Johnson's Island, Ohio	Barracks with high fence	1862–65	3,256	235
Alton, Illinois	Existing prison	1862–65	1,891	1,508

MAJOR CONFEDERATE PRISONS

PRISON	TYPE	YEARS OPEN	MOST PRISONERS HELD	DEATHS
Andersonville, Georgia	Barren stockade	1864–65	32,899	12,919
Richmond, Virginia (fifteen locations)	Existing prison and converted buildings	1861–65	13,500	200+
Belle Isle, Virginia	Barren stockade	1862–64	10,000	300+
Camp Ford, Texas	Barren stockade	1863–65	4,900	232+
Libby Warehouse, Virginia	Converted buildings	1862–65	4,221	20+

Source: Speer, *Portals to Hell.*

UNION PRISONS

General Orme, in his series of prison inspections in November 1863, just before he became commander at Camp Douglas, provides a snapshot of Union prisons at that time. Prisons included in his reports were Camp Douglas, Alton Penitentiary, Camp Chase, Rock Island, Camp Morton and Johnson's Island.

General Orme summarized his findings as follows:

> *There is, however, a want of uniformity in the treatment of the prisoners at the different prisons, at some more privileges being allowed them than at others, while at all places, however, they are kindly treated and well supplied with food. The whole number of prisoners that I visited is about 16,300, and taking into consideration that these men have been gathered from all parts of the Southern States, have endured immense hardships and fatigue, and have been exposed to all kinds of weather and finally compelled to change climate by being removed as prisoners to the Northern States, the present sanitary condition of them is in my opinion very good. At all the prison camps the commandants have taken from the prisoners large amounts of Confederate money, which they hold without any special orders. At several of these camps I found large numbers of Union soldiers under sentence of courts-martial. Although not within the purview of this report, I cannot help from suggesting that there are many fine soldiers who have already been punished sufficiently and who would render good service if sent back to their commands. Some good plan of cooking for the prisoners at all these large camps should be adopted, by means of which the Government could save very largely in expense, both in rations and fuel.*[522]

Common in General Orme's report were mentions of food and its preparation, sanitation, escapes, death and medical facilities. Orme's observation of generally good sanitation is contrary to many other inspections made of Union prisons. Sanitation was usually found to be in need of improvement. Similarly, the quality and quantity of food was often criticized in other inspections.

The following is a summary of major Union prison camps.

Point Lookout, Maryland[523]

Point Lookout opened as a prison camp in 1863 and would become the largest prison in the Union system. The camp was located at the junction of the Potomac River and the Chesapeake Bay. Point Lookout consisted of approximately forty acres, and all prisoners were housed in tents.

In July 1863, the camp opened to 4,000 prisoners. By September, the population had grown to 9,000. Ultimately, the prison population would reach over 20,000, nearly twice the number of the next-largest prison. Total deaths in Point Lookout were reported as 3,584.

The camp was plagued with a lack of bedding, and many prisoners slept on bare ground. There was constant flooding, causing muddy conditions, and poor policing of prisoner areas and tents and inadequate toilet facilities were also noted frequently. Rations were barely adequate. The guard force, consisting of regular and Veteran Reserve Corps, was supplemented by U.S. Colored Troops. Poor training and brutal treatment of prisoners was noted at Point Lookout. By April 1865, there were twenty-two thousand prisoners remaining in the camp. By June 30, 1865, all prisoners had been released.

Fort Delaware, Delaware[524]

By mid-1863, Fort Delaware had earned the reputation of being the most dreaded prison in the Union. The camp was known for unusual cruelty, including hanging prisoners by the thumbs and requiring them to stand for extended periods on barrel tops. The guard force, which consisted of mostly regular troops and National Guard units, was especially brutal. Army leadership appeared to turn a blind eye to this treatment.

Barracks that had been hastily constructed in 1862 soon became dilapidated, contributing to primitive conditions in the camp. Poor sanitary conditions and the lack of adequate water resulted in high instances of illness and death; smallpox was widespread throughout the camp's existence. Rations were generally poor, and a lack of vegetables caused scurvy to become a major problem. Population of the camp ranged from 3,000 to 9,000 and reached a peak of over 12,500 in July 1863. From that point on, the average prison population was approximately 9,000.

In spite of an eight-hundred-bed hospital, nearly 1,000 prisoners were sick in the camp in 1863–64. Death was excessive, and Fort Delaware is the only prison camp in which those who died were not identified by name.

Over eight thousand prisoners remained in Fort Delaware in April 1865. The last prisoners remained in the camp until July 1865.

Elmira, New York[525]

In May 1861, the Elmira Depot camp was opened in an abandoned barrel factory. Approximately seventy wooden barracks were soon constructed, along with support facilities. These facilities could accommodate ten thousand soldiers, and nearly twenty-one thousand Union soldiers passed through the camp when it operated as a reception center. These facilities continued to receive Union soldiers through 1864.

In May 1864, work began to convert Elmira's Barracks No. 3, also known as Camp Rathbun, to receive prisoners. Barracks No. 3 was located a mile west of Elmira near Foster's Pond, which provided water for washing and bathing. Barracks No. 3 could house two thousand men and could be expanded to accommodate an additional one thousand. With the addition of tents, Elmira could hold ten thousand prisoners.

On July 6, 1864, the first 400 prisoners arrived at Barracks No. 3. Within a week, the prison population had quickly climbed to 1,150. Poor sanitary conditions with sinks too near Foster's Pond caused concerns about increased illness. Poor-quality rations and the lack of vegetables plagued Elmira with increased cases of scurvy.

In 1864, chilly winter temperatures and a lack of prisoner clothing contributed to illness and led to an inordinate amount of deaths. Smallpox was of significant concern in Elmira.

Deaths in the camp were high as a result of poor sanitary conditions. Other factors contributing to a high death rate were severe weather conditions and inadequate medical care. At 24 percent, Elmira had the greatest percentage of deaths of any Union prison (the death percentage at Camp Douglas was 15 percent).

By July 1865, most of the prisoners had been released. The prison population at Elmira peaked at nearly ten thousand.

Camp Chase, Ohio[526]

Camp Chase was located four miles west of Columbus, Ohio, and was originally used to receive Union troops. The first Confederate prisoners arrived in April 1862. As with Camp Douglas, the immediate question was who was responsible for the camp, the state or the U.S. Army.

The camp consisted of three separate units surrounded by a stockade fence with guard stations and was rated for 3,500 to 5,000 prisoners, although the population peaked at over 9,000. Sanitary conditions were unacceptable, with sinks being little more than open trenches. Drainage was poor, and the camp was filled with mud most of the time.

Smallpox was epidemic in mid-1864, with a total of 2,260 prisoners dying at the facility. Food was poor as well, with control over quality and quantity very lax. The final prisoners were released in July 1865.

Rock Island, Illinois[527]

The Rock Island prison was located on an island on the Mississippi River at a facility that had been a U.S. military installation since 1812. Developed as a prison in November 1863, Rock Island had a capacity to hold over ten thousand prisoners in wooden barracks.

The first prisoners arrived on December 3, 1863, in extremely cold weather with snow covering the ground. Of the 5,592 prisoners arriving, 94 had smallpox and 150 others were ill. By November, the population had increased to 8,000, with 325 having died during the month. Cold weather and the poor conditions of troops upon arrival created a situation of extremely high sick calls with inadequate medical facilities. Poor drainage and excessive mud added to the poor conditions of the camp.

Water was provided by pumps from the river; however, these pumps frequently failed, leaving water extremely scarce. The quality and quantity of rations were less than desired.

A total of 12,400 prisoners were confined at Rock Island during its twenty-month existence. The most held at any one time was slightly over 8,600, and 3,000 prisoners were exchanged in January and February 1865. The last prisoners were released in July 1865.

These top five Union prisons, along with Camp Douglas, provided a representation of the conditions present in most Union prisons. Common among all were poor sanitary conditions, overcrowding, high incidents of illness (especially smallpox), inadequate and poor-quality rations and ill-trained guards.

Confederate Prisons

Specific details of inspections and other information on Confederate prisons are difficult to obtain. Much of the information is based on postwar writings from former prisoners and Union authorities.

Andersonville, Georgia[528]

Andersonville, officially known as Camp Sumter, was the most infamous prison of the Civil War. To a great extent, Andersonville was unlike any other prison in either the Confederacy or the Union. In operation for only fourteen months, Andersonville housed about forty thousand prisoners, with nearly thirteen thousand dying. Located in southwestern Georgia near the small rail depot town of Andersonville, the camp initially consisted of sixteen and a half acres but later expanded to twenty-six acres. A branch of the sluggish Sweet Water Creek ran west–east across the southern part of the camp. Andersonville was an open area with virtually no protection from rain or heat. A fifteen-foot-high stockade fence surrounded the camp. Guard posts were located approximately eighty-eight feet apart along the stockade fence and were covered with wooden roofs. A "dead line" was outlined inside the stockade fence. An earthen fort with cannons pointing toward the camp was located near the southwestern corner of the camp. Other forts were located on the other corners of the camp. A hospital, which initially consisted of about two acres and later increased to five acres of tents, was located directly south of the compound.

The first five hundred prisoners arrived on February 25, 1864, from Belle Isle prison. By May 1864, more than thirteen thousand prisoners had arrived. The population continued to increase via the transfer of prisoners from other Confederate prison camps until it peaked in August 1864 at nearly thirty-three thousand. In September 1864, the first group of prisoners left Andersonville for Charleston and Florence, South Carolina. These transfers were a result of the threat of a possible raid on the camp as General Sherman marched toward Atlanta. By November 1864, fewer than two thousand prisoners were housed at Andersonville. What was left of the camp was liberated by Union forces in May 1865.

Prisoners were without shelter and required to construct huts and lean-tos, known as "shebangs," from items they brought with them, such as blankets and overcoats. Some brush, logs and limbs were available early in

Camp Sumter in Andersonville, Georgia. *National Archives.*

the camp's existence. Some prisoners chose to burrow into the ground for shelter. None of the shelters provided protection from the heat, rain and mud. There was no organization of the shelters, and this hodgepodge of streets made policing the area impossible. The increase in filth contributed to illness and death.

Criminal elements among the prisoners, while not unknown in other prisons, were especially troublesome at Andersonville. This group of thieves, robbers and murderers in Andersonville were known as the "Raiders." Organized under a number of leaders, they terrorized other prisoners from the opening of the camp. Eventually, four hundred or five hundred prisoners were engaged in robbing, berating and killing fellow prisoners. These predators would often depose prisoners of their shelter and steal anything of value.

The prisoners finally appealed to Captain Henry Wirz, prison commander, to rid the camp of the terrorists. Captain Wirz moved fifty identified Raiders out of the camp in late June 1864. They were returned to the camp for a trial authorized by General William Winder on June 30. The trial, conducted by Union prisoners, resulted in a few being required to wear a ball and chain, while others were placed in stocks or strung up by their thumbs. Six were convicted of murder and were executed by hanging on July 10, 1864. This ended one of the most deplorable chapters in the life of Union prisoners.

While drinking water was available from the branch of Sweet Water Creek, this water soon became putrid from latrines dug near the creek and human waste deposited directly into the creek. Unfortunately, some prisoners continued to drink this disease-filled water. Other prisoners dug wells to provide better (but still not good) quality water. Inadequate raw food was provided to prisoners early in the camp's operation. A lack of firewood for prisoners to cook food caused the camp's administration to provide a reduced amount of cooked food.

Medical treatment was very poor. The hospital area consisted of ragged tents with little or no bedding available to the patients. The lack of medicine and a patient-doctor ratio of one hundred to one resulted in a total failure of medical support. Epidemics of disease, such as smallpox, diarrhea and dysentery, were beyond the coping ability of the medical facilities.

Inadequate shelter, poor rations, unsanitary conditions, ineffective medical care and the behavior of the prisoners themselves all contributed to Andersonville having the greatest number of deaths (12,919) of any Civil War prison camp.

Captain Henry Wirz was the only Confederate officer tried and executed after the war for war crimes. Andersonville was an anomaly among Civil War prison camps. Comparing this prison with other prisons, Confederate or Union, is extremely difficult and will likely lead to erroneous conclusions.

Richmond, Virginia (fifteen locations)[529]

The fifteen prisons spread throughout Richmond were, for the most part, converted factory or storage buildings. Existing jail facilities were used but almost immediately filled. These prisons lacked any facilities that would comfort the prisoners, including toilets and lights. Few blankets and little bedding material were available. Food, consisting of bread and small amounts of beef, was eaten with the hands.

Belle Isle, Virginia[530]

Belle Isle was a small island in the James River within sight of Libby Prison. The camp, believed to be capable of handling three thousand prisoners, reached that level within two weeks of opening in June 1862. By July, there were five thousand prisoners on the island. The maximum number of prisoners held there during the war was ten thousand. The prisoners lived in tents surrounded by three-foot-high earthworks. Frequently, there were insufficient tents available, requiring prisoners to live in holes to protect themselves from the elements.

Unusually cold weather during the winter of 1863 caused serious problems for prisoners on Belle Isle. Pneumonia, typhoid and smallpox were common during this time. Rations consisted almost exclusively of corn bread and sweet potatoes. Some bread was provided, and bacon was issued until 1864, when it was too difficult to obtain. Beginning in early 1864, prisoners were transferred to prisons in Georgia. The prison was closed in March 1864, when the last prisoners were transferred to Andersonville.

Camp Ford, Texas[531]

Camp Ford, established in Tyler, Texas, in July 1863, was originally a reception center for Confederate troops from East Texas. No shelter was provided, but sufficient water was provided from a spring in the camp.

Conditions in the prison were generally good through 1863. As the population increased to over two thousand in the summer of 1864, the few remaining shade trees were cut down, and conditions continued to deteriorate. Sanitation suffered, and disease increased. Because of an inadequate diet, scurvy was the number-one killer at Camp Ford.

It is estimated that 6,000 prisoners passed through Camp Ford, with the average monthly prisoner count at 4,700. The last prisoners left the camp in April 1865.

Libby Warehouse, Virginia[532]

Libby Prison in Richmond, Virginia, was located in a four-story warehouse that had formerly housed a ship chandler. Prisoners were held in six rooms on the upper two floors. These rooms, which measured forty-five feet by ninety feet, contained no furniture and could accommodate one hundred prisoners each. The prison had running water (of questionable quality) that was pumped in directly from the James River. Natural light was limited, and the building had no internal lights.

The prison received its first prisoners, who had been moved from other Richmond prisons, on March 26, 1862, and within three days was housing seven hundred prisoners. By 1863, the population had grown to four thousand, with an average of four hundred prisoners per each room. Some prisoners were moved in 1863 to reduce crowding. The guards at Libby Prison were especially brutal. Cold weather, broken windows and lack of heat made the prison extremely uncomfortable. Prisoners also lacked adequate blankets and sleeping material. Scurvy, dysentery and typhoid were the most common diseases in the camp. By 1863, rations had been reduced to a small portion of meat, a half pound of bread and a cup of rice or beans per day.

Libby operated as a prison until the spring of 1864, when prisoners were transferred to Macon, Georgia.

Confederate prisons were less developed than those of the Union. Many had limited or no permanent housing facilities. Others were poorly converted warehouses lacking proper heat, lighting and toilet facilities. Food and water were limited and of poor quality. Like Union prisons, disease and poor sanitation were constant problems.

Disease and sanitation concerns in prisons mirrored the concerns in all military units. Rations in most prison camps were not unlike what was available to the average soldier; thus, all Civil War prison camps can be characterized as unsanitary, ill-prepared, poorly managed and overcrowded facilities of despair.

Epilogue

Summary of Prisons

It is easy today to criticize Civil War prison camps for their poor conditions and brutal treatment of prisoners. However, it is often forgotten that these twenty-first-century attitudes and values gave us Abu Ghraib and Guantanamo, along with waterboarding and sleep and food deprivation.

Civil War prison camp life, like the war itself, was primitive and lacked basic sanitation, adequate food and proper medical treatment. Much of the conditions criticized during the war and in the prison camps was typical of nineteenth-century life. Meager housing, minimal food and being subjected to harsh weather were common during the period. While conditions in Camp Douglas could have been improved, for a variety of reasons, timely actions were not taken by U.S. prison authorities.

Camp Douglas and other Union prison camps are often compared to Andersonville. The use of titles like James Gillispie's *Andersonvilles of the North* might sell books, but this comparison is unfair. Andersonville was an anomaly, even among Confederate prisons. Given the short amount of time (fifteen months) Andersonville was in existence relative to Camp Douglas (two and a half years), comparing weather conditions, shelter or medical treatment between the two adds nothing to our full understanding of Camp Douglas or other prison camps. Calling Camp Douglas or any other Union prison camp an "Andersonville of the North" is not only unjustified but also inappropriate.

Each prison camp was different. Food, shelter, sanitary conditions, weather and other factors differed from one prison to another. The personality of command also varied greatly, affecting how prisoners were treated.

Prison camps should be evaluated by analyzing the camp's ability to provide prisoners with basic food, shelter, sanitation and medical care. These must be judged within the knowledge and experience of the nineteenth century. Just as important, camps should be evaluated on the leadership's ability to identify shortcomings in meeting basic needs and to take corrective actions.

Camp Douglas Site after the War

The history of Chicago following the Civil War is partly responsible for Camp Douglas being forgotten. By the end of the Civil War, Chicago had become the fastest-growing city in the nation. Priority for this growth was principally in the north and west sections of the city. The south section, including the Camp Douglas site, was annexed into the city in 1863 and began slow but steady growth. Most of the remainder of the southern part of Chicago, south of Thirty-fifth Street, was not annexed until 1889.

The Great Fire of October 8, 1871, forever changed the face of Chicago and delayed the development of the city's southern section. Recovery from the Great Fire required that most of the city be devoted to rebuilding the central business district and much of the northern section of the city. The area around the site of Camp Douglas received many German Jews who had been burned out of the downtown area. By 1880, the population was again increasing, with elegant homes and small cottages lining the major streets. The southern portion of the city did not receive significant attention until near the opening of the 1893 World's Fair, held some five miles southeast of the Camp Douglas site.

As World War I approached, some development began at the Camp Douglas site. The "Great Migration" of African Americans from the South to Chicago was the next factor in forgetting Camp Douglas's history. Limited by restrictive covenants of city laws, African Americans were required to live in what would soon be identified as Bronzeville. These restrictive covenants were not overturned until the U.S. Supreme Court's *Hansberry v. Lee* decision in 1940. The Illinois Central Railroad that had once served Camp Douglas was now the primary transportation of the African Americans participating in the Great Migration.

With this population growth in Bronzeville, land was at a premium for building multiple-family residences. A majority of the construction on and around the site of Camp Douglas was completed by 1915. Bronzeville became famous for prosperous African American businesses and as the center for jazz and blues in Chicago. As the population continued to grow, the housing stock rapidly deteriorated into desperate slums by the late-1930s. The next factor to change Chicago's priorities was World War II.

After the end of World War II, priorities were shifted to provide housing and job opportunities for the returning veterans. This began the period of urban sprawl in the Chicago metropolitan area and "white flight" to the suburbs. Not until about 1950 did urban renewal come to Bronzeville. The City of Chicago razed blocks and blocks of slum buildings that were in deplorable condition. Property was to be developed by public and private enterprises. Major public housing was developed a few blocks west of the Camp Douglas site, and a major development, Lake Meadows, including a shopping center, was constructed on what had been White Oak Square, South (or Hospital) Square and Garrison Square. The Prisoners Square area was developed as single- and multiple-

An archaeological excavation being performed by DePaul University, 2014. *Author's collection*

family homes and public buildings such as churches and schools. This is the configuration that remains today.

Finally, at the beginning of the twenty-first century, interest in history and Camp Douglas began to increase. Efforts by the Camp Douglas Restoration Foundation, supported by Bronzeville organizations and institutions, have led to increased knowledge of the importance of Camp Douglas in the history of Bronzeville and the city. The foundation's activities include emphasis on education in Chicago schools, presentations on Camp Douglas to community organizations and sponsorship of archaeological investigations of the campsite.

Camp Douglas Summary

Camp Douglas, quickly built with inferior-quality material on a hastily selected site, was one of the longest-operating prison camps in the Union. As a prison and reception and training center, Camp Douglas was the most significant Civil War military facility in Chicago. Next to the Western Theater staging area at Cairo, Camp Douglas was probably the largest military facility in Illinois.

Poor sanitary conditions, the poor condition of arriving prisoners and severe Chicago winter weather contributed to illness and death at Camp Douglas. With the dubious distinction of having more deaths than any other Union prison, the camp faced ultimate and unjustified comparisons with Andersonville.

Camp Douglas was neither better nor worse than any other Union prison camp. While different from Confederate prisons, Camp Douglas shared the problems of poor sanitation and medical treatment with these institutions.

In December 1865, Camp Douglas was razed, with nothing remaining of the two hundred buildings that once made up the camp. Today, a century and a half later, there is little understanding of the existence of the camp in the city of Chicago other than a historic marker on King Drive near Thirty-third Street.

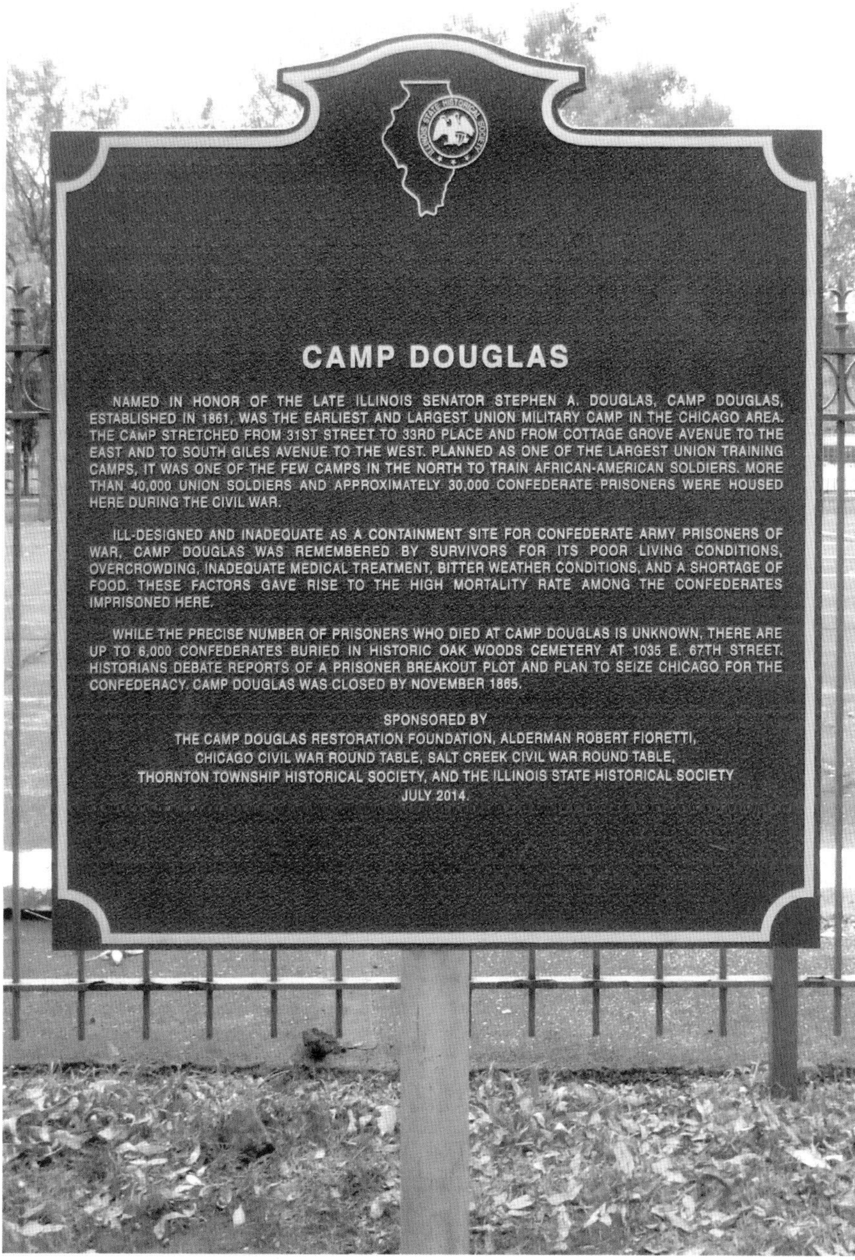

This historical marker was erected on the site of Camp Douglas at Thirty-third Street and King Drive in 2014. *Author's collection.*

EPILOGUE

Final Thought

In his introduction to the 2011 revision of Ovid Futch's *History of Andersonville Prison*, Michael Gray noted that the study and understanding of Civil War prison camps has been slow in developing. Until the 1990s, very little writing was devoted to the study of prison camps. Both micro-study and macro-monographs have increased since 1990, providing significant additional information on Civil War prisons and prisoners. Hopefully, this book adds to that knowledge. This book has offered a view of Camp Douglas based on facts gleaned from historic records. More importantly, the tone and feeling of the camp is told in the written words of prisoners who lived the experience. Robert Bagby, Curtis Burke, John Copley, William Huff and James Mackey documented nearly every day of the camp's existence, were of different circumstances and told their stories from their own unique perspectives. Thanks to their writing, Camp Douglas has more than just numbers, reports and orders—it possesses an enduring personality.

Appendix I

Timeline

1861 April 14	Fort Sumter evacuated
June 12	General Montgomery Meigs identifies the need for prison camps
September 20	Camp Douglas opens; camp commanded by Colonel Joseph Tucker
October 3	Colonel William Hoffman named commissary of prisoners
1862 February 14	Colonel James Mulligan is named commander of Camp Douglas but refuses; Tucker continues in command
February 16	Fort Donelson surrenders to the Union
February 20	First prisoners arrive at Camp Douglas
February 22	James Taswell Mackey, Forty-eighth Tennessee Infantry, arrives at Camp Douglas
February 26	Mulligan assumes command of the camp
February 28	Prison population reaches 3,900
March 31	Prison population reaches 5,000
June 14	Colonel Daniel Cameron assumes command of the camp
June 19	Tucker resumes command of the camp
July 8	Martial law declared near camp
July 22	Dix-Hill Cartel approved
August 28	First prisoners sent for exchange
September 7	James Mackey leaves camp in an exchange

September 28	Paroled Union soldiers from Harpers Ferry arrive at camp
September 30	General Daniel Tyler assumes command of camp; the prison population is 51
November 20	Colonel Cameron assumes command of the camp
December 15	Last paroled Unions soldiers leave camp
1863 January 6	General Jacob Ammen assumes command of the camp
January 27	Robert Anderson Bagby, First Northwest Missouri Cavalry, arrives at camp
February 18	Prison population is 3,900
April 3	Prisoners sent for exchange
April 7	Prisoners exchanged (including those with smallpox)
April 10	Captain John Phillips assumes command of the camp
April 24	General Order 100 regarding prisoner treatment issued by President Lincoln
May 4	Last prisoners, except sick, exchanged
May 12	Captain J.S. Putman assumes command of the camp
June 3	Prison population is 52
August 18	General Charles DeLand assumes command of the camp Curtis R. Burke, Lexington Rifles, Morgan's Raiders arrives at camp
August 27	Exchange of prisoners suspended by the U.S. government
August 31	Prison population reaches 3,200
October 4	William F. Huff, Thirteenth Louisiana Volunteer Infantry, arrives at camp
October 31	Prison population reaches 6,100 Wooden sewer completed
November 6	Major work on running water and sewer in camp finished
December 16	General William Orme assumes command of the camp
December 31	Prison population is 5,900
1864 January 28	New Prisoners Square opens
March 1	Colonel James Strong commands prisoners
March 31	Prison population is 5,700
May 2	Colonel Benjamin Sweet assumes command of the camp
June 20	Prison population is 5,300
September 30	Prison population is 7,600
October 30	The three-inch water line is replaced with a six-inch line

APPENDIX I

November 6	Colonel Sweet arrests "conspirators"
December 5	John Copley, Forty-ninth Tennessee Infantry, arrives at camp
December 31	Prison population reaches 12,082, the highest number of prisoners at one time
1865 February 13	First prisoner exchange since April 3, 1863, begins
March 2	Curtis Burke takes the oath and leaves camp
March 27	Robert Bagby takes the oath and leaves camp
March 31	Prison population is 9,300
May 3	William Huff takes the oath and leaves camp
June 20	John Copley takes the oath and leaves camp
June 30	Prison population is 4,100
July 30	Prison population is 32
August 2	Officials begin to close the camp
September 29	Colonel Sweet resigns
October 1	Captain E.C. Phetteplace assumes command of the camp
December 24	Last buildings sold and camp remnants destroyed
1866 March 20	Camp officially closed
1867 April 13	Removal of bodies from City Cemetery to Oak Woods Cemetery begins
April 27	Final bodies removed and reinterred at Oak Woods Cemetery
1895 May 30	President Grover Cleveland dedicates the Confederate Mound monument at Oak Woods Cemetery

Appendix II

Camp Douglas Principal Commanders

BRIGADIER GENERAL MONTGOMERY MEIGS was appointed quartermaster general of the U.S. Army on June 16, 1861, and had overall responsibility for all U.S. prison camps.

LIEUTENANT COLONEL WILLIAM HOFFMAN was appointed commissary of prisoners on October 3, 1861. He retained that office until the end of the war and was promoted to colonel and later brevet (temporary) brigadier general.

COLONEL JOSEPH H. TUCKER, Sixtieth Illinois State Militia, was

Top: Brigadier General Montgomery C. Meigs. *Library of Congress*.

Right: Lieutenant Colonel William Hoffman and staff. *Library of Congress*.

Colonel James A. Mulligan. *Library of Congress.*

designated by Governor Yates to construct the camp. He commanded the camp from September 20, 1861, to February 28, 1862, and again from June 19, 1862, to September 30, 1862.

COLONEL JAMES A. MULLIGAN, Twenty-third Illinois Infantry (Irish Brigade), commanded the camp from February 28, 1862, to June 14, 1862.

COLONEL DANIEL CAMERON, Sixty-fifth Illinois Infantry, commanded camp from June 14, 1862, to June 19, 1862, when Colonel Tucker assumed command again.

Colonel Daniel Cameron. *U.S. Army Heritage and Education Center.*

General Daniel Tyler. *Library of Congress.*

GENERAL DANIEL TYLER, who had been designated to bring the Union parolees from Harpers Ferry to Camp Douglas, commanded the camp from September 30, 1862, to November 30, 1862.

COLONEL CAMERON commanded the camp from November 30, 1863, until January 6, 1863.

BRIGADIER GENERAL JACOB AMMEN commanded the camp from January 6, 1863, to April 10, 1863.

Brigadier General Jacob Ammen. *U.S. Army Military History Institute.*

Colonel Charles DeLand. *New York State Library.*

CAPTAIN JOHN PHILLIPS commanded the camp from April 10, 1863, to May 12, 1863.

CAPTAIN J.S. PUTMAN commanded the camp from May 12, 1863, to August 18, 1863.

COLONEL CHARLES V. DELAND, First Michigan Sharpshooters, commanded the camp from August 18, 1863, to December 16, 1863.

BRIGADIER GENERAL WILLIAM W. ORME, commander of the Northern District of Chicago, including Camp Douglas, commanded the camp from December 16, 1863, to May 2, 1864.

Brigadier General William Orme. *U.S. Army Military History Institute.*

Colonel James C. Strong. *U.S. Army Military History Institute.*

COLONEL JAMES C. STRONG, Fifteenth Regiment of the Invalid Corps, commanded the prison portion of the camp from December 16, 1863, until nearly all Confederate prisoners were released in 1865.

COLONEL (BREVET BRIGADIER GENERAL) BENJAMIN J. SWEET commanded the camp from May 2, 1864, until nearly all Confederate prisoners were released in 1865.

Colonel Benjamin J. Sweet. *Chicago History Museum.*

CAPTAIN E.C. PHETTEPLACE assumed command on October 1, 1865, and remained commander until the camp was officially closed on March 20, 1866.

Appendix III

U.S. Army Units Mustered in at Camp Douglas and Guard Units at Camp Douglas

Unit	Commander	Muster-in Date	Comment
19th Infantry	Colonel John Turchin	5/4/1861	Camp Long
23rd Infantry	Colonel James A. Mulligan	6/15/1861	Irish Brigade/Guards
24th Infantry	Captain T.G. Pitcher	7/8/1861	Two companies
42nd Infantry	Colonel William Webb	7/22/1861	
44th Infantry	Colonel Charles Knoblesdorf	9/13/1861	Camp Ellsworth
45th Infantry	Colonel John E. Smith	12/25/1861	Lead Mine
51st Infantry	Colonel Gilbert W. Cumming	12/24/1861	Chicago Legion
53rd Infantry	Colonel William Cushman	2/27/1862	National Guards
55th Infantry	Colonel David Stuart	10/31/1861	
57th Infantry	Colonel Silas D. Baldwin	10/1861	Quartered at Camp Douglas
58th Infantry	Colonel William F. Lynch	2/11/1862	
65th Infantry	Colonel Daniel Cameron	5/1/1862	Paroled to Camp Douglas/Guards
67th Infantry	Colonel Roselle M. Hough	6/13/1862	Guards
69th Infantry	Colonel Joseph H. Tucker	6/14/1862	Guards
71st Infantry	Colonel Othniel Gilbert	7/26/1862	
72nd Infantry	Colonel Fredrick Starling	7/23/1862	First Board of Trade
82nd Infantry	Colonel Frederick Hecker		Concordia Guards
88th Infantry	Colonel Forest Sherman	10/4/1862	2nd Irish Brigade
89th Infantry	Colonel John Christopher	8/27/1862	Rail Road
90th Infantry	Colonel Timothy O'Meara	9/7/1862	Irish Legion/Guards
93rd Infantry	Colonel Holden Putam	10/13/1862	

APPENDIX III

Unit	Commander	Muster-in Date	Comment
96th Infantry	Colonel Thomas E. Champion	9/6/1862	Camp Fuller
105th Infantry	Colonel Daniel Dustin	9/2/1862	Quartered at Camp Douglas
113th Infantry	Colonel Giles A. Smith	11/6/1862	Camp Hancock
127th Infantry	Colonel John Van Armin	9/6/1862	Guards
29th USCT	Lieutenant Colonel John Bross		Company B
9th Cavalry	Colonel Albert G. Brackett	11/30/1861	
13th Cavalry	Colonel J.W. Bell	12/1861	
Battery B, 1st Light Artillery	Captain Bouton; Captain Miller	12/19/1861	
Battery L, 2nd Light Artillery	Captain Bolto; Captain Phillips	8/29/1862	
Board of Trade Artillery	Captain J. Christopher	8/1/1862	37th and Stanton
Chicago Mercantile Artillery	Captain P.H. White	8/29/1862	
Winnebago County Guards	Captain Enoch	6/5/1862	
Rockford City Guards	Captain Hull	6/5/1862	
Washington Light Infantry	Lieutenant Crane	6/5/1862	
Peoria Guards	Captain Oakely	6/5/1862	
Corcoran Guards	Captain Scanlon	6/5/1862	
Anderson Rifles	Captain Reed	6/5/1862	
Ellsworth Zouaves	Captain Heilig	6/5/1862	Guards
Woodworth Rifles	Captain Burroughs	9/3/1862	

Sources: Illinois State Archives, "Illinois Adjutant General's Report"; Haynie, *A History of Camp Douglas*, 13–14; *Chicago Tribune*, June 5, 1862, and September 3, 1862.

APPENDIX III

GUARD UNITS

23rd Illinois Infantry (Irish Brigade)
48th Illinois Infantry
65th Illinois Infantry
67th Illinois Infantry
69th Illinois Infantry
90th Illinois Infantry
93rd Illinois Infantry
105th Illinois Infantry
127th Illinois Infantry
9th Vermont Infantry
1st Michigan Sharpshooters
104th Illinois Infantry
8th Regiment Invalid Corps (Veteran Reserve Corps)
11th Regiment Invalid Corps (Veteran Reserve Corps)
12th Regiment Invalid Corps (Veteran Reserve Corps)
15th Regiment Invalid Corps (Veteran Reserve Corps)
196th Pennsylvania Infantry
48th Missouri Infantry
24th Ohio Independent Battery, 2nd Regiment Home Guards
Ellsworth's Zouaves, Light Guard

Appendix IV

Camp Douglas Prison Population

Date	Beginning plus new	Died, transferred, escaped, released	Ending Prisoners
1862			
March			5,000
July	7,850	197	7,653
September	7,407	7,356	51
1863			
February	3,884	444	3,440
April	380	41	339
July	49	2	31
August	3,203	7	3,196
October	6,115	142	5,973
December	5,874	213	5,661
1864			
February	5,607	93	5,514
April	5,462	83	5,379
July	6,803	55	6,748
October	7,525	126	7,399
December	12,082	380	11,702
1865			
February	11,239	1,973	9,266
April	7,168	1,060	6,108
July	30	30	0

Source: Eisendrath, "Chicago's Camp Douglas," 37–63 (compiled from *Official Records* Ser. II, Vol. VIII, 986).

Notes

Chapter 1

1. Schneider, *Old Man River*, 267–71.
2. Campbell, *Fighting Slavery in Chicago*, 14, 22.
3. Ibid., 30.
4. Cook, *Bygone Days in Chicago*, 68.
5. Grossman, Keating and Reiff, *Encyclopedia of Chicago*, 839.
6. Mahoney, "Black Abolitionists," 32.
7. Ibid., 22.
8. Campbell, *Fighting Slavery in Chicago*, 84.
9. Ibid., 51.
10. Bross, "History of Camp Douglas,"17; Levy, *To Die in Chicago*, 97; *Chicago Tribune*, August 6, 1862, and November 3, 1863.
11. Cook, *Bygone Days in Chicago*, 50. See Chapter 11 for details of the 1864 Conspiracy.
12. Cook, *Bygone Days in Chicago*, 48, 74.
13. Mahoney, "Black Abolitionists," 37.
14. Howard, *Illinois*, 287–98.
15. Cook, *Bygone Days in Chicago*, 28.
16. Karamanski, *Rally 'Round the Flag*, 224–26.
17. Ibid., 226.
18. Ibid., 191–95; *Chicago Tribune*, June 4, 1863, and June 22, 1863.
19. Mackey, "Diary."
20. Howard, *History of the Prairie State*, 319.
21. Ibid.
22. *Camp Douglas News* (Spring 2011).
23. Illinois State Archives, "Regimental and Unit Histories."
24. Kogan and Wendt, *Chicago*, 94.
25. Howard, *History of the Prairie State*, 320.
26. Spinny, *City of Big Shoulders*, Tables 1 and 4.

27. Swan, *Chicago's Irish Legion*, 2.
28. McPherson, *Battle Cry of Freedom*, Appendix A.
29. *Camp Douglas News* (Summer 2011); Cavanaugh and Marvel, *Petersburg Campaign*.
30. Spinny, *City of Big Shoulders*, 57.
31. Ibid., 74.
32. Ibid., 54.
33. Ibid., 74.

Chapter 2

34. United States Agricultural Society, "Seventh National Exhibition."
35. *Official Records of the Union and Confederate Armies* (*OR*), Series II, Volume V, 588.
36. Bross, "History of Camp Douglas," 164; Howard, *History of the Prairie State*, 10–12.
37. Andreas, *History of Chicago*.
38. National Archives RG 77-2.
39. Goodspeed, "Old University of Chicago," 52–57; Grossman, Keating and Reiff, *Encyclopedia of Chicago*, 845.
40. Levy, *To Die in Chicago*, 31.
41. National Archives RG 92, Entry 800, Box 64. Letter dated October 26, 1865, by Office of Quartermaster Department, Chicago, to U.S. quartermaster general.
42. Ibid.
43. Haynie, *History of Camp Douglas*, 4.
44. Swan, *Chicago's Irish Legion*, 15.
45. Haynie, *History of Camp Douglas*, 4; Illinois State Archives, "Regimental and Unit Histories"; see also Appendix 3.
46. *OR* Ser. II, Vol. IV, 186.
47. Levy, *To Die in Chicago*, 31, 34.
48. Doyle, *Voices from Captivity*, 20; Sanders, *Hands of the Enemy*, 162.
49. This foundation was uncovered and identified in June 2012 during an archaeological investigation sponsored by the Camp Douglas Restoration Foundation, conducted by Northern Michigan and Loyola Universities and financed by the Abraham Lincoln Bicentennial Foundation.
50. Haynie, *History of Camp Douglas*, 5.
51. Burke, "Civil War Journal," August 18, 1863.
52. Ibid.
53. *OR* Ser. II, Vol. VI, 434, 461.
54. Ibid.
55. Huff, "Diary," October 4, 1863.
56. Ibid., February 14, 1864.
57. *Chicago Tribune*, April 30, 1862.
58. Levy, *To Die in Chicago*, 148.
59. Haynie, *History of Camp Douglas*, 5.
60. *Chicago Tribune*, February 25, 1864.
61. Bagby, "Civil War Diary," 30.
62. *Chicago Tribune*, December 1, 1862.
63. Bagby, "Civil War Diary," 30.

64. Levy, *To Die in Chicago*, 333.
65. Haynie, *History of Camp Douglas*, 5.
66. Kelly, "History of Camp Douglas," 84.
67. Ibid., 82.
68. Ibid.
69. National Archives RG, 77-2.
70. Burke, "Civil War Journal," April 16, May 12 and November 25, 1864.
71. Copley, "Reminiscences of Camp Douglas," Chapter V.
72. Huff, "Diary," June 1864.
73. Burke, "Civil War Journal," April 3, 1864.
74. Copley, "Reminiscences of Camp Douglas," Chapter. V.
75. *OR* Ser. II, Vol. VII, 694, 1027; Burke, "Civil War Journal," November 22, 1864.
76. Burke, "Civil War Journal," April 10, 1864, and October 15, 1863.
77. Copley, "Reminiscences of Camp Douglas," Chapter. V.
78. Burke, "Civil War Journal," March 14, 1864.
79. Haynie, *History of Camp Douglas*, 5.
80. Spear, *Portals to Hell*, 304; Pucci, *Camp Douglas*, 104.
81. Sanders, *Hands of the Enemy*, 165.
82. Levy, *To Die in Chicago*, 165, 187.
83. Spear, *Portals to Hell*, 222.

Chapter 3

84. Illinois State Archives, "Regimental and Unit Histories."
85. *Chicago Tribune*, October 4, 1862.
86. Ibid., January 15, 1862.
87. Ibid.
88. Swan, *Chicago's Irish Legion*, 16.
89. Ibid.
90. *Chicago Tribune*, October 4, 1862.
91. See Chapter 7 for details on Dix-Hill and the parole and exchange of prisoners.
92. Doyle, *Enemy in Our Hands*, Appendix 2.
93. Peckenpaugh, *Captives in Grey*, 70; *Chicago Tribune*, October 6, 1862.
94. *OR* Ser. II, Vol. IV, 600.
95. *Chicago Tribune*, October 4, 1862.
96. Ibid., October 29, 1862, and December 1, 1862.
97. *OR* Ser. II, Vol. IV, 645.
98. Brown, Civil War Letters.
99. *Chicago Tribune*, October11, October 18 and November 22, 1862.
100. Ibid., April 6, 1863.

Chapter 4

101. Yale Law School, "General Orders No. 100."
102. Doyle, *Enemy in our Hands*.
103. Sanders, *Hands of the Enemy*.
104. Gillispie, *Andersonvilles of the North*.

105. Doyle, *Voices from Captivity*, 38.
106. Clausewitz, *On War*, 309–11.
107. Doyle, *Enemy in Our Hands*, 12, 13.
108. Ibid., 12.
109. Ibid., 23.
110. Ibid., 30.
111. Ibid., 19.
112. Doyle, *Voices from Captivity*, 30.
113. Ibid., 12, Appendix 2.
114. Ibid., 43.
115. Ibid., 16; Sanders, *Hands of the Enemy*, 21.
116. Doyle, *Enemy in Our Hands*, 4, 90.
117. Doyle, *Voices from Captivity*, Appendix 4.
118. Spear, *Portals to Hell*, xvi.
119. Gillispie, *Andersonvilles of the North*, 29.
120. Cloyd, *Haunted by Atrocity*, 27.
121. Gillispie, *Andersonvilles of the North*, 4.
122. Ibid., Appendix A; Medical and Surgical History of the War of the Rebellion, Volume 1 Part 111, 30 & 46. There have been no meaningful studies on other factors, such as the Union blockade and availability of medicine, that may have affected recovery at Chimborazo Hospital.
123. Gillispie, *Andersonvilles of the North*, 66.
124. McPherson, *Battle Cry of Freedom*, 802.
125. Ibid., 38, 89, 793; Sanders, *Hands of the Enemy*, 152, 158.
126. Gillispie, *Andersonvilles of the North*, 87.
127. McPherson, *Battle Cry of Freedom*, 793; Cloyd, *Haunted by Atrocity*, 44.
128. Cloyd, *Haunted by Atrocity*, 56.
129. Ibid., 77.
130. Sanders, *Hands of the Enemy*, 300.
131. Ibid., 52, 199.
132. Ibid., 245.
133. *OR* Ser. II, Vol. VII, 367.
134. Sanders, *Hands of the Enemy*, 311.
135. Ibid., 187, 255.
136. Ibid., 170.
137. Billings, *Hardtack and Coffee*, Chapter VIII.
138. Yale Law School, "General Orders No. 100."

Chapter 5

139. *OR* Ser. II, Vol. III, 315–16.
140. *Chicago Tribune*, February 22, 1862, and February 28, 1862.
141. Karamanski, *Rally 'Round the Flag*, 134.
142. Spear, *Portals to Hell*, 72.
143. Levy, *To Die in Chicago*, 41.
144. Peckenpaugh, *Captives in Grey*, 20.

145. *Chicago Tribune*, February 22, 1862.
146. Ibid.
147. Ibid., February 24, 1862.
148. Levy, *To Die in Chicago*, 50.
149. *Chicago Tribune*, February 27, 1862, and February 28, 1862.
150. Haynie, *History of Camp Douglas*, 9.
151. *Chicago Tribune*, April 15, 1862.
152. Ibid., April 19, 1862.
153. Ibid., September 6, 1862, and September 16, 1862.
154. Bagby, "Civil War Diary," January 27, 1863
155. Burke, "Civil War Journal," August 17, 1863.
156. Huff, "Diary," October 4, 1863.
157. Burke, "Civil War Journal," July 16, 1864.
158. Ibid., August 24, 1864.
159. Ibid., December 23, 1864.
160. Bagby, "Civil War Diary," 31.
161. Copley, "Reminiscences of Camp Douglas," 75–78.
162. *Chicago Tribune*, May 13, 1862, and May 17, 1862.
163. Ibid., January 27, 1863.
164. Ibid., March 11, 1862; Levy, *To Die in Chicago*, 56.
165. *OR* Ser. II, Vol. VI, 339.
166. Bagby, "Civil War Diary."
167. *OR* Ser. II, Vol. IV, 102–03.
168. *Chicago Tribune*, March 1, 1862.
169. Ibid., March 2, 1862.
170. Ibid., March 20, 1862.
171. Ibid., March 26, 1862.

Chapter 6

172. Peckenpaugh, *Captives in Grey*, 2.
173. Warner, *Generals in Blue*, 318.
174. Ibid., 587.
175. *OR* Ser. II, Vol. VI, 30.
176. Peckenpaugh, *Captives in Grey*, 3.
177. Warner, *Generals in Gray*, 340.
178. Sanders, *Hands of the Enemy*, 46.
179. *OR* Ser. II, Vol. V, 686.
180. Ibid., Vol. III, 301.
181. Ibid., Vol. IV, 432; *Chicago Tribune*, August 29, 1862.
182. *OR* Ser. II, Vol. V, 686.
183. Levy, *To Die in Chicago*, 59.
184. Spear, *Portals to Hell*, 73; *Chicago Tribune*, June 23, 1862.
185. *Chicago Tribune*, June 12, 1862.
186. Ibid., June 26, 1862.
187. *OR* Ser. II, Vol. IV, 172, 182.

188. *Chicago Tribune*, July 24, 1862, and July 25, 1862.
189. *OR* Ser. II, Vol. IV, 154.
190. *Chicago Tribune*, August 6, 1862.
191. *OR* Ser. II, Vol. IV, 339.
192. Levy, *To Die in Chicago*, 79–81.
193. *Chicago Tribune*, September 22, 1865.
194. Ibid., October 4, 1862; Doyle, *Enemy in Our Hands*, 339, Appendix 2.
195. Warner, *Generals in Blue*, 514.
196. *Chicago Tribune*, October 1, 1862.
197. Ibid., October 5, 1862.
198. Ibid., October 10, 1862.
199. Warner, *Generals in Blue*, 6.
200. *Chicago Tribune*, January 28, 1863, and January 31, 1863.
201. Bagby, "Civil War Diary," January 28, 1863.
202. *Chicago Tribune*, February 21, 1863.
203. *OR* Ser. II, Vol. V, 344.
204. Ibid.
205. Ibid., 131; *Chicago Tribune*, January 31, 1863.
206. *Chicago Tribune*, January 31, 1863, and February 10, 1863.
207. Ibid., April 16, 1863.
208. Kelly, "History of Camp Douglas," 51.
209. *Chicago Tribune*, August 19, 21 and 24, 1863; September 1, 1863.
210. *OR* Ser. II, Vol. VI, 434, 461.
211. Spear, *Portals to Hell*, 222.
212. *OR* Ser. II, Vol. VI, 390, 434, 632, 637; Ibid., Vol. V, 686.
213. New York State Division of Military and Naval Affairs, "Col. James C. Strong."
214. Warner, *Generals in Blue*, 350.
215. *OR* Ser. II, Vol. VI, 660.
216. Burke, " Civil War Journal," March 7, 1864.
217. Ibid., February 27, March 7 and March 12, 1864.
218. Ibid., March 14, 1864.
219. Ibid., April 3, 1864.
220. *OR* Ser. II, Vol. VII, 57.
221. Ibid., 58.
222. Donald, *Lincoln*, 60, 83–86, 185.
223. *OR* Ser. II, Vol. VI, 461–64.
224. Burke, " Civil War Journal," October 21, 1863.
225. *OR* Ser. II, Vol. VI, 490.
226. Ibid., 804.
227. Wisconsin Historical Society, "Benjamin Sweet."
228. Billings, *Hardtack and Coffee*, 146.
229. Karamanski, *Rally 'Round the Flag*, 155.
230. *OR* Ser. II, Vol. VII, 428.
231. Ibid., 503.
232. Ibid., 664.

233. Ibid., 694, 767, 1063, 1067, 1083, 1084.
234. Ibid., 897.
235. Levy, *To Die in Chicago*, 239.
236. *OR* Ser. II, Vol. VII, 767.
237. Ibid., 954.
238. *OR* Ser. II, Vol. VIII, 538.
239. Jean Cooper (archivist at the Lombard Historical Society) in discussion with the author, April 17, 2014.

Chapter 7

240. Bagby, "Civil War Diary"; Burke, "Civil War Journal"; Copley, "Reminiscences of Camp Douglas."
241. *OR* Ser. II, Vol. IV, 266–68.
242. Ibid., Vol. III, 156.
243. Ibid., 157.
244. Ibid., Vol. IV, 278.
245. Ibid., 458.
246. Haynie, *History of Camp Douglas*, 10.
247. *OR* Ser. II, Vol. V, 449, 495, 686.
248. McPherson, *Battle Cry of Freedom*, 793; Sanders, *Hands of the Enemy*, 152, 158; Gillispie, *Andersonvilles of the North*, 38, 89.
249. *OR* Ser. II, Vol. V, 671–87.
250. Burke, "Civil War Journal," January 8, 1864.
251. Bagby, "Civil War Diary," February 27, 1864.
252. Burke, "Civil War Journal," May 27, 1864.
253. Copley, "Reminiscences of Camp Douglas," 204.
254. Bagby, "Civil War Diary," January 17, 1865.
255. Burke, "Civil War Journal," September 14, 1864.
256. *Chicago Tribune*, February 6, 1864.
257. Ibid., March 21, 1863; March 25, 1863; and August 14, 1862.
258. Mackey, "Diary," August 28, 1862.
259. Copley, "Reminiscences of Camp Douglas," 147–57.
260. Burke, "Civil War Journal," August 26, 1864.
261. *OR* Ser. II, Vol. VIII, 538.

Chapter 8

262. Fold 3.com, "Civil War Records: Card Number 46045291."
263. Burke, "Civil War Journal," November 24, 1864; Copley, "Reminiscences of Camp Douglas," 147.
264. *Chicago Tribune*, February 24, 1863.
265. Burke, "Civil War Journal," March 7, 1864.
266. Copley, "Reminiscences of Camp Douglas," 101.
267. Burke, "Civil War Journal," July 2, 1864.
268. Bagby, "Civil War Diary," January 15, 1865; Copley, "Reminiscences of Camp Douglas," 77.

269. Bagby, "Civil War Diary," January 15, 1865.
270. Ibid., January 22, 1865.
271. *OR* Ser. II, Vol. IV, 458.
272. Huff, " Diary," April 1864.
273. Burke, "Civil War Journal," December 4, 1863.
274. Ibid., April 14, 1864.
275. Ibid., June 5, 1864.
276. Mackey, "Diary," June 23, 1862.
277. Burke, "Civil War Journal," April 15, 1864; Copley, "Reminiscences of Camp Douglas," 116.
278. Burke, "Civil War Journal," October 21, 1864.
279. Ibid., March 28, 1864; Copley, "Reminiscences of Camp Douglas," 171.
280. Copley, "Reminiscences of Camp Douglas," 170.
281. Burke, "Civil War Journal," February 26, 1865.
282. Huff, "Diary," June 1864.
283. Ibid., November 11, 1863; Burke, "Civil War Journal," April 19, 1864.
284. Haynie, *History of Camp Douglas*, 14.
285. Burke, "Civil War Journal," April 19, 1864, and April 20, 1864.
286. Haynie, *History of Camp Douglas*, 14.
287. Burke, "Civil War Journal," February 22, 1864; *Chicago Tribune*, March 25, 1862.
288. Mackey, "Diary," March 25, 1862.
289. Burke, "Civil War Journal," March 25, 1863.
290. Copley, "Reminiscences of Camp Douglas," 163–65.
291. Burke, "Civil War Journal," October 2, 1863.
292. Mackey, "Diary," March 22, 1862.
293. Copley, "Reminiscences of Camp Douglas," 171.
294. Burke, "Civil War Journal," October 5, 1863.
295. Flyer in the collection of the Tennessee State Library and Archives.
296. Burke, "Civil War Journal," November 24, 1863.
297. Ibid., March 21, 1861.
298. *Prisoners Vidette*, Chicago Public Library.
299. Burke, "Civil War Journal," April 10, 1864.
300. Ibid., July 4, 1864.
301. Copley, "Reminiscences of Camp Douglas," 115.
302. Burke, "Civil War Journal," April 20, 1864.
303. Mackey, "Diary," July 26, 1862.
304. *OR* Ser. II, Vol. IV, 103.
305. Ibid., Vol. VI, 1036.
306. Copley, "Reminiscences of Camp Douglas," 167–69.
307. Bagby, "Civil War Diary," October 1 1864.
308. William R. Paul, Company H, Fifteenth Tennessee Cavalry, to Mrs. Winnie Paul, October 28, 1864, and January 24, 1865.
309. *OR* Ser. II, Vol. VII, 496.
310. Copley, "Reminiscences of Camp Douglas," 89.

311. *OR* Ser. II, Vol. IV, 103; Kelly, "A History of Camp Douglas," 95.
312. *OR* Ser. II, Vol. VII, 57.
313. Kelly, "A History of Camp Douglas," 96.
314. *OR* Ser. II, Vol. VII, 954, 1006.
315. Ibid., 57.
316. Burke, "Civil War Journal," September 11, 1863.
317. Kelly, "A History of Camp Douglas," 97.
318. Burke, "Civil War Journal," March 24, 1864.
319. William R. Paul to Mrs. Winnie Paul, January 24, 1865.
320. Burke, "Civil War Journal," 390–91.
321. Kelly, "A History of Camp Douglas," 98.
322. *OR* Ser. II, Vol. VI, 142.
323. Ibid., 475; Sanders, *Hands of the Enemy*, 300; McPherson, *Battle Cry of Freedom*, 797.
324. *OR* Ser. II, Vol. VI, 476.
325. Ibid., 183.
326. *OR* Ser. II, Vol. V, 344; Vol. VI, 372, 660; Vol. VII, 57, 1083.
327. *OR* Ser. II, Vol. VII, 975.
328. *Chicago Tribune*, November 18, 1862.
329. *OR* Ser. II, Vol. III, 549.
330. *Chicago Tribune*, August 19, 1862.
331. *OR* Ser. II, Vol. VI, 390.
332. Ibid., 489.
333. Ibid., 490.
334. *OR* Ser. II, Vol. VII, 390, 694.
335. Copley, "Reminiscences of Camp Douglas," 124.
336. Ibid.,121.
337. Ibid., 29.
338. Ibid., 69.
339. Huff, "Diary," June 1864 and August 14, 1864.
340. Mackey, "Diary," February 28, 1862.
341. Bagby, "Civil War Diary," January 28, 1863.
342. Burke, "Civil War Journal," August 17, 1863.
343. Ibid., December 25, 1863.
344. Ibid., December 25, 1864.
345. Ibid., April 28, 1864.
346. Ibid., September 28, 1864.
347. Spear, *Portals to Hell*, 183.
348. Gray, *Business of Captivity*, 40–41.
349. Whitaker, "Part of War and Prison Life," 6.
350. Burke, "Civil War Journal," January 21, 1864.
351. *OR* Ser. II, Vol. VI, 778.
352. *Camp Douglas News* (Summer 2010).
353. *Medical and Surgical History Vol. I.*
354. *OR* Ser. II, Vol. VII, 954, 1006.
355. Copley, "Reminiscences of Camp Douglas," 30, 76.

356. *Chicago Tribune*, February 22, 1862.
357. *OR* Ser. II, Vol. VI, 372.
358. Ibid., 778.
359. Ibid., 799.
360. Ibid.
361. Burke, "Civil War Journal," October 19, 1864; Huff, "Diary," January 1, 1864
362. Burke, "Civil War Journal," September 16,1864.
363. Warner, *Generals in Gray*, 21.
364. Peckenpaugh, *Captives in Grey*, 223–25; *OR* Ser. II, Vol. VII, 1122, 1279–83, 1288–91.
365. Burke, "Civil War Journal," December 12, 1864.
366. *Chicago Tribune*, February 19, 1863.
367. *OR* Ser. II, Vol. V, 48, 347, 588, 686.
368. *OR* Ser. II, Vol. VI, 371.
369. Ibid., 434, 461.
370. Burke, "Civil War Journal," April 11, 1864.
371. Copley, "Reminiscences of Camp Douglas," 88; Burke, "Civil War Journal," September 11, 1863.
372. Burke, "Civil War Journal," March 11, 1864, and June 22, 1864.
373. Ibid., March 14, 1864.
374. OR Ser. II, Vol. VII, 57.
375. Ibid., 1083.
376. Huff, "Diary," October 4, 1863; Haynie, *History of Camp Douglas*, 5.
377. Haynie, *History of Camp Douglas*, 5.
378. Copley, "Reminiscences of Camp Douglas," 158.
379. Ibid., 88.
380. Bagby, "Civil War Diary," January 28, 1863.
381. *OR* Ser. II, Vol. VI, 187.
382. Copley, "Reminiscences of Camp Douglas," 100.
383. Bagby, "Civil War Diary," January 13, 1865.
384. Copley, "Reminiscences of Camp Douglas," 100.
385. Ibid., 103–09.
386. Ibid., 187.
387. Ibid., 110.
388. Burke, "Civil War Journal," April 3, 1864.
389. Copley, "Reminiscences of Camp Douglas," 138.
390. Ibid., 96.
391. Ibid.
392. Ibid., 188.
393. Ibid., 101.
394. Burke, "Civil War Journal," October 2, 1863.
395. Ibid., September 16, 1864.
396. Ibid., January 1, 1864.
397. Ibid., December 15, 1864.
398. Copley, "Reminiscences of Camp Douglas," 79.

399. Ibid., 175.
400. Huff, "Diary," October 29, 1864.
401. Copley, "Reminiscences of Camp Douglas," 142.
402. Burke, "Civil War Journal" April 3, 1864.
403. Copley, "Reminiscences of Camp Douglas," 130.
404. Mackey, "Diary," March 30, 1862.
405. Copley, Reminiscences of Camp Douglas, 114.
406. Mackey, "Diary," May 23, 1862.
407. Burke, "Civil War Journal," August 18, 1864.
408. Ibid., April 10, 1864.
409. Ibid., April 12, 1864.
410. Copley, "Reminiscences of Camp Douglas," 133–36.
411. Burke, "Civil War Journal," November 22, 1863.
412. Copley, "Reminiscences of Camp Douglas," 136.
413. Burke, "Civil War Journal," January 31, 1864.
414. Bagby, "Civil War Diary," February 1, 1865.
415. Burke, "Civil War Journal," November 3, 1863; April 19, 1864; and July 4, 1864.
416. *Chicago Tribune*, April 30, 1862.
417. Billings, *Hardtack and Coffee*.
418. Mackey, "Diary," July 21, 1862.
419. *Chicago Tribune*, May 15, 1862.
420. Ibid., May 30, 1862.
421. Stone, *"Morgan's Men."*
422. Ibid.
423. *OR* Ser. II, Vol. IV, 278.
424. Ibid., Vol. VI, 278; *Chicago Tribune*, July 25, 1862.
425. *Chicago Tribune*, May 17, 1862.
426. *OR* Ser. II, Vol. IV, 323.
427. *Chicago Tribune*, July 24, and 25, 1862; Huff, "Diary," June 1864.
428. Huff, "Diary," June 1864.
429. *Chicago Tribune*, September 23, 1863.
430. Ibid., February 21, 1863.
431. Ibid., September 9, 1863.
432. Ibid., November 13, 1863.
433. Burke, "Civil War Journal," September 7, 1863.
434. *OR* Ser. II, Vol. VI, 637; *Chicago Tribune*, December 4, 1863, and December 6, 1863.
435. Bagby, "Civil War Diary," December 7, 1864.
436. Huff, "Diary," April 1864, August 9, 1864.
437. Burke, "Civil War Journal," February 28, 1864.
438. Bagby, "Civil War Diary," October 16, 1864.
439. Camp Douglas General Order 96, September 28, 1864.
440. Levy, *To Die in Chicago*, 332.
441. Haynie, *History of Camp Douglas*, 15.
442. Bagby, "Civil War Diary," December 18, 1864.
443. Burke, "Civil War Journal," May 6, 1864.

Chapter 9

444. *Chicago Tribune*, December 1, 1861.
445. Kelly, "History of Camp Douglas," 84.
446. *OR* Ser. II, Vol. V, 588.
447. Ibid., Vol. IV, 371.
448. Ibid., Vol. VI, 463.
449. Ibid., 798.
450. *OR* Ser. II, Vol. VII, 496.
451. Copley, "Reminiscences of Camp Douglas," 197.
452. *OR* Ser. II, Vol. IV, 371.
453. Ibid., Vol. VI, 798.
454. Burke, "Civil War Journal," October 22, 1863.
455. Ibid., August 7, 1864.
456. *Chicago Tribune*, March 11, 1862.
457. Ibid., March 14, 1862.
458. Ibid.
459. Burke, "Civil War Journal," July 26, 1864.
460. Ibid., August 7, 1864.
461. Bagby, "Civil War Diary," January 29, 1863; February 2, 1863; and February 21 1864.
462. Copley, "Reminiscences of Camp Douglas," 196.
463. Ibid., 198.
464. *Chicago Tribune*, March 12, 1863.
465. Ibid., January 29, 1864.
466. Burke, "Civil War Journal," March 11, 1864, and March 12, 1864.
467. *OR* Ser. II, Vol. VII, 52.
468. Burke, "Civil War Journal," February 14, 1864, and September 7, 1864.
469. Copley, "Reminiscences of Camp Douglas," 198.
470. Ibid., 196.
471. Burke, "Civil War Journal," October 5, 1864.
472. Ibid., October 7, 1864; October 9, 1864; October 13, 1864; and October 18,1864.
473. Bagby, "Civil War Diary," February 6, 1863, and October 1, 1864.
474. Ibid., November 21, 1864.

Chapter 10

475. Faust, *This Republic Is Suffering*, 266.
476. Sanders, *Hands of the Enemy*, 1.
477. Levy, *To Die in Chicago*, 349–61.
478. *Chicago Tribune*, February 16, 1863.
479. Levy, *To Die in Chicago*, 349–61.
480. Urbanski, "Story of Two Confederate Soldiers Named Jonathan Bond," http://graveyards.com/IL/Cook/oakwoods/confederate-names/tablet008.jpg.
481. Bagby, "Civil War Diary"; Mackey, "Diary"; *Camp Douglas News* (Spring 2012).
482. *Camp Douglas News* (Spring 2012).

483. Faust, *Death and the American Civil War*, 31.
484. Mackey, "Diary," 1862.
485. Bagby, "Civil War Diary," February 1, 1863.
486. Mackey, "Diary," July 26, 1862.
487. Bagby, "Civil War Diary," September 30, 1864.
488. Mackey, "Diary," April 6, 1862.
489. Ibid., May 31, 1862.
490. Ibid., March 19, 1862.
491. Bagby, "Civil War Diary," October 9, 1863.
492. Ibid., February 11, 1863.

Chapter 11

493. *Chicago Tribune*, November 3, and 9, 1863.
494. Starr, *Colonel Grenfell's Wars*, 180.
495. *Chicago Tribune*, March 11, 1864.
496. Bagby, "Civil War Diary," October 1, 1864.
497. Starr, *Colonel Grenfell's Wars*, 187.
498. Bagby, "Civil War Diary," November 5, 1864.
499. Ibid., November 9, 1864.
500. Ibid., December 5, 1864.
501. Ibid.
502. Burke, "Civil War Journal," November 7, 1864.
503. *OR* Ser. I, Vol. IXL, Part III, 678.
504. *Atlantic Monthly*, "The Chicago Conspiracy," 108, 110, 114.
505. Ibid., 111.
506. Bross, "History of Camp Douglas," 15.
507. Ibid., 17.
508. Ibid., 24.
509. *Chicago Tribune*, January 26, 29, and 30, 1864; February 12, 1864; and March 11, 1864.
510. Ibid., April 25, 1864.
511. *OR* Ser. I, Vol. XLI, Part 1, 1076–81.

Chapter 12

512. Sanders, *Hands of the Enemy.*
513. Gillispie, *Andersonvilles of the North.*
514. Peckenpaugh, *Captives in Grey.*
515. Doyle, *Enemy in Our Hands.*
516. *Camp Douglas News* (Spring 2014). The death rate for Morgan's Raiders is based on the assumption that between 2,000 and 2,500 were incarcerated at the camp, with deaths based on names contained on the monument at Oak Woods Cemetery. Exact figures for the number at the prison and deaths are unknown.
517. Gott, *Where the South Lost the War*, 260.
518. Mackey, "Diary."
519. Copley, "Reminiscences of Camp Douglas," 68–80.

520. McDonough, *Nashville*, 150.
521. *OR* Ser. II, Vol. VI, 343; Vol. VI, 390, 799; Vol. VI, 660.

Chapter 13

522. *OR* Ser. II, Vol. VI, 660.
523. Spear, *Portals to Hell*; Peckenpaugh, *Captives in Grey*.
524. Ibid.
525. Gray, *Business of Captivity*.
526. Spear, *Portals to Hell*; Peckenpaugh, *Captives in Grey*.
527. Ibid.
528. Futch, *History of Andersonville Prison*; Spear, *Portals to Hell*; Peckenpaugh, *Captives in Grey*.
529. Spear, *Portals to Hell*.
530. Ibid.
531. Ibid.
532. Ibid.

Bibliography

Books

Andreas, A.T. *History of Chicago*. Vol. 2. Chicago: A.T. Andreas, 1885.

Bernstein, Arnie. *The Hoofs and Guns of the Storm: Chicago's Civil War Connection*. Chicago: Lake Claremont Press, 2003.

Billings, John D. *Hardtack and Coffee*. New York: Konecky & Konecky, 1887.

Campbell, Thomas. *Fighting Slavery in Chicago: Abolitionists, the Law of Slavery and Lincoln*. Chicago: Ampersand Inc., 2009.

Cavanaugh, Michael A., and William Marvel. *The Petersburg Campaign: The Battle of the Crater*. Lynchburg, VA: H.E. Howard Inc., 1989.

Cloyd, Benjamin C. *Haunted by Atrocity: Civil War Prisons in American Memory*. Baton Rouge: Louisiana State University Press 2010.

Cook, Francis Frederick. *Bygone Days in Chicago: Recollections of the "Garden City" of the Sixties*. Chicago: A.C. McClurg and Co., 1910.

Donald, David Herbert. *Lincoln*. New York: Simon & Schuster, 1995.

Doyle, Robert C. *The Enemy in Our Hands*. Lexington: University Press of Kentucky, 2010.

———. *Voices from Captivity*. St. Lawrence: University Press of Kansas, 1944.

Faust, Drew Gilpin. *This Republic Is Suffering: Death and the American Civil War*. New York: Vintage Books, 2008.

Futch, Ovid L. *History of Andersonville Prison*. Revised ed. Gainesville: University Press of Florida, 2011.

Gillispie, James M. *Andersonvilles of the North: The Myths and Realities of Northern Treatment of Civil War Confederate Prisoners*. Denton: University of North Texas Press, 2008.

Gott, Kendall. *Where the South Lost the War: An Analysis of the Fort Henry–Fort Donelson Campaign, February 1862*. Mechanicsburg, PA: Stackpole Books, 2003.

Gray, Michael P. *The Business of Captivity: Elmira and Its Civil War Prison*. Kent, OH: Kent State University Press, 2001.

Grossman, James R., Ann Durkin Keating and Janice L. Reiff, eds. *The Encyclopedia of Chicago*. Chicago: University of Chicago Press, 2004.

Haynie, I.N. *A History of Camp Douglas: A Prisoner of War Camp at Chicago, Illinois, 1861–1865*. Little Rock, AR: Eagle Press, 1991.

Howard. Robert P. *Illinois: A History of the Prairie State*. Grand Rapids, MI: William B. Eerdmans Publishing Co., 1972.

Karamanski, Theodore J. *Rally 'Round the Flag: Chicago and the Civil War*. Chicago: Nelson-Hall Inc., 1993.

Karamanski, Theodore J., and Eileen M. McMahon, eds. *Civil War Chicago: Eyewitness to History*. Athens: Ohio University Press, 2014.

Kogan, Herman, and Lloyd Wendt. *Chicago: A Pictorial History*. New York: Bonanza Books, 1958.

Levy, George. *To Die in Chicago: Confederate Prisoners at Camp Douglas, 1862–65*. Gretna, LA: Pelican Publishing Company, 1999.

McDonough, James Lee. *Nashville*. Knoxville: University of Tennessee Press, 2004.

Mcilvaine, Mabel. *Reminiscences of Chicago During the Civil War*. Chicago: R.R. Donnelley and Sons, 1914.

McPherson, James M. *Battle Cry of Freedom: The Civil War Era*. New York: Ballantine Books, 1989.

———. *The Negro's Civil War*. Urbana: University of Illinois Press, 1982.

Orendorff, H.H., ed. *Reminiscences of the Civil War from Diaries of Members of the 103rd Illinois Volunteer Infantry*. Chicago: J.F. Leaming and Co., 1904.

Peckenpaugh, Roger. *Captives in Grey: The Civil War Prisons of the Union*. Tuscaloosa: University of Alabama Press, 2009.

Pucci, Kelly. *Camp Douglas: Chicago's Civil War Prison*. Charleston, SC: Arcadia Publishing, 2007.

Sanders, Charles W. *While in the Hands of the Enemy: Military Prisons of the Civil War*. Baton Rouge: Louisiana State University Press, 2005.

Schneider, Paul. *Old Man River: The Mississippi River in North American History*. New York: Henry Holt & Co., 2013.

Spear, Lonnie R. *Portals to Hell: Military Prisons of the Civil War*. Lincoln: University of Nebraska Press, 1997.

Spinny, Robert G. *City of Big Shoulders: A History of Chicago*. De Kalb: Northern Illinois University Press, 2000.

Stanley, Dorothy, ed. *Autobiography of Sir Henry Morton Stanley*. Boston: Houghton Mifflin Co., 1909.

Starr, Stephen Z. *Colonel Grenfell's Wars*. Baton Rouge: Louisiana State University Press, 1971.

Stone, Henry Lane. *"Morgan's Men": A Narrative of Personal Experiences Delivered before George B. Eastin Camp, No. 803, United Confederate Veterans, at the Free Public Library, Louisville, KY, April 8, 1919*. Louisville, KY: Westerfield-Bonte Co., 1919.

Swan, James B. *Chicago's Irish Legion: The 90th Illinois Volunteers in the Civil War*. Carbondale: Southern Illinois University Press, 2009.

Turner, Bernard C. *A View of Bronzeville*. Chicago: Highlights of Chicago Press, 2002.

Von Clausewitz, Carl. *On War*. London: Penguin Books, 1968.

The War of the Rebellion: A Compilation of the Official Records of the Union and Confederate Armies. 128 vols. Washington, D.C.: U.S. Government Printing Office, 1880–1901.

Warner, Ezra J. *Generals in Blue: Lives of Union Commanders*. Baton Rouge: Louisiana State University Press, 1964.

———. *Generals in Gray: Lives of Confederate Commanders*. Baton Rouge: Louisiana State University Press, 1959.

Zimm, John, ed. *This Wicked Rebellion: Wisconsin Civil War Soldiers Write Home*. Madison: Wisconsin Historical Society Press, 2012.

Diaries, Journals and Letters

Adams, William Henry (Company G, Third Kentucky Cavalry, CSA). Wartime letters.

Bagby, Robert Anderson. "Civil War Diary, 1863–1865." Transcribed by David L. Keller, Camp Douglas Restoration Foundation, 2013.

Brown, William Liston. Civil War Letters. Chicago History Museum.

Burke, Curtis R. "Civil War Journal, 1862–1865." Dictated in Indianapolis, Indiana, in 1915 and edited by Kathryn Wilmont, Indiana Historical Society, in 2007.

Copley, John M. "A Sketch of the Battle of Franklin, Tennessee, with Reminiscences of Camp Douglas." Austin, TX: Eugene Von Boeckmann, 1893.

Huff, William D. "Diary, October 4, 1863–May 4, 1865." Chicago History Museum, MSS Alpha 2 H.

Mackey, James Taswell. "Diary of Lieut. James Taswell Mackey of Maury County, in the 48th Regiment Tennessee Infantry, 1861–65." Museum of the Confederacy, Richmond, Virginia.

Moses, Jefferson (Company G, Ninety-third Illinois Volunteers). "Journal, Mustered in at Camp Douglas," 1911.

Paul, William R. (Company H, Fifteenth Tennessee Cavalry). Letters to Mrs. Winnie Paul, October 28, 1864, and January 24, 1865.

"Taylor Family Correspondence." Notre Dame University, 1864.

Whitaker, William. "A Part of War and Prison Life." Allen's Laurel Hill Sutlery.

Williams, Robert Thomas. "The Diary of Robert Thomas Williams: Marches, Skirmishes and Battles of the 4th Regiment, Texas Militia Volunteers, October 1861 to November 1865." Compiled and transcribed by Connie Ragan Seelke.

Websites

Camp Douglas Restoration Foundation. http://www.campdouglas.org.

City of Paris (KY). "Morgan's Raiders, 2nd Kentucky Cavalry, CSA." http://www.paris.ky.gov/Morgan.htm.

The Civil War in Morgan County. "Kentucky Confederate Troops." http://civilwar.morganco2.freeservers.com/conftroops.htm.

Fold3.com. "Civil War Records." http://go.fold3.com/civilwar_records.

Illinois in the Civil War. "Search Rosters." http://www.illinoiscivilwar.org/searchsos.html.

Illinois State Archives. "Illinois Adjutant General's Report: Regimental and Unit Histories, Containing Reports for the Years 1861–1866." http://cyberdriveillinois.com/departments/archives/databases/reghist.pdf.

———. "Illinois Civil War Muster and Descriptive Rolls." http://www.ilsos.gov/isaveterans/civilmustersrch.jsp.

New York State Division of Military and Naval Affairs. "Col. James C. Strong, 38th New York Infantry." http://www.dmna.state.ny.us/historic/reghist/civil/infantry/38thInf/38thInfPersonStrong.htm.

Wisconsin Historical Society. "Benjamin Sweet." http://www.wisconsinhistory.org/dictionary.

Yale Law School. "General Orders No. 100." Avalon Project. http://avalon.law.yale.edu/19th_century/lieber.asp.

Other

Atlantic Monthly. "The Chicago Conspiracy." July 1865.

Bross, William A.M. "Biographical Sketch of the Late Gen. B.J. Sweet: History of Camp Douglas: A Paper Read before the Chicago Historical Society, Tuesday Evening, June 8, 1878." Chicago: Jansen McClurg & Co., 1878.

Clingman, Lewis B., Jr. "History of Camp Douglas." Master's thesis, DePaul University, June 1942.

Cloyd, Benjamin Gregory. "Civil War Prisons in American Memory." PhD thesis, Louisiana State University, June 2005.

Eisendrath, Joseph L., Jr. "Chicago's Camp Douglas, 1861–1865." *Journal of the Illinois State Historical Society* 53, no. 1 (Spring 1960): 37, 63.

Goodspeed, Edgar J. "The Old University of Chicago in 1867." *Journal of the Illinois State Historical Society* 3, no. 2 (July 1910): 52–57.

Grant, Catherine M. "Public Opinion in Chicago During the Civil War." Master's thesis, DePaul University, June 1937.

Kelly, Dennis. "A History of Camp Douglas, Illinois, Union Prison, 1861–1865." United States National Park Service, Southeast Regional Office, August 1989.

"Kentucky Confederates Buried at Camp Douglas, Illinois." *Register of the Kentucky Historical Society* 46, no. 154 (January 1948): 404–09.

Kubalanza, Joan Marie G. "A Comparative Study of Conditions at Two Civil War Camps: Camp Douglas, Chicago Illinois, and Camp Sumpter, Andersonville, Georgia." Master's thesis, DePaul University, 1979.

Long, E.B. "Camp Douglas: 'A Hellish Hole.'" *Chicago History* (Fall 1970).

Mahoney, Olivia. "Black Abolitionists." *Chicago History* (Spring and Summer 1991).

Map of Chicago by Charles Shober, 1863.

Map of Chicago by Rufus Blanchard, 1957.

National Archives. "Statistical Reports of Hospitals in Virginia, 1862–1864." Record Group 109, Ch. 6, Vol. 151., 43–44.

Richmond Sentinel. June 21, 1864.

United Confederate Veterans. "Register of Confederate Soldiers Who Died in Camp Douglas, 1862–65, and Lie Buried in Oak Woods Cemetery." Cincinnati, OH: Cohen & Co., 1892.

United States Agricultural Society. "Seventh National Exhibition to be Held in the City of Chicago, September 12th, 13th, 14th, 15th, 16th and 17th, 1859." Chicago: Press & Tribune Job Printing Office, 1859.

Urbanski, Theodore. "A Story of Two Confederate Soldiers Named Jonathan Bond." Unpublished.

Index

R

S

T

U

W

Y

About the Author

David Keller founded the Camp Douglas Restoration Foundation in 2010 and has been involved in the education on and recognition of Camp Douglas for many years. Retired from the banking industry, David has been a prolific writer and speaker on both the banking industry and his second passion, soccer refereeing. He is a docent at the Chicago History Museum and a popular speaker on Camp Douglas and the Civil War. The Camp Douglas Restoration Foundation has conducted four archaeological excavations on the site of Camp Douglas and has a major objective to develop and operate a museum on the site. David and his wife, Linda, are longtime residents of Chicago.